Lone Star J. R.

The Autobiography of Racing Legend Johnny Rutherford

*by Johnny Rutherford
and David Craft*

TRIUMPH
BOOKS
CHICAGO

Library of Congress Cataloging-in-Publication Data
Rutherford, Johnny, 1938-
      Lone Star J. R. : the autobiography of racing legend Johnny Rutherford / by
Johnny Rutherford and David Craft.
         p. cm.
      ISBN 1-57243-353-1
      1. Rutherford, Johnny, 1938- 2. Automobile racing drivers—United States—
Biography.
      I. Craft, David. II. Title.

GV1032.R87 A3 2000
796.72'092—dc21
[B]   00-036422

This book is available in quantity at special discounts for your group or
organization. For further information, contact:

Triumph Books
601 South LaSalle Street
Suite 500
Chicago, Illinois 60605
(312) 939-3330
Fax (312) 663-3557

Printed in the United States.

ISBN 1-57243-353-1

Book design by Patricia Frey.
Jacket design by Salvatore Concialdi.

To my dad, John Rutherford Jr., who started me on the journey; to my wife, Betty, who has walked beside me on the journey; and to my children, John and Angela, who will continue the journey.

☆ Table of Contents ☆

☆ FOREWORD ☆

When Johnny Rutherford asked me to write a foreword for his book, I was honored. Johnny and I have been friends for a very long time; we've been through a lot of good times together, and some bad times, too.

Johnny has always been a great ambassador for racing. He is polished and knows the right thing to say in any situation. I think he did a lot for the sport in that way. And he still does a lot for the sport in the way he is guiding and advising the young drivers coming into Indy car racing today. I have helped young drivers but I think Johnny is better at getting his point across and leaving the drivers' egos intact.

I admire Johnny's ability to say the right thing (something I've never been known for), but I admire his courage even more. He's been through some pretty tough accidents but he always came back strong. He had a bad one when he flipped a sprint car at Eldora, Ohio, and broke both his arms.

But the one I remember was at Phoenix, where he got third degree burns on his right hand and burned his feet. During the race Johnny spun in oil when one of the Unsers lost an engine. Roger McCluskey hit the oil and spun and then Mario Andretti came along, hit the oil, and crashed into McCluskey and Rutherford. The hit ruptured Johnny's fuel tank. When Johnny got out of the car, he complained about his feet being hot. The emergency crew was taking care of McCluskey, whose bell had been rung. I got there and when I saw the condition of Rutherford—his feet were almost smoking and his right hand was really burnt—I asked McCluskey to get off the stretcher so Rutherford could get on. People say I yanked Roger off the stretcher, but I don't remember doing that.

I went with Johnny to the hospital and waited until they bandaged him up, and then I drove him back to the hotel where my wife Lucy and I were staying. We kept checking on him that night to make sure he was okay. Rutherford always makes a big deal out of it, but I just figured he needed help. It was no big deal to me. He was my friend, plain and simple. Friends take care of friends . . . plus he lived in Texas.

When I think back over the years and remember the good times, Johnny Rutherford is one of the guys who always comes to mind. He and his wife Betty have been good friends and we've shared some great times when racing was about racing and not about money and politics. I know you can't ever go back to those days, but sometimes it's enough just to remember them once in a while . . .

A. J. Foyt

☆ PREFACE ☆

Johnny and Betty Rutherford are exemplary people in our sport of auto racing. He won our Indianapolis five hundred-mile race three times, but it's what he has done outside of the race car that makes him special to me.

I just think he is a wonderful example of how a race driver can become involved in the community. I always remember him being involved in the 500 Festival activities that surround our race in May. He always attended the mayor's breakfast—you could always count on him.

And Betty always took a leading role with CARA, the wives' auxiliary, and all of the charities they work with.

One of my favorite projects each May at the Indianapolis Motor Speedway is the "Save Arnold" barbecue. We invite Special Olympics youth from around Indiana to the track to participate in a variety of games. Joining each team is a guest celebrity, usually a driver. Johnny is a three-time winner of the race, but he is always hitting balls, shooting baskets, posing for pictures, and signing autographs. His participation has helped us raise thousands and thousands of dollars for the Special Olympics.

I've gotten to know him much better since he retired. He came to the Speedway in 1963 when I was winding down as a car owner. I know his first victory in 1974 was very popular, and his victories in 1976 and 1980 made him one of the very few to have won that many times.

I also know that he met Betty at the track and that they have shown a good example of family life. They are an ideal family. Even today you see both of them at the races.

And Johnny keeps giving back to the sport. He drives the pace car at the Northern Light Indy Racing Series events. He and four-time Indy winner Al Unser Sr. have been very helpful in bringing new drivers to the league. I feel safe with him there. He's an asset to the league.

Johnny drove in twenty-four Indy 500s—that's fourth on the all-time list. But what I admire was his tenacity. He never won until his eleventh race. He could have given up, but he kept coming back. And finally his perseverance paid off. However, Johnny remained the same person when he became a winner as he was during all of those struggling years. His easygoing, friendly nature belied the intense desire inside of him.

It was hard for him to retire, just as it was for other Indy greats like A. J., Mario, Al Sr., and Mears. Yet eventually he did it gracefully. But he felt he still had much to contribute to the sport. That's why he chose to add his expertise and status to the Indy Racing League.

He's always set a good example. He's a credit to the sport. He's a good role model for other drivers to follow.

I'm proud that he and Betty represent our sport and our speedway in such a fine fashion. Every business needs people like them, and we're lucky to have Johnny and Betty. Thanks to both of you.

Mary Hulman George
Chairman
Indianapolis Motor Speedway
Spring 2000

☆　☆　☆

Across the Short Chute and into the Turn

As my generation has mellowed, the cherry bomb industry has gone into a downward slide. It's definitely suffering from a depressed market.

I have enjoyed my journey thus far, and I deeply appreciate the windows of opportunity I have stepped through. I still believe no one remembers who finished second, and that luck is where opportunity meets preparation.

Thank God I have had a wonderful career, a wonderful family, and wonderful friends. I look forward to the future. As Jimmy Stewart said, "It's a wonderful life."

I have always liked Ernest Hemingway's observation that "The only true sports are mountain climbing, bullfighting, and auto racing. The rest are just games."

☆ INTRODUCTION ☆

from Johnny:

Never did I imagine that I would write an autobiography. All that I ever wanted to do was drive a race car—anytime, anywhere. When I retired from active driving, intellectually I knew it was time, but in my heart I still wanted to race more than anything. To survive this most life changing of decisions, I had to find something to keep me so occupied that I did not have time to feel sorry for myself—something I suspect most retirees experience to some degree. Fortunately, I found I could still be involved in racing, contribute to my community, and even have some time to experiment with new adventures.

While I had experienced fleeting thoughts of writing an autobiography, it wasn't until Milton Kahn of Milton Kahn Associates urged me to take the first step by introducing me to literary agent Rhonda Winchell. She listened to my thoughts and advised me to consider writing my autobiography with David Craft, a pro in writing sports profiles. Finally the last part of the team signed on when Mitchell Rogatz of Triumph Books agreed to publish this book. They felt, as did my family, that the time was right for me to put my life on paper—perhaps before I forgot all the details. David insisted that this was to be my book with his guidance and assistance. To his credit, I must thank him for remaining calm through all of my storms.

During the compiling and taping of the bits and pieces of my life, I began to realize that this effort not only was going to be a very labor-intensive task, but one of many choices. During the third and fourth edit, those choices became very difficult. Every day of my life has contributed to the whole adventure, and to choose only some of the special or important events for this book was very difficult indeed. It seems to me that all of those insignificant details of one's life help tie that life together. Even choosing photos from thousands that Betty has so carefully kept in chronological order in hundreds of albums became a chore. I certainly have gained a new respect for authors during this process. Writing a book is very difficult, and the stress levels reached in meeting deadlines can be numbing. What a great way, though, to examine one's life and in the process relive the good and the not so good. For me it was a great journey—even this second time around.

While the following reminiscences are in no way a complete history, I must admit that too much of anything is not healthy, and I doubt that anyone would want to read thousands of pages detailing my entire life. I have tried to give you enough to show my love for the sport of auto racing and still allow the forces that drove me in my passion to shine through.

My everlasting gratitude and love to Betty for all of the editing sessions and deadlines that she so ably helped me survive. She also deserves hugs and kisses for keeping a scrapbook on my life and career—she has compiled six newspaper-sized books, each approximately six inches thick. I cannot tell you how many arguments those books have settled. I very much appreciate all of the support I have received from my family and friends throughout writing this book, and I am especially grateful to Mari George and A. J. Foyt for their contributions.

Thanks to Dick Jordon of USAC, Buz McKim of NASCAR, Craig Agan of the National Sprint Car Hall of Fame and Museum, Donald Davidson of the Indianapolis Motor Speedway, Pete Hylton of SCCA, T. E. McHale of CART, Bethany Gentry of Professional Sports Car Racing (formerly IMSA), George Signore of IROC, and everyone else who has been involved for all their help in compiling the stats on my career. Unfortunately, some of the IMCA records were lost and those stats as well as the records of the modified races are not as complete as the rest. For all of you young racers, start to keep your records now. It will make your life much easier when you entertain thoughts of writing your autobiography.

I have enjoyed being able to bring together some of the major people and events in my life to share with you. I hope each of you enjoys the read and that you are able to gain some insight into my life and my passion for auto racing. I am proud to have reached a significant level of success during my lifetime, and have enjoyed being a champion and winning races. Mostly, I have enjoyed being a positive role model not only for my own children, John and Angela, but for the many other children and young people that I have met during my long and successful racing career.

Even though I basically feel that luck is where opportunity meets preparation, I also think that I have been extremely fortunate throughout my life. That lucky charm, the ladybug, has been riding on my shoulder almost always. My life continues to be rewarding and a "work" in progress—stay tuned!

DETERMINATION

There is no chance, no destiny, no fate,
Can circumvent or hinder or control
The firm resolve of a determined soul.
Gifts count for nothing; will alone is great;
All things give way before it, soon or late.
What obstacle can stay the mighty force

Of the sea-seeking river in its course,
Or cause the ascending orb of day to wait?
Each well-born soul must win what it deserves.
Let the fool prate of luck. The fortunate
Is he whose earnest purpose never swerves,
The one great aim.
Why, even Death stands still,
And waits an hour sometimes for such a will.

Ella Wheeler Wilcox

from David:

There are three things you should know about this book: first, Johnny Rutherford is a superb storyteller; second, Betty Rutherford is not the unsung hero in this project (because I'm about to sing her praises); and third, I am not a ghostwriter.

Let's take these elements in reverse order.

Johnny and I first met at the Indianapolis Motor Speedway three weeks before the 1999 Indianapolis 500. Something amazing happened less than a minute into our conversation. We realized that we had, independently of each other, hit on the idea of beginning this book with a dramatic episode from his racing career and then segueing into more of a chronology.

From the dozens of hours of personal interviews we did, from his countless handwritten notes in the margins of several distinct versions of the manuscript, and from the various correspondence we sent back and forth, Johnny and I truly collaborated on this book. Best of all, *Lone Star J. R.* is, to the greatest degree we could make it, in Johnny's own words.

Betty also put in many long hours on the project. She read for content and factual correctness. On three or four occasions when I was writing and editing well into the morning, my fax machine would start whirring away. It would be a fax from Betty, sending me new or revised information to incorporate into the manuscript. I appreciate her efforts more than I can express here. Betty, like this book's two coauthors, worked tirelessly to "get it right." Thank you, Betty.

Johnny ranks high on my list of bright, well-spoken athletes who possess the ability to tell great stories in great detail. In these pages, the legendary race car driver and Renaissance man shares a wealth of stories that run the gamut of emotions. This book will draw you into the world of one of professional auto racing's great gentlemen, a well-rounded individual who continues to live life to the fullest and maintains a so-called "retirement" schedule that rivals that of a busy corporate executive.

I am grateful for the opportunity I had to work with the Rutherfords and thank them for their graciousness and generosity during my visits to Indianapolis and their Fort Worth home. To Johnny, I would like to say thanks again for taking me for a spin—but not a spinout—around the Brickyard in your passenger car. What an honor and a privilege. (Though I'm not given to hyperbole, I think that as I retell the story years from now, our top speed that day is likely going to be in the neighborhood of 160 mph rather than the true speedometer reading, *whatever* it was.)

I also wish to thank my family—especially Karen—and friends—including Milt Kahn and Rhonda Winchell—for their enthusiastic support of my work on this book. My thanks, also, to the patient and supportive people at Triumph Books.

☆ CHAPTER 1 ☆

Quitting Was Never an Option

April 3, 1966, was "Johnny Rutherford Day" at Eldora Speedway, and the track officials found me slumped over in my car with my hands in my lap.

I was a mess: my goggles were down around my mouth and my flip shield was hanging off the back of my helmet. At least that's what they told me later. I don't remember anything, because after it happened I was in a daze.

As I came to, I could hear the rocks being kicked up by the guys leaping over the guardrail and running down the embankment toward me. I can even remember the voice of the first man who reached me, my old friend, Roy Reed.

"John! John! Are you okay?!"

Confused and groaning, I somehow mumbled, "I think my arms are broken. They hurt like hell, and I can't see."

Because of all the ruptured surface blood vessels in my head, I had temporarily lost my vision. It felt as if a couple of handfuls of sand had been thrown into my eyes. My eyes were irritated and every time I blinked it hurt, so I kept them closed as best I could.

The guys unhooked my belts and started to pull me from the car so they could lay me on a stretcher. It was a heck of a way to celebrate a day in my honor. There I was, the reigning United States Auto Club's National Sprint Car Champion of 1965, carrying the number "1" on my car for the 1966 season, and I was being carried out on a stretcher while thousands of fans, including my wife of three years, Betty, watched. It was only the second race of the new season, a season, as it turned out, in which I wouldn't race again.

The first race of the '66 season had been at Reading, Pennsylvania. It was cold that day and I was driving a brand new car. The owner, Wally Meskowski, had built the car for me earlier that winter, and he had put Mario Andretti in the car in which I had won the title the year before. I was excited about having a new sprint car, but it was March, and I didn't know yet how the changes Wally had made to the new car would affect its handling on the track.

The crew prepared the car for warm-up laps at Reading, but in all the excitement, the crewman whose job was to change the gears and put things together in the center section of the rear end forgot to replace the lubricant. When I went out to drive some slow warm-up laps, the car didn't feel right. It was kind of sluggish. I returned to the pits, and when we checked the car we found that the lack of lubricant had caused the ring gear and pinion in the rear end of the car to overheat. They were ruined, and our race day was over before it began. I had no idea what the car would be like in an actual race; it was still brand new.

The race at Eldora Speedway in Rossburg, Ohio, came a week later. Track conditions were typical of Eldora in the spring, coming into a thaw. A lot of rocks in the dirt came to the surface in the spring, so the racetrack was unpredictable and always rough. In fact, I heard that Earl Bates, the track promoter and owner would have the track plowed and then he'd take a potato picker out to the track and pick the rocks out himself.

The racetrack was built on the side of a hill, and the dirt was pushed from the infield and built up to create the backstretch of the track. This formed about a sixty-foot drop from the guardrail to the normal terrain level outside the track. A small creek ran along the bottom of that sixty-foot bank.

I really liked the Eldora racetrack. It's a half-mile, high-banked, dirt track that is fast and a lot of fun to run. I had done fairly well there over the years. In 1964 I won my first USAC sprint car race at Eldora, and I set a new track record there in '65 when I won the title. I was confident about returning to Eldora. Plus, I had the extra incentive of racing there on "Johnny Rutherford Day." Boy, was it ever.

The car was not handling well, but I was able to make the feature event. I had barely made the feature through my heat race, a qualifying race. I was running about seventh in the field of eighteen cars that had started the feature event. Mario was behind me, driving the car I had been so successful with the previous year.

Wally Meskowski was on the front straightaway, giving us hand signals to tell us "You're stretching the guy out" or "He's closing in on you." Wally stepped out to where I could see him and signaled me to move up. I thought, *Well, I can't see what everybody else is doing, but he sees something,* so I moved up a little bit. When I did, my car hooked a rut and I bounded around slightly as Mario drove by me on the inside.

I came around again and let Wally know with my own hand signals what I thought of his moving me up. I went into the first turn and then ran a couple more laps. On lap thirteen I was closing in on Mario, trying to set myself up to pass him, when his car kicked up a rock or dirt clod. Whatever it was, it hit me right between the eyes and gained my undivided attention.

I had my goggles on, of course, and attached to my helmet was a shield made of clear, heavy, acetate plastic. I would throw the shield over the front of the helmet to protect my eyes from the rocks, clods of dirt, and mud that would fly up during the early stages of a race. When the shield became too dirty to see through, I'd just flip it back over my helmet. I'd still be protected by my goggles, which had what were called stack-ups—extra lenses on elastic straps. When they became covered with mud and dirt, I would just pull a stack-up down to expose a clean lens. That's the routine over the course of a dirt race.

I had just flipped my shield back when that rock or clod struck my face just above the bridge of my nose. It must have knocked me unconscious for a moment. At the very least I was stunned. The impact of that rock was the beginning of the end of my day at Eldora Speedway. The right rear of the car bounced as I hooked a rut. In that split second, when I relaxed and my foot came off the throttle—which is a cardinal sin in dirt track racing, because in the rough stuff you have to keep the back wheels churning and buzzing so you can work through those tough spots—my car hooked the rut and was jerked into the air.

As a result of that movement the tail of my car turned toward the infield, and then the car hooked another rut. Because the car was set up statically, with extra weight in the left rear wheel of the car, the wheel dug in and the car started flipping. The right-side tire hit the top of the guardrail post. The car bounced like a beach ball when the tires struck the railing.

My car soared out of the racetrack, flipping in the air at a height of twenty-five to thirty feet, higher than a nearby light pole. Then, after nose-diving down the sixty-foot embankment, the car landed on its wheels in a shallow creek bed. Later, a full-page photo in *Life* magazine caught me extended out of the car by approximately a foot, hanging by my seat belt and shoulder harness with my arms dangling above my head, when the car, nose down, was at its gyrating peak, higher than the light pole.

When the car nose-dived into the ground, my outstretched arms came down hard on top of the windshield, breaking both arms virtually in the same place. The right arm was more badly damaged because of a dislocation and fracture of the elbow.

The race had to be red-flagged—stopped—because all the emergency equipment was located on the infield, with access at the third-turn gate on the track.

Dr. Ward Dunseth, a sprint car owner from Illinois, was also racing at Eldora that day. Occasionally Dr. Dunseth served as our unofficial track physician. Seconds after my car landed in the creek, he was at the scene and quickly examined me. He suspected that I had suffered a basal skull fracture.

I vaguely remember Dr. Dunseth looking at me, firmly but gently holding my head, and saying, "Now, you may have a head injury, so John, for God's sake, don't move your head." Of course, being an animated person I nodded my head yes and said, "Okay." Right away I could feel his hands start to hold my head a little tighter.

An ambulance took me to the hospital in Greenville, Ohio, thirteen miles south of Rossburg on Highway 127. The doctor on call was not pleased to be called in to treat, of all people, "a stupid race car driver." I was later told he was most unpleasant, and that although he diagnosed my broken right arm, he completely missed my broken left arm until Betty brought it to his attention. Betty and Dr. Dunseth requested that X-rays be taken, but the attending doctor refused their request. He asked Betty to move me to a Dayton hospital immediately, as he did not wish to accept the responsibility of tending to my injuries.

Betty refused to move me anywhere.

As a registered nurse, she knew how serious my condition was and that if I did have a basal skull fracture there could be further complications if I were moved. She was more concerned about my possible head injury, and she knew what needed to be done—she called Indianapolis to talk with Dr. Ted Luros, a neurological surgeon with whom she had worked, and related my condition and symptoms over the phone.

Given the Greenville doctor's unpleasant behavior, Dr. Luros recommended that I be transferred to Dayton and called a doctor there to see me on arrival. Dr. Luros even offered to fly to either Greenville or Dayton if needed.

Betty knew that a fellow driver, Donnie Davis, had died as a result of a basal skull fracture suffered in a sprint car mishap in New Bremen, Ohio, not far from Rossburg. Because of insufficient emergency equipment and lack of skilled medical staff at the scene, Donnie was transported in a florist's truck to a Dayton hospital. He didn't have a chance of surviving his injury.

Betty was absolutely terrified at the thought of my being taken to Dayton in my condition, and she rode in the ambulance, holding my head for the entire thirty miles.

In the hospital I looked like one massive bruise. I was yellow and green and blue and purple. The white in my eyes was gone; they were solid red. While in the hospital, a doctor who had worked with NASA told me that I had had a "red-out." That's what happens when you pull in an excess of ten negative g's, which forces the blood to the head and causes many surface blood vessels to rupture. My eyes did not return to normal until about six to eight weeks after the accident.

At the hospital, surgeons placed a plate in my right arm to hold a wedge-shaped fragment of bone in place at the fracture site in my badly broken ulna, the large bone in the forearm. A second surgery was performed on my radius, the small bone in the forearm, which was dislocated at my elbow. Because of scar tissue and the dislocation, I neither can straighten my right arm nor turn my palm up or down. I only have about seventy percent mobility in my arm, but through the years I have learned to make small adjustments in the way I accomplish everyday tasks. For racing, my crew simply modified the car's steering wheel by moving it closer to me.

After I arrived at Dayton, Wally Meskowski, Mario Andretti, and Don Branson came to the hospital to check on me. Don was a friend and teammate of mine. I always called him "Teamie."

Betty was in the hall outside the emergency room when Don arrived. She told him, "Don, I want you to do something for me. When you go in there to see him, don't tell him who you are. Just stand beside him. Johnny said he couldn't see when they brought him in."

Don walked to my bedside and Betty said, "Look who's here to see you, Johnny."

I turned and opened my eyes slightly and said, "Oh, hi, Teamie."

Betty later told me that that was one of the biggest reliefs she experienced during our whole ordeal. I was getting my sight back. I was still in trauma, but I was recovering, however slowly. During the first two to three days I saw double images, but I could see, and I was improving.

It was going to be a long, hard pull. My fortunes had changed. One moment I was out doing what I loved to do and the next thing I knew I was bedridden at Good Samaritan Hospital in Dayton.

It was a violent crash, and I was fortunate to have survived and to have remembered little of the accident. Thank God the creek wasn't very deep, because if I had landed upside down I might have drowned before emergency crews could reach me.

Practice for the Indianapolis 500 was less than a month away, and when I saw the newspaper headlines—"Rutherford out of '500' "—Betty said I pitched a fit because I did not intend to miss the 1966 Indianapolis 500. But in truth, I would miss the race that year because my injuries were more complicated than I thought.

Examining my uniform after the accident, I found a red stain on the right shoulder and on the entire length of the sleeve. On the race car itself, the upholstery had been cut as if by a knife, just below where my right shoulder would have been. I found out later that the guardrail at Eldora was painted with red oxide primer, which seemed to solve the mystery of the red stain. The right-side tires had come down on top of the guardrail post and I must have slammed my shoulder and arm into the guardrail as the car bounded off the railing. The top of the guardrail apparently was sharp enough to cut right through the upholstery next to my arm. Luckily, my arm wasn't severed in the accident.

It's possible that the car's collision with the guardrail caused the dislocation of my elbow, which was later broken when the car made its final impact. That mystery remains unsolved.

Convalescing in the hospital gave me plenty of time to ponder what happened out there on the track. But for the life of me I couldn't understand how I lost control of my car and flipped as I did. That piece of the puzzle was still missing. I'd ask Betty, "What happened?" and she'd answer me as best she could, based on what she knew as a witness to the whole thing. After the first day or two that she stayed with me in the hospital, she tired of hearing me ask, "What happened?" But I needed to know what really took place out there.

Of course, when you suffer a head injury like that, it's devastating. You don't just bounce back right away. My short-term memory was gone for a while after the accident, but soon returned once the cause of my puzzling accident was discovered.

When I was moved to Good Samaritan Hospital in Dayton, Pete Wales, the owner and promoter of Winchester Speedway, one of the country's most famous high-banked racetracks, and his wife, Dottie, asked Betty to stay with them at their place, which wasn't far from the hospital.

At their house, Betty was getting some luggage out of the trunk when she found my helmet, my gloves, my goggles, and the uniform that had been cut from me after the accident. She looked at the goggles and immediately thought she knew what really started the accident.

At that time, race drivers always taped their lenses in with black electrical tape to provide shade from the sun and to hold the lenses in place if anything hit them. The rock that hit me split the tape and shattered the lens right at the point of impact.

The next day, when Betty came to visit me at the hospital, she handed me the goggles and told me what she had figured out. I still have those goggles in my trophy case at home. The goggles—which are the same type of shatter-resistant goggles used by fighter pilots in World War II— were shattered at the place where the rock hit them.

Even though it was discovered at the hospital that I did not have a basal skull fracture, I was devastated after the accident, both physically and psychologically, because it knocked me out of the Indy 500 that year and out of racing for the entire season.

After about a month in the hospital I was released, and Betty and I returned to Indianapolis to our new apartment. I was up and mobile but still pretty weak.

Immediately, I went over to the Indianapolis Motor Speedway to visit with everybody, and I watched in agony as somebody else drove my car in the time trials—the car I would have been in and should have been in—for the 1966 Indy 500. That was tough, very tough. I knew I was in no condition to be driving in the Indy 500, but I still wanted to be out there on that legendary track. I was miserable. I decided to never again step over the dollar to pick up the dime.

Because I was out with two broken arms, I was approached to do the color commentary on the race, and I agreed. I was partnered with announcers Charlie Brockman and Chris Economacki, and I did the expert commentary on the first closed-circuit television coverage of the Indianapolis 500. Fans could go to their local movie theater, pay an admission price, and watch live coverage of the Indianapolis 500.

I was still suffering physically from the aftermath of the accident. Immediately following my surgery I had started running a low-grade fever, an indication of possible infection. After a month of antibiotics, the medical staff saw little improvement in my condition. My cast was removed and cultures were taken of the nonhealing incision. All sorts of blood tests were done. The new diagnosis: I had a staph infection in my right arm. That infection kept me out of racing for more than a year. I should have healed in the usual three or four months and been back in action by midseason or so, but the medical staff just could not get rid of that staph infection.

I was in real danger of losing my right arm. I decided not to return to Dayton, and transferred instead to Dr. Hugh Williams, one of the doctors on the medical staff at the Indianapolis Motor Speedway. He examined my right arm and immediately started treatments to try to bring the staph infection under control and then destroy it.

During the first operation Dr. Williams inspected the metal plate that held the wedge of bone in place in my arm, and things looked pretty grim. Though it should have started knitting by then, the wedge of bone fell out when he took the plate off. The infection had interrupted the healing process.

Six surgeries later, Dr. Williams succeeded in treating the staph infection. Then I had to wait six long weeks before undergoing bone graft surgery. Two days before Christmas, in 1966, I was in the hospital for my ninth surgery, the final one. Bone was removed from my hip and placed into my arm, which hurt more than breaking my arms ever did.

Roger McCluskey, who had had sprint car-induced arm injuries two years prior to mine, called me every day to tell me jokes. He managed to make me laugh at least once a day. He was a delightful "cuss" and a good friend.

As the weeks passed, my right arm finally started healing, and in May of 1967 I ran my first race in thirteen months—the Indianapolis 500.

☆　☆　☆　☆　☆

I called on my spiritual beliefs during those times when life was hard. A person must have faith in those beliefs to help answer the haunting questions of "Why me?" and "Why do these things happen?"

I had to develop the attitude that it was part of God's plan, that there was a reason for what happened to me and that some day I would understand it. I had to accept that and move ahead, just as I learned to accept whatever comes as a result of my own actions. I take life one day at a time.

I never entertained thoughts of quitting racing, the profession I loved so much. I've had many doctors tell me that race car drivers heal faster than anyone else, and I believe that's because we have such an intense, burning desire to get back into the competition.

We tend to do things that help us heal quicker, from our willingness to undergo intensive physical therapy to our mental and emotional strength—a mind-over-matter ability to block out pain. Whatever it is, it is at the core of our beings.

Anytime I had a debilitating injury, I never once said, "Man, I'm never going to do this again. I could get killed out there." It's just not part of my makeup, nor is it a trait you'll find in race car drivers as a whole. Racing on the edge is not a death wish. It's living life to the max.

Betty never once broached the subject of my leaving the sport and doing something else for a living. I think she has always understood my drive to win, to be the best. She was my biggest supporter, my biggest fan. She was, and is, my rock.

A few years after my Eldora accident, when we were seeing some retired drivers returning to the cockpit only to experience disastrous results, Betty offered me some cautionary advice: "If you ever declare your retirement, don't you ever go back on your word and come out of retirement later on, because I will have gotten used to the idea of us not having that element of danger in our lives. I don't want you to do that to me, your family and friends, and more importantly, yourself. I will fight to make you keep your word."

Despite my love for my job, a few frustrating moments late in my career, from 1989 through 1992, made me question getting behind the wheel. It was during these moments when I would ask myself, "What's going on? Why is this happening to me? I never had this kind of problem before. Is it me? The car? The team? Or some combination of those things that seems to be creating problems for me on the track and more often than I'm comfortable with? I've got to evaluate my situation and decide what to do next."

When circumstances began to stack up against me, human nature tended to make me doubt my own ability. As I matured, I realized that perhaps that was not always true. Those moments were as close as I ever got to thinking about moving on and doing something other than driving race cars.

You need to understand something about race car drivers. An incident happens very quickly when you're behind the wheel of a race car that's flying around a track at super-high speeds. The scariest moments of racing only exist after the fact, when you've had some time to think about what could have happened.

I've impacted the wall at more than two hundred miles per hour, and it hurts. But it happens so fast that, if the driver is killed instantly, he never knows what happened. It's over.

I know, Al Unser knows, A. J. Foyt knows, and Mario Andretti knows that if a driver meets "the end" in a race car accident, that driver will not be scared nor feel the pain of approaching death—selfish feelings, perhaps, for drivers to possess, but realistic nonetheless.

After racing at Indianapolis for twenty years, I had my first run-in with the wall in 1983. With the newer cars and the higher speeds, if the car suffers a failure or a driver commits an error on the racetrack, the slamming crash into the wall at speeds between 180 and 200 mph is going to hurt like heck. And it certainly did!

However, if you look up and can still see daylight, if you recognize people, if you can unhook the seat belts and get out of that pile of wreckage that just moments before had been a half-million-dollar race car, and still walk away from it, then your violent crash is something that has happened. It's past tense. Don't even worry about *that*. Let's find out what happened, why it happened, and what we as a team can do to prevent a recurrence. That's the attitude that has to prevail or you'll go crazy and won't be able to perform to the best of your ability.

I did not win a single Indy car race until '65, when I won in Atlanta. The following year I broke my arms in the sprint car race at Eldora. It was like starting over. I had to regain my confidence and prove to others in racing that I still possessed the assets and the ability to again become a winner and a champion.

It took years, from 1965 to 1970, for me to get close to my dream of having a chance at winning the Indianapolis 500. In 1970 I nearly sat on the pole in the closest pole run in Indy history, which really boosted my stock there.

That fire in my belly was always there, and in time I managed to win at Indy. But I experienced one failure after another, one frustration after another, year after year.

It was a long road back from the Eldora accident in '66, and during that time I gained a better feeling for the big picture. I knew what could happen and how fragile life can be. Maturity was a key factor to my understanding; perseverance became my code. Support from family and friends was essential to my success. Through it all, Betty was there. She was as much a part of my racing team as anyone.

I want to make it clear that it was always my philosophy not to be a dare-devil. It's important that you know that about me. Yet I've always been a believer, maybe because of the nature of what I did for a living—drive all kinds of race cars while literally and figuratively going to the edge—that if you don't go to the edge and look over now and then, it gets pretty boring around here.

By nature I'm a risk-taker who will accept any challenge, and I'm sure I inherited that trait from my dad, an adventuresome sort who was responsible for sparking my interest in auto racing when I was a young boy.

☆ CHAPTER 2 ☆

Many Friends, Too Many Places

I was born John Sherman Rutherford III on March 12, 1938, in Coffeyville, Kansas, a small town located about seventy miles north of Tulsa, Oklahoma, right on the Oklahoma-Kansas border. Coffeyville is noted for its connection to outlaws Frank and Jesse James and the Dalton boys. In fact, Coffeyville is where the Dalton Gang met their end trying to rob the Condon National Bank.

I was named after my granddad and my dad. To help eliminate some of the confusion resulting from having three Johns in the family, Lee Ferguson, my dad's best friend in Coffeyville, called me "one-eleven," a variation on the Roman numeral at the end of my name. Since my youth I've been called "Johnny", and when I was making a name for myself in racing and earning some success along the way, I earned the nickname "Lone Star J. R." People sometimes call me "John," but since my son, John Sherman Rutherford IV, prefers to be called that, it still causes some confusion. In the end, "Johnny" is the name that has stuck with me both personally and professionally.

My parents, John Sherman Jr. and Mary Henrietta Brooks Rutherford, separated when I was about three years old and soon afterward divorced. After the divorce, my mother moved from Coffeyville to California. I didn't see her again until I was nearly twelve years old. Mary married Norm Vediner, one of the finest gentlemen I've ever known. He worked in the Long Beach shipyards during World War II, and after the war he worked for Union Oil as a pipe fitter in the plant. Mary and Norm lived and raised their family in Fullerton, California.

Mary and I had a close relationship. Throughout my adult life I always visited her whenever I was in California to race, conduct business, or visit friends. Mary passed away in February of 1997, Norm in September of 1999. Both are greatly missed. But I still get out to California, and I truly enjoy visiting with my half brothers, Mike and David, and half sisters, Judy and Jan, and their families.

Prior to and during World War II, my dad was in the Army Air Corps and was stationed stateside. However, his work as an instructor in the service meant he had to travel from base to base and that he was absent a lot when I was young. During the war years, I would take wagonloads of scrap metal to the redemption center in Coffeyville where we lived. The war introduced many different things to our lives: war bond drives, conserving fuel, rationing, victory gardens, eight-by-eight-inch white flags trimmed in black and gold and bearing a blue star for each relative at war. Across the United States people pitched in and did what needed to be done to help the war effort.

Even though I was only three at the time, I remember my grandparents listening to President Roosevelt declare war on Japan after the Japanese bombed Pearl Harbor on December 7, 1941. I remember the intensity on their faces when the president made his announcement before a joint session of Congress. Even now, when I hear a recording of that address or see the film clip on TV, I'm always taken back to that historical moment. It's difficult to forget a declaration of war when your dad is in the military.

I lived with my paternal grandparents, John S. and Ida Bell England Rutherford, in Coffeyville while my father traveled. In fact, my grandmother had custody of me from when I was three to five years old.

The arrangement was fine with me—I loved being with my grandparents, and I can honestly say that my childhood was perfectly normal. I led a stable life and wasn't shuffled from one relative to another. I was so young when my parents separated that I didn't realize what it actually meant, and thus it didn't have the effect on me that it might have had if I'd been older.

My dad remarried and was granted custody of me when I was five. His second wife, Doris Jean Mayfield Rutherford, became my stepmother and assumed command of me. She raised me and I've always thought of her as my mom. Dad met Doris while he was stationed in Abilene, Texas, and I was living in Coffeyville. After Dad and Mom married in 1943, I moved to Abilene, and about a year later we moved back to Coffeyville for a short period of time before we moved to Fort Sill, Oklahoma. During Dad's time with the Air Corps we lived off base except when we lived in Fort Sill. From there we moved to Oklahoma City, where my dad was stationed at Tinker

Field. When World War II ended in 1945, Dad remained in the Air Force as a warrant officer.

Then it was on to Tulsa, Oklahoma, in 1946. Since my dad was in the Air Corps our family had to move often. I made friends easily enough and was always outgoing and something of a practical joker, but in each town in which we lived I had to accept the fact that one day I would move to another town. To me, moving was just a part of my life and sometimes even an adventure.

Oddly enough, moving around didn't so much alter the basic "me." I remained the same person wherever we lived, though I realize now that had we moved during my teen years it would have been much tougher, because of the strong friendships I was beginning to form and the activities in which I was becoming involved.

It was in Tulsa that I attended my first racing event. Dad came home one summer evening in 1947 and announced to Mom and me that he was taking us to see something special. I was nine years old and full of curiosity.

Mom put our dinner on simmer and Dad drove us to the Tulsa Fairgrounds. It was an old place with a big, wooden, covered grandstand. A few people were going inside, and though at first I had no idea what was happening, I soon learned why we came.

When we got inside I saw these beautiful little cars warming up and racing around a dirt track. It was an amazing sight for an impressionable nine year old: the brightly colored cars with numbers painted on them, the glint of the cars as they sped under the track's lights, the shiny chrome exhaust pipes and the nerf bars, the dirt kicked up by the tires—it was the first time I'd ever seen a race car on a dirt track. I thought that it would be a thrill to drive one.

I was mesmerized by the quick movement of the cars around the quarter-mile track, the smells of hot exhaust wafting through the air, and the sound of that place—the engine noise.

What a scene! I was wide-eyed and energized, an instant fan of midget racing.

It wasn't a real race—there probably were no more than half a dozen cars out there practicing that night. But I didn't care that it was only a practice session. I just imagined how great it would be to one day sit in the cockpit, to take the wheel of one of those little cars and race against the other drivers. The thrill of that thought and all those little race cars sparked my imagination. That moment marked the beginning of my lifelong love affair with racing and race cars.

Because this was just a practice for the drivers and their cars, the grandstand was largely empty. We were able to walk down the steps to seats that were close to the track so I could really be near the action. All too soon for me, Dad said it was time for supper. But who could eat after all that excitement?

It was all I could talk and think about. In my mind I kept seeing those little brightly painted cars racing around that dirt track. I was hooked. From then on, I looked forward to watching the midget cars race every weekend. I saved up my allowance money to buy pictures of my favorite drivers, Bud Camden, Clarence Merritt, and George Bennie, and Dad took me to the track so I could ask them to sign the pictures. I still have those photos proudly displayed on my shop wall. It was a great time for Dad and me.

Peaches Campbell, one of the famous car owners of the '20s, '30s, and '40s, had a "big car." That was the name given to the forerunner of the modern championship car that ran in the Indianapolis 500 during the 1950s and 1960s.

One afternoon, Dad and I went to the Tulsa Fairgrounds track to watch Campbell's "big car" during some test runs. After watching midgets run on a quarter-mile track right in front of the grandstand, where I could see all the exciting action, I wasn't overly impressed watching a "big car" on the larger mile track. At least I wasn't initially impressed. But that "big car" was fast. I noticed that almost immediately.

It was then that I was introduced to another aspect of racing—speed. My education in motor sports had begun, and my interest in race cars grew more intense.

But my passion was still for midget racing. I know that many people shared my enthusiasm for the sport, and in the half-century since that all-too-short evening my parents and I spent at the Tulsa Fairgrounds I gained an even greater appreciation for midget racing and its place in history.

Midget racing began in the 1930s during the Great Depression and was an instant hit with people whose lives were mired in personal and professional struggles. Midget racing was fast-paced entertainment on a quarter-mile, oval dirt track, but it could be adapted for longer distances. It was something that could, at least for a few hours on any given day or night, take people's minds off their worries.

By the late 1930s, midget racing was a huge success. I've been told that in some parts of the country these little cars were racing seven nights a week. The most successful drivers could make several thousand dollars a month, which was good money at the time. But when the United States entered World War II in late 1941, midget racing, like many things, was forced to go on a hiatus.

After the war, midget racing was still popular, but it had a lot of competition for the wage-earner's dollar and free time; stock car racing, television, baseball, and motion pictures were each coming into their own. But when my folks and I went to the fairgrounds during that summer of 1947, midget racing was still rowdy, noisy fun for the whole family.

Midget race cars are essentially scaled-down versions of sprint cars, which in turn are essentially scaled-down versions of championship Indy cars. When I raced them, midget cars even had their own miniature Offenhauser engines, which from the '30s through the '60s was the racing engine of note. Midgets had tubular frames, torsion-bar suspension in the rear, and other features found on sprint and championship cars.

They were designed for dirt track racing, and were thus fast and fun to drive. The Indianapolis Motor Speedway Hall of Fame and Museum showcases more than seventy-five legendary racing cars, including midgets. A comparison of the midgets' size with that of the sprints or the Indy cars might conjure up some images of what it was like to fly down the straightaways at eighty or ninety miles per hour—and that was on rutty dirt.

Watching and listening to half a dozen midget cars in their practice runs on a short, dirt track at the fairgrounds in Oklahoma may not seem very exhilarating, but to a nine-year-old boy with a vivid imagination, it was captivating, and a pivotal moment in my life.

Only a few years later, I began experimenting racing tricks on my younger half brother, Evan Wayne. I was an only child until the age of seven when my half sister, Beverly Jean, was born. Evan Wayne was born when I was nine. Wayne was a tag-along towhead. When he was five years old, I built him a little race car—having "borrowed" the wheels of Beverly's baby buggy—and a ramp.

I would run as fast as I could behind Wayne and push him in the car. One last mighty shove would send him and his car up the ramp on two wheels—in the style of the thrill shows—and cause the car to roll over and crash onto the ground. I know he was just a little kid, but in my defense I'd like to point out that I did fashion a protective helmet for him to wear. Occasionally, Wayne thanks me for contributing to his "craziness," and we can still have a good laugh recalling those days.

My sister, brother, and I didn't do a lot of things together because of our age differences. Mom often stayed home on Saturday nights to take care of them while Dad and I went to watch the midget cars race at the fairgrounds. Dad would always take me to a particular section of the grandstand and then he'd go off to the pits to talk engines and racing with the other mechanics at the track. He often would volunteer to help in the pits, where his talents as a mechanic were welcome. He'd give me a quarter to buy some popcorn and a soft drink, and when the race was over he expected me to be where he left me. I was fairly responsible for a ten-year-old boy, and the desire to continue to come watch the race cars was good incentive to mind my father.

Mom has been an important part of my life, as well. She, as much as anyone, instilled in me what we've come to call "family values." Mom taught me, as a youngster, to understand church and the Ten Commandments; to respect one's elders; always to be honest, courteous, and straightforward; and always to have a sense of fair play. The values my parents instilled in me helped me as an adult in a variety of situations: in dealing with the media, in making personal appearances, in public speaking, and in cultivating sponsors for my racing career.

Being raised as a Southern Baptist meant that I went to Sunday school and/or church services on Sundays and attended Bible school every summer. During Sunday services, Beverly, Wayne, and I had an affinity for choosing the most inopportune moments to make noise and generally disturb those around us—which, of course, included our parents. I remember the three of us getting pinched regularly in church for our misbehavior. Of course, our yips would be even louder than our giggling and noisemaking was.

As I grew older, I went in a different direction for a while, skipping church because I was so busy, especially with Sunday races. Now Betty and I attend University Christian Church when we can, and in recent years we have been able to attend traveling chapel services at all the racetracks. I like to think that I still embody all the qualities my parents instilled in me.

Our family is still very close. Wayne lives in Fort Worth and I see him, his wife, Sandy, and their three daughters, Tobi, Regan, and Sidney, quite often. Beverly and her husband, Benny, who is a conductor for CSX Railroad, live in Tennessee, but we talk on a regular basis and visit as often as possible. I feel blessed that God has given me three brothers and three sisters.

My dad passed away more than twenty-five years ago. Mom met Bill Booth, a fine gentleman who attends her Fort Worth church, several years later. After a respectful courtship, Mom and Bill were married.

Bill is now my stepfather, and although he is eighty-nine, he is spry and sharp. I just hope I can be like him when I reach that age. Bill is one heck of a role model; he was a successful businessman in Fort Worth and is still going strong. I was certainly thrilled to see my mom find somebody with whom she could be happy and with whom she could enjoy traveling the world.

I was not very big as a child; I actually was somewhat frail. As a young child I experienced many ear infections and ruptured eardrums and I suffered from asthma, although I outgrew it by the time I was about six or seven. When I was four, I nearly died of scarlet fever. Being a sickly child meant that I didn't go outside much; in fact, I didn't get to play in the snow until I was six years old because of my constantly inflamed tonsils.

Once I had my tonsils removed, my life was almost immediately different. I was healthy again; I started growing and filled out just like my peers. As a healthy youngster I went fishing with Grandma Rutherford. I also played pee-wee baseball and pickup games of softball and sandlot football. In Tulsa we lived not far from a park, and during the winter I would go there with my friends to either ice skate or play hockey on the frozen pond. I even enjoyed swimming at the YMCA, though I almost drowned during my first attempt. (Unlike myself, my dad was a championship swimmer; in the early 1930s he challenged gold medalist swimmer Johnny Weissmuller to a race and won.)

I was a Cub Scout, and I loved tree houses, playground swings, catching crawdads at the nearby pond, and playing with friends who, like me, were fascinated by race cars and motorcycles. We would clothespin several playing cards or baseball cards to our bicycle spokes to create the clicking sound of an engine. It was an idyllic life for a youngster and his school chums in Tulsa in 1946.

My family lived in Tulsa until 1950, when we moved to Alexandria, Louisiana, where Dad's squadron was being prepared for service in Korea. Because of a hangar accident in Tulsa, in which he severely hurt his back, Dad experienced extreme back pains and finally decided to muster out of the service. By that time, he had thirteen or fourteen years of service in the Army Air Corps and Air Force. Dad left the military just before the Korean War in late 1950. Once again, we moved back to Coffeyville for a short time before we made our final move to Fort Worth, Texas, in early 1951. I had attended thirteen different schools by the time I had finished the sixth grade—three in the sixth grade alone.

Dad went to work for Consolidated Vultee in Fort Worth, where he helped build B-36 bombers. I'm not just being a proud son when I say that my dad was a mechanic of the first order. Over the years I've encountered many of my dad's friends, and they all tell me that he was the best engine man they have ever known. When it came to an aircraft engine, John S. Rutherford Jr. could simply listen to it and tell you what was wrong. Up until the introduction of the jet engine, my dad worked on just about any kind of aircraft you can name.

Dad always had a knack for maintenance and engine work. He was good with his hands. While his talents were mainly directed at aviation, Dad could work on anything, it seems, that had an engine in it.

My dad was so good at what he did that he was held in high esteem by his superiors in the service. In fact, in 1944, although Dad's orders were cut and he was about to board ship for Europe to work with the P-38 Lightnings' photo recon squadron, he was called out during roll call and given a new set of orders: to stay in Oklahoma and become an instructor in engine school. He had exceptional talent as a mechanic and the military felt they would be better served if he remained stateside, so he didn't board that ship. We learned later that the ship was torpedoed and sunk on the voyage. Everyone aboard perished.

Dad's best friend, Evan Graham, for whom my half brother was named, was on that ship. It still gives me an eerie feeling to imagine losing Dad on that ship he was supposed to board. That was the one time I was grateful to the Army Air Corps for giving Dad new orders and forcing him to live and work somewhere else.

Dad sought adventure. He had race cars or boats or an airplane at the airport. Once, while in Tulsa, Dad even did some midget car racing just for fun. There was always something different he was working on, something new he wanted to show me.

When we lived in Tulsa and Dad was still in the service, another phase of my life took root. Dad was chief of maintenance for the 125th Fighter Squadron, Oklahoma Air National Guard. They flew P-51 Mustangs and I fell in love with those warbirds. I would go to the hangar to climb all over them. *Nothing* sounds like the P-51 Rolls Royce–Merlin engine.

In 1974 I found a P-51 Mustang in the civilian registry. It was listed for sale by its owner, a dentist in Dallas, Texas, and I bought it. Three years later I found another P-51 that was completely disassembled on a flatbed trailer in California. I had it rebuilt from the ground up—everything was zero-fresh on it. Those two P-51 Mustangs gave me a total of about 130 hours of pure, joyous flying time. Betty proudly reminds friends that, when I flew the P-51s over Fort Worth, there was neither an ME 109 nor a Zero spotted flying in the area.

It's ironic, or at least interesting to note, that my dad's life was aviation and his hobby was race cars, while my life has been race cars and my hobby has been aviation. When Dad was in his early twenties, before I was born, he and his buddies would race motorcycles for fun. Like me, he was always fascinated with speed and power. But he also was dead-set against me having a motorcycle as a boy because he knew how dangerous a boy on a motorcycle could be. Thus, I didn't have a motorcycle until I was old enough to buy my own.

Although I was an adult when I earned my pilot's license and began flying my own airplanes, I was introduced to aviation very early in life; my birth mother, Mary, told me that once, just before I was born, she and I flew with Dad.

Shortly after the war, when I was eight, Dad and Lee bought some World War II surplus primary trainers. Dad fixed them up and sold them for a profit.

Dad and I had an episode involving one of those planes, a Fairchild PT-19, an open-cockpit, tandem-seat trainer that was painted blue and yellow—like the airplanes were then—and bore the Army Air Corps star with the red-dot center. Dad flew this Fairchild PT-19 back and forth from Tulsa to Coffeyville. On one of those trips to Coffeyville, he decided that I could go with him. I put on my helmet and goggles, zipped up my jacket, and climbed into the backseat of the airplane, where Dad hooked up my seat belt and shoulder harness and strapped me in good and tight. I sat on a seat cushion but I still was sitting too low in the airplane to see over the sides of the cockpit.

Dad said, "Now don't touch anything, just sit there and ride along, okay?"

He taxied out and lifted the plane off into the blue, and we headed off for Coffeyville.

A small town called Nowata, Oklahoma, lies between Tulsa and Coffeyville. Dad had friends at the airport there, so he put the plane into a dive, pulled it up, and did a roll.

Just as Dad flipped the plane, he remembered I was in the backseat and suddenly worried that I might have unhooked my seat belt. He turned around frantically as he righted the plane.

A couple of days prior to the airplane trip with my dad, Mom took me to the store and bought me a new pair of tennis shoes. Now, in the plane, without anything to do in the backseat and being unable to see over the sides of the cockpit, I had my feet up on the instrument panel so I could look at my new tennis shoes.

When he was struck by that sudden panic, Dad leaned forward and looked under the seat to make sure my feet were hanging down—but they weren't.

My God, I'm sure he thought, *I've just dumped my kid out over Nowata, Oklahoma.*

He broke out in a cold sweat, quickly unhooked his seat belt, turned around, and got on his knees to look into the backseat area. There I was, looking up at him, grinning and waving.

He told me later that seeing me still strapped into that seat belt and waving to him was the best sight he'd ever seen in his life. He turned back around in his seat, refastened his seat belt, and flew on, straight and level, to Coffeyville, where he landed the plane.

Dad was protective of me but he wasn't overbearing. He just expected me to listen to him, my mom, and my grandparents. He was a good listener himself, and was always interested in what I was doing and what was on my mind. My granddad was the same way. He was a very stately looking gentleman and for a time was a county judge in Oklahoma. He also worked for Chevrolet and I still have some of the trophies that he won in sales and maintenance at the Chevrolet dealership where he was employed, as well as from the Chevrolet corporate headquarters. Imagine—another competitive Rutherford involved with automobiles.

☆ CHAPTER 3 ☆

The First Step

After we moved to Fort Worth my life stabilized somewhat. I attended Castleberry Elementary School for my sixth-grade year and then moved on to the new junior high school—Irma Marsh Junior High. After I graduated from Irma Marsh I went on to attend North Side High School.

School sports helped raise my level of confidence, because even though I was friendly and outgoing at school, I could also be quiet and more of a dreamer. I enjoyed baseball a lot—I played in the outfield, at second base, and some as catcher—and I also ran low hurdles and long distance races for the track team during the spring season.

I played a little football for the North Side High "Steers" team, though I was never very good because I wasn't big enough—128 pounds, give or take a pound. Football was and is an important sport in Texas, and the guys in the "in" group at school always were involved in football. My senior year I mostly played at defensive end, but I also did some running in the backfield as a half-back. I guess you could say I was a combination of end, guard, and tackle: I sat at the *end* of the bench, I would *guard* the water bucket, and I would *tackle* anybody who came near it.

In high school, the guys in sports were a close-knit group. At North Side High there was a great sense of tradition and duty. I, along with my group of friends, joined the Marine Corps Reserves because it seemed like the right thing to do at the time. Looking back, I am confident it was.

Jerry L. Sadler, the North Side High School football team line coach, was also the commandant of the Third 105 Howitzer Battery, United States Marine Corps Reserve, in Fort Worth. On Halloween night in 1955, about eight of my buddies and I decided to attend a Reserve meeting at Coach

Sadler's invitation. We ended up joining the Marine Corps Reserve. I was seventeen.

Peer pressure may have had something to do with my decision to enlist, although I surely wouldn't compare it to going downtown and getting a tattoo. After all, I could change my mind and get a tattoo removed, but when I signed up with the United States Marine Corps, there was no going back. Once a Marine, always a Marine. Semper fidelis—"Always faithful"—the motto of the U.S. Marine Corps is in your blood forever.

The Marine Corps is a tremendous organization. I have enjoyed and cherished my affiliation with the Marines. My enlistment came along at a time in my life when I needed to understand the meaning of loyalty and traditions, how I could earn the respect of others by doing the right things, and why I should work with others for the common good.

I was in the Marine Reserve for six years, after Korea and before Vietnam, during a period in our nation's history when joining the military didn't mean you'd be shipped off to war.

We trained for two weeks each summer at Camp Pendleton in Southern California near San Clemente. At the end of my first summer training, I boarded a train to Fullerton to visit my birth mother, Mary, and her husband, Norm. I had not seen my mother since I was twelve, and knew little of her life in California. I had a chance to meet my two half sisters, Judy and Jan, and my two half brothers, Michael and David. That visit filled a gap in my life and answered a lot of questions for me.

While staying in Fullerton I borrowed the family car and drove to Glendale to visit the Kurtis Kraft plant where Frank Kurtis and his staff designed and built midget and championship race cars. It was quite a thrill. Frank Kurtis was the premier car builder of the time and to visit his shop, where some 550 midget race cars and several Indy winners' cars were built, was a dream come true. Then I went to A. J. Watson's shop, where he was building his first Watson roadster.

As the story goes, Watson competed in races with a Kurtis Kraft car for several seasons. A. J. cut out and disposed of whatever broke on the chassis, and when he was through he had the Watson roadster. It was lighter and faster. So if you wanted to win or be competitive in the late '50s or '60s, you had to have a Watson roadster.

I visited a few more shops and then had an opportunity to go to Western Speedway in Gardena, California, a beautiful little third-of-a-mile dirt track.

The drivers gave a demonstration sprint car race that afternoon. One of the drivers competing in the jalopies that day was Parnelli Jones, a racer who has been a great friend to me throughout my career. I saw him take his first ride in a sprint car that day; a few years later we became friends and raced sprint and Indy cars together. Chuck Hulse, who also became a good friend and fellow racer, also competed that day.

I spent a week out in California before saying goodbye to my family and boarding a Santa Fe Railroad passenger train home. Back in Fort Worth, I met with my unit every other Monday night. We'd learn about military law, the traditions of the Marine Corps—everything you needed to know to be in the service. We also learned the basics of electronics with radio maintenance and practiced marksmanship, an essential element of our Marine training. As an artillery outfit, we were taught how to dismantle a 105mm howitzer.

My stint in the Marine Corps Reserve was important to my development because it taught me discipline. It came at the right time in my life. It wasn't that I had problems; my teenage years were very normal. The Marine Reserves simply helped me grow up.

As teenagers, my friends and I never lacked for something to do; if we weren't playing sports of some kind, we were swimming at Burger's Lake. I was an average student for the most part, though sometimes my teachers would catch me drawing pictures of race cars and airplanes instead of studying in class. Perhaps I knew even at that age that the three—cars, airplanes, and art—would become a big part of my adult life.

Despite those times my mind wandered into areas unrelated to my lessons and classroom studies, I graduated from high school in 1956 as planned.

Upon graduation, I considered going to work out at Consolidated Vultee in the mechanical drawing department. Even though I had not had any extensive art training, I had taken a few mechanical drawing and technical art courses. With that training I could draw blueprints or become a technical illustrator.

Both my granddad and my dad had artistic ability. Each had an artistic eye but seldom created much beyond doodles and cartoons. I carried my artistic talent forward with oil paintings, portraits, pencil sketches, and water colors. My son, John, has artistic abilities as well and earned a college degree in art and design. Perhaps artistic talent is just a natural ability in the genes of the John Rutherfords.

But instead of getting a job, I decided to go to college. I started at Texas Christian University in the fall of 1956, just a few months after I graduated from North Side High School.

I lasted almost a semester at TCU. I came home during Thanksgiving break, pitched my books onto the bed, approached my folks, and blurted out that I didn't want to attend college anymore. College just wasn't for me. In my heart I knew I wanted to race cars—and sooner rather than later.

Only one other career had come close to gaining my attention. As a young-ster growing up in Tulsa, I had entertained thoughts of one day becoming a geologist, specifically a petroleum engineer. Tulsa at that time was considered by many to be the oil capital of the world. As a kid, the idea of looking for oil was intriguing, but by the time I was old enough to really think about pursu-ing that option, driving race cars had captured my full attention. Becoming an engineer no longer appealed to me.

I had made up my mind that the profession I wanted to pursue was racing. But before I could race cars I had to learn how to drive them. I had been steer-ing a car since I was eight years old, when I would sit in my dad's lap as we drove down the highway. I would steer and Dad would work the pedals and the stick shift. Once I was able to reach the pedals and learn the proper foot action, I put it all together quickly. Getting behind the wheel and driving a car felt like a natural act for me.

When I got my learner's permit at age thirteen, I *lived* to drive Mom to the store on Saturdays and the whole family to church on Sundays in the family car, a 1949 Chevrolet Deluxe fastback—a "torpedo back," as it was called. When I was thirteen, Dad bought me an old 1931 Ford Model A coupe, which we kept in the yard at the side of the house. The yard behind our house was wide and more than an acre long, and I would drive the '31 Ford to the back lot to hone my driving skills. I especially enjoyed driving after it had rained because I could slide that coupe around like a race car taking the turns on a dirt track. I learned how to shift, steer, brake, and turn under various conditions. A typical teenager, I searched for any excuse to get behind the wheel and go driving. I received my driver's license when I was fourteen, after failing the written test twice.

My dream of actually racing cars at a track was realized a few years later. We had moved from Tulsa to Fort Worth and my dad, who was the Bardahl dis-tributor for Fort Worth, took me to Riverside Raceway to watch the early-model stock cars race on Saturday nights. The stock cars were not as fast and exciting as the midget cars, and did not pique my interest the way the midget cars had. However, stock cars had a fan following; people loved to watch the stock cars crash into each other.

When I was a teenager in high school my priorities were sports and girls—though not always in that order—and then academics. Racing, always a constant part of my life, was not always a top priority during that time. However, after I graduated from high school in 1956, I joined a local hot rod club, the Idlers, and was a member for three years.

Having saved nearly every cent I had earned from various odd jobs during high school and the summer after I graduated, I was able to buy a 1932 five-window Ford coupe for about $150. The car was in excellent condition except for the interior. I replaced the car's four-cylinder Model B engine with a '56 V-8 Chevrolet engine I had bought for eighty-five dollars. I also installed a three-speed '37 Ford transmission. It was my street rod, and the Idlers occasionally helped me work on it.

Nationally organized drag racing was in its infancy in 1956. As now, drag racing on city streets was at that time both illegal and unsafe. In an attempt to keep us and other hot rod enthusiasts off the street and out of trouble, the Fort Worth Police Department staged drag races at the National Guard base northwest of Fort Worth near Eagle Mountain Lake. The Idlers scheduled drag races there a couple of times a month. The police department's cautionary statement was: "Brag about smokin' somebody during the week, but don't race on the street. Come out here and prove your point."

Their offer worked. Staged drag racing was fun, organized, and it helped strengthen the relationship between the police, the city, and the growing number of hot rodders in the area. Being a member of the Idlers was a great experience for me. I participated in a lot of events with the Idlers, including poker runs with the other clubs in Fort Worth. Poker runs involved traveling in your hot rod to designated areas throughout the city, and then drawing a card from a deck of cards. The best poker hand won some small prize but the real fun of those runs was getting to drive around the area and show off our street rods.

Club members helped one another work on their cars and offered suggestions to help solve problems. We even started building our own rail job—a dragster with exposed, bare-frame rails and little body work. The design really reduced the weight of the dragster, but the aerodynamics suffered because of it.

At one time we probably had fifteen or twenty club members. They ranged in age from the late teens to the late twenties and early thirties. One of the members was a welder by trade, so he had the equipment we needed for our various projects. Our clubhouse was the garage of one of the mainstays of the Idlers, Bobby Lloyd, whose folks let us use their garage. Bobby now has a body shop in River Oaks and has remained a friend. We are both still street rodders and are working on our current street rods—Bobby has a '32 Ford highboy roadster, which has no fenders and is powered by a Pontiac V-8 engine, and I have a 1934 Ford coupe.

I have remained a street rodder since those halcyon days of my youth. "Street rodder" is the familiar term for someone who takes an old car and, with modern equipment, completely rebuilds the car as a street rod. The street rod is an American way of life, an American icon, one might say. There are many street rod devotees, and I am one of them.

My 1934 Ford coupe was advertised locally in Fort Worth, and Betty bought it for me one Christmas. I'm completely redoing the frame, working extensively on the body, and putting new floorboards into the car. It's great fun and very relaxing for someone who likes to weld and pound on metal.

As I pursued my dream of racing professionally, I worked a number of different jobs to support myself after high school. Over time, I saved up enough money to make a down payment on a new 1957 Chevrolet. The '57 Chevy was a popular model then, and in the years since it first came out, it has attained "classic car" status.

One night in 1958, during our regular Idlers club meeting, one of the members said, "I've got to leave a little early tonight to go help my brother put the engine into his dirt track car."

I sat straight up and said, "*Dirt track car?*"

He said, "Yeah, they race every Friday night over in Dallas at the Devil's Bowl Speedway."

The next day they were going to take the car out and run it. I found out where and when, and planned to meet them. My friend's brother had taken the body off his car; just the roll cage on the frame and an engine remained. It was a real hybrid with a V-8 Chevy engine in it. Thinking about that car now, I suppose I should have gotten a tetanus shot before I went to meet them.

My friend's brother ran the car up and down a dirt road out in the country a few times and then asked if I'd like to try it.

He didn't exactly have to twist my arm.

I got into the car and drove it down to the end of the run. I didn't have any experience with a locked rear end in a car—meaning that both rear-drive wheels are turning the same way because the spider gears have been welded together in the rear end, making it a straight axle.

When I got to the end of the run, I didn't know how to turn the car around. It had a transmission and I could put it into reverse, but with a locked rear end it's a difficult task. There wasn't a lot of maneuvering space in which to turn around, so I finally drove it a little farther up the run, locked it up, and made a bootlegger turn. I spun the car out in the middle of the road and then came back in the other direction.

During all this jockeying to turn the car around, I had bent the throttle pedal slightly. It wasn't very sturdy to begin with, and when I mashed the throttle down to come back up the road, it stuck. When I got close to my stopping point I eased my foot up but the car kept going. Of course, I didn't know the car well enough and wasn't familiar with its switches. To make matters worse, I saw that the road forked up ahead. One fork of the road went off to the side and one went straight ahead.

If I had just gone straight I might have had time to figure out how to turn the switch off or do *something*. But by the time I made the decision to go straight, it was too late. I hit the center island. I drove through a patch of tall weeds that were dry and dusty. I hit a dirt mound just right and the car became airborne for a few feet before hitting the ground on its front wheels and bouncing a couple of times. The throttle had come unstuck and I was hard on the brakes.

But I wasn't home free yet. In my rush to get into the car moments earlier, I had neglected to fasten my seat belts. When the car struck the dirt mound, the impact nearly bounced me out of the car. Finally, I ended up back in the seat, got things under control, and stopped the car.

That was my first ride in a race car.

My friend and his brother ran over to me and said, "Oh, boy, we didn't know if you were going to make it or not!" They said that when the car hit the fork in the road and became airborne, they saw me come up out of the seat. When the car landed on its front wheels and kicked up a cloud of dust, all they could see was my butt sticking up through the roll cage. I was still hanging on to the steering wheel, thank God. What a wild ride!

That whole escapade was the shot of incentive I needed. I decided to sell my '57 Chevy and go looking for a race car to build, one that I could run at the Devil's Bowl on Friday nights. I virtually gave away my brand new car, making just enough from the sale to buy a '53 Buick Roadmaster hardtop for cheap transportation.

My search for a race car ended when I found a '32 Chevrolet coupe in Grapevine, Texas, that had actually been a race car at one time. There was much work to be done to make it conform to the rules then in effect. With the help of the guys in the Idlers, I built my race car in the winter of 1958–59. When I finished building the car, it was the realization of a longtime dream. I started racing in April of 1959 at the Devil's Bowl Speedway in Dallas. I was twenty-one and had no idea where this first step would take me.

The start of a bad day at Eldora Speedway—Rossburg, Ohio, April 3, 1966.

My heart-stopping ascent over the guardrail at Eldora Speedway, April 3, 1966.

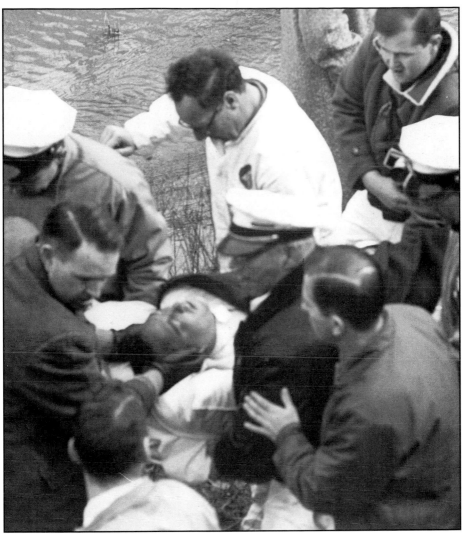

Dr. Ward Dunseth holds my head as they take me from the car to the ambulance moments after the crash.

Me and Don Branson, a.k.a. "Teamie."

On the road to recovery: clowning around with A. J. Watson at the Indianapolis Motor Speedway.

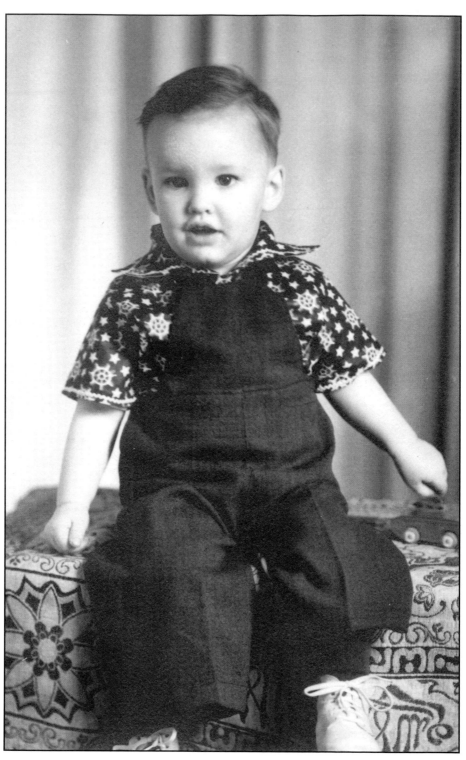

Me at about eighteen months.

Me, at age three, in my Army Air Corps uniform (1941).

Sister Beverly, age four, in an orange-crate 2 x 4 midget racer I built while living in Abilene, Texas.

Nine years old, sitting in my dad's midget car in Tulsa, Oklahoma.

With Wayne, in September 1956.

Semper Fidelis: in my Marine Corps Reserves uniform, 1956.

Idlers Auto Club Headquarters.

The Idlers Auto Club, 1957. I'm in the back row, third from left.

Sanding down a dragster in the Idlers Club garage, November 1957.

*Me in the
first race car
I ever built
at the
Devil's Bowl
Speedway, in
Dallas,
Texas, 1959.*

In Charlie Cleveland's super-modified from Covington, Kentucky (Lawrenceburg, Indiana in July 1960).

Me in the first sprint car I ever drove (owned by Merle Heath), New Bremen, Ohio, 1960.

☆ CHAPTER 4 ☆

On My Own

The thought of racing a car on a dirt track like those I had seen as a little boy seemed as exciting as ever to me. I decided that it was what I wanted to do, despite the fact that the financial rewards registered at the bottom of the scale.

To be able to race cars, I had to find a salaried job. From the late 1950s through the early 1960s, I held a number of odd jobs to support myself as I worked my way up the ranks of racing.

Early in my racing career, art helped sustain me during the off-season winter months. I landed a job as a commercial artist, making silk screens and signs for a family business, May Advertising. It was my first and only pursuit of art—which has always been just a hobby—as avocation. As much as I enjoyed the creative environment and working at May, I knew it could never replace my desire for a racing career.

In 1959, before the end of my first season of racing, I went to work for Moe Meador, an Oldsmobile dealer in Fort Worth. We developed a friendship while I worked in his dealership that has lasted to this day. I was employed at Meador Olds in the new car "make-ready" area. When new cars were unloaded off the trucks and brought in to the dealership, another worker and I would clean the cars and prepare them for display on the showroom floor or the sales lot. Believe me, there's a lot to be done to a car even when it's new. They're not shiny and clean when they come in from the factory; in fact, they are rather dirty.

In 1960 I again changed jobs. For a brief time I was what was called a "hot-shot." I worked with a number of other young people on the second floor of the Montgomery Wards store in Fort Worth, filling catalog orders. I'd take written orders, roller skate to the area where the items were stored, pull the orders, and then skate back to a central station. There the orders would be processed and sent down to the customers. Because I was a pretty good skater, I was a natural for the job—one of the most entertaining jobs I've ever had.

Yet all that time, I was angling for my dream of racing as a full-time profession, though I didn't know exactly how to go about it. I had just enough money to live on, and I had saved some thanks to the grubstake I earned when I sold my first race car.

When I started driving on the professional level, racing was everything I thought it would be. I certainly didn't know all I needed to know about driving a race car when I first started: I wasn't familiar with the car's energy forces or how to maintain control of them, and I had to learn how to drive and handle the car as I went. But when I flung an eighteen hundred- to two thousand-pound car into a corner on wet dirt, I learned real quick. It was a baptism by fire.

I was green, but man how I loved it—the smell of the burning fuel and smoking tires, the roar of the engines, the flying dirt clods and dust so thick it choked you, the bugs in the lights, the feel of my heart pumping hard as I narrowly avoided clipping another driver or allowing a driver to clip me.

Running on the dirt—pitching the car, sliding it around the turns, and then accelerating hard down the straightaways—just felt natural to me. Learning the intricacies of the car, how to read the track, which tires to use on different kinds of tracks, which gears to use and when—these things I picked up over time. I relished every moment of it. I devoured it all. It was my life.

While some dirt drivers prefer a hard, slick, smooth track that they can drive like they can a pavement track with sand, I, like most dirt drivers, liked a heavy track. I always enjoyed the cushion of a moist track, which allowed me to really get a hold of the track and propel the car faster. Plus, the technique racers used on a heavy track was a little more on the edge than the technique used on a hard, slick track.

Forty years ago, promoters would sometimes have their crews spread calcium chloride on the track's surface before they watered it. The dirt would then absorb the calcium chloride. The evening races would begin, and at sundown, just when it seemed the track was drying out, the temperature would drop and the higher humidity would cause the calcium chloride to act as a moistening agent. The track would once again be moist—the way most drivers liked it. Grounds crews today still wet the tracks, but it doesn't last long in most cases. If it's a hot summer night, the moisture evaporates quickly. Most of the tracks these days don't use calcium chloride—they are primarily hard-slick. Sprint cars today have a wing on top, similar to an upside-down airplane wing, that creates a downforce and helps the car grip the ground. Now there's no real need for the heavy, moist tracks I ran on, although most drivers still prefer them.

Track preparation is not what it used to be. When I was dirt track racing, the grounds crew would start preparing the track at noon Friday for a Saturday night race. They would wet the track down, disc it up, scarify it, water it, and then start wheel-packing it. During the day on Saturday they'd disc and water it again. In the evening the push trucks for the cars would show up, along with the teams in their trailers, and everybody would wheel-pack— drive clockwise around the track, the opposite direction that the cars raced. We did this because tires tend to push the mix of mud and soft dirt out in waves, so that when the tires on the race cars would spin, they didn't dig up the track. This technique kept the track smoother longer. There's a real art to setting up a dirt track. I learned this art running on so many dirt tracks early in my career and watching crews prepare them.

In those first few weeks of racing professionally I decided to let a veteran driver race my car. A veteran could check the car out to see how it was handling and could advise me on what I could do to make the car better. The veteran I chose was Clyde Daniels, whose car had had problems early in the afternoon and wasn't quite ready for the next race.

After I ran my car well enough in the heat race to qualify for the feature, Clyde agreed to drive my car in the race.

I put Clyde in the car, and when they dropped the green flag I got a charge out of watching my own creation running around on that dirt track. I had put a V-8 Chevrolet engine in my '32 Chevrolet coupe and had set the battery inside a frame that I strapped in behind the driver's seat. Evidently my welding skills were not as sharp as my racing abilities, because the battery fell out of the car. It was hanging by the cables off the posts and was bouncing between the car and the dirt track. I watched in horror as the battery broke up, the car shut down, and Clyde pulled the car in. The battery was just hanging there out of the car, nothing more than bits and pieces.

The next weekend, another driver came up to me, holding what appeared to be a brand new pair of Levi's. They had little holes all over them—it looked like someone had shot them up with a twelve-gauge. Billy Jack Casper, the driver, looked me in the eye and said, "You owe me a pair of pants."

Billy Jack had been driving behind Clyde when the battery came apart and fell out of my car. The battery acid had sprayed back—all over Billy Jack's brand new Levi's. It had just *ruined* them. That was my first casualty in racing—a pair of Levi's that belonged to Billy Jack Casper.

Dad came to see me race a few times at the Devil's Bowl, but Mom wouldn't attend. It was tough to sell her on my racing. Years earlier she had seen a driver killed on the track in front of us at the Tulsa midget car races. We were sitting near turn 4, right in front of the grandstand. In the middle of turns 3 and 4, the driver's car flipped, crashed, and stopped no more than two hundred feet from us. It was not a pretty sight.

Racing is dangerous. Mom didn't have to hear it from her friends or read about it in the newspapers to understand that. And despite the low opinion some people had of race car drivers, she was concerned more for my safety than about a few of her friends perceiving her older son as "one of those dirt track bums." Even after I started to enjoy modest success, I think she was still hoping I'd outgrow my desire to race cars for a living. She was openly critical of my career choice, plain and simple.

My dad, realizing that I was an adult and that I would make my own choices, helped ease the situation. He said to her, "Either we're gonna join him or lose him."

I think Dad secretly loved every minute of my racing—after all, I was very much like him—but he would never admit that to Mom. Dad knew I had no thoughts of turning back. He understood that I loved racing and that I wanted to make a career of it.

Mom gradually mellowed about my career choice. The more years I raced without being seriously injured, the less tense she seemed to be about it. I doubt that she ever really stopped hoping that I would quit racing. She just wasn't vocal about it. Instead of hearing, "Don't you think you want to do something else?" all the time, I simply heard the occasional sigh whenever the subject of my racing came up.

Despite her criticism of my decision to race cars for a living, Mom was always among my biggest supporters. She was a mother whose son happened to be hurtling around a racetrack at breakneck speeds. It was natural for her to be concerned.

I raced at the Devil's Bowl Speedway every Friday night for a season and a half. But the thrills didn't come cheap, and finally I decided that operating my own race car was too expensive. In 1960 I parked my car and started driving for Aubrey Hodge, a car owner from Dallas. It was a whole new experience for me.

Hodge's car usually had a lot of troubles with its engine—an International six-cylinder pickup truck engine. I'd always heard that this type of engine was tough because International would pour the engine blocks, get them all set up and machined, and then dump them into a field for a couple of years. Pure nature was used to harden the blocks; in the summer heat the blocks would expand and in the winter cold they would contract. The steel would harden like this over a period of several years. When they peaked, the folks at International would finish all the machining and then build the engines. These engines were strong, having been made with really "seasoned" blocks. I don't know how long International has been using this system, but the method has its supporters.

Aubrey took his International engine block to a local machine shop to have it bored—have the cylinders cleaned out. But he had to go from one machine shop to another to get the job done. Why? Because the steel in every cylinder was so hard that it would break their boring bars. At every shop they told him to take his damn block out of their shop and never come back. It took eight machine shops to finally get all six cylinders bored.

But when Aubrey got it right, that thing would fly. I don't recall ever winning a feature race with the car, but I did win some heat races. Not only did that experience give me confidence, it also taught me things about technique and handling that by today's standards one might call primitive; but it was grass roots, dirt track racing.

I also helped maintain the car. I trailered it to Dallas every week, and Aubrey would meet me at the track, tune it, and work on it. I'd race it at the old Devil's Bowl Speedway and on occasion in Waco, Houston, and even Texarkana.

I drove for Aubrey for half a season. The time I spent at the Devil's Bowl Speedway in 1959 and 1960 allowed me to form many friendships, friendships based on a mutual love of racing and cars. It also brought in a little money—from $4.50 to $10 per race. Those were some big paydays, huh?

One of the first people to befriend me was Shady McWhorter, another racer who had a shop in nearby Haltom City, where he fixed automatic transmissions. After I first learned about the races at the Devil's Bowl Speedway, Shady's shop was one of several places I'd frequent just to see race cars. I would look at the other guys' cars and study how they were built. I cataloged that knowledge and applied it when I was building my own race car with the help of the Idlers.

Shady was always happy to talk with me and offer tips on what I could or should do. He would let me sit in his car and observe where everything was placed, how it was made, and how it all worked. Shady was a generous guy, and a very smooth driver himself. He undoubtedly could have made it in big-time racing, and, in my opinion, would have been very good. However, he never pursued more than local racing because he liked staying home and running his transmission shop. Sadly, Shady passed away a few years ago after suffering a heart attack.

I met another driver, Jimmy McElreath, through Shady, and though I was just an inexperienced kid and Jimmy had years of racing experience behind him, we developed an instant and lifelong friendship. Jimmy started racing in 1945, so when I first met him in '59 he was one of the top drivers at the Devil's Bowl Speedway. He lived in Arlington, between Dallas and Fort Worth. Although later Jimmy and I became rivals on the racetrack, we traveled around together early in my career.

Halfway through the 1960 season, Jimmy and I left the Devil's Bowl Speedway for the Midwest to make our fame and fortune. Our decision to pursue racing in the Midwest turned out to be a good career move. I even began to make some money—not a lot, but enough for me to live on. The financial rewards would get better and better. It just took time.

☆ CHAPTER 5 ☆

My Scuffling Days

Jimmy McElreath and I wanted to break into racing's big time, and because the Midwest was a hotbed of racing activity in the early 1960s, going there seemed like the right move for the veteran and the rookie to make.

In May of 1960, I was given my first opportunity to race in the Midwest. I secured a ride in a super-modified stock car and raced at Eldora Speedway in Rossburg, Ohio. The car owner, who also owned a machine shop in St. Marys, Ohio, didn't have a driver, so I convinced him to let me drive his car that afternoon.

The day started off on a strange foot. The car I was set to drive was parked in the infield, where the pits were situated, in the third turn. I drove Jimmy's truck around back and parked between the track and the main grandstand. I got out of the car and started disrobing to put on my driver's suit. When I stripped down to my skivvies, I heard these faint cheers, whistles, and catcalls. I thought, *What in the world is going on?* I turned around and looked up into the third turn, where a group of people was watching me undress.

I then realized that the promoter had terraced the grounds outside the racetrack so the fans could park their cars and trucks and campers just as they would at a drive-in theater. Folks had a great view from up there, and they were all watching me change my clothes, just smiling and waving at me. All I could do was smile weakly, wave back, and put on my uniform.

Welcome to the Midwest, Johnny Rutherford.

Before Jimmy and I began our odyssey on the dirt tracks of the Midwest, we took a little side trip to Indianapolis in May of 1960. Jimmy and I, along with Jimmy's wife, Shirley, and some of the other racers and car owners associated with the Devil's Bowl Speedway in Dallas, went to the Indy 500.

About three or four days prior to the great event I attended the Little 500—which is almost an institution in Indiana—as a spectator. The Little 500 is run in conjunction with the Indianapolis 500 and is held in Anderson, a few miles northeast of Indianapolis. The starting field consists of thirty-three sprint cars that run five hundred laps around a quarter-mile, high-banked, paved racetrack. That's a lot of laps around a little racetrack. But the word *little* hardly begins to describe the annual event. It's a great spectator race.

The 1960 Indy itself was some race. I watched from the infield on the backstretch as Rodger Ward, Jim Rathmann, and Johnny Thompson battled it out for the checkered flag. The lead kept shifting throughout the race, and several times in the last twenty or thirty laps. Thompson's engine finally gave up with ten laps to go and then Jim and Rodger really dueled. Rathmann edged out Ward for the win with just a few laps to go. It was a close, hard-fought race.

During the 1960 Indy a temporary scaffolding built for viewing in the infield collapsed during the pace lap before the start of the race. Seventy-five to one hundred people were on the three-level scaffolding that day—some were killed and several others were injured. Unbeknownst to me at the time, Betty was there and was pressed into action in her capacity as a nurse.

Jimmy McElreath and I started racing super-modifieds and whatever else we could get rides in after we arrived in Covington, Kentucky, just across the Ohio River from Cincinnati. There were no contracts in my earliest days in racing; it was a handshake deal. You maintained your position on the team by performing well.

Jimmy, a bricklayer by trade, and I were hired to do some work for a construction company whose owner, Charlie Cleveland, fielded the race car I would drive. For a couple of months, Jimmy drove a car for Charlie's brother, Fred Cleveland. We raced on tracks throughout southern Indiana and Ohio with minor success.

The super-modifieds were similar to sprints, but they weren't as agile. Super-modified cars have tubular frames like those used in sprint cars, but they also have abbreviated car bodies and roofs. A super-modified is an open-wheeled, single-seat race car powered by a domestic V-8 engine. Some of the nicknames we gave them reflected their looks and their power: "bugs," "super-bugs," and even "super-bombs."

Even though I was racing with little success, I was learning a great deal during those early days in the Midwest. During a race in Lawrenceburg, Indiana, I got a little too high on the track while chasing the leader. The track did not have a guardrail and the right side of the car slipped over the edge, dug in, and began flipping. I was slammed around in the cockpit, and the watch my parents gave me when I graduated high school was smashed to bits. I still have the pieces to remind me to never wear a watch while racing.

In mid-August of 1960, Jimmy was offered a sprint car ride in Oskaloosa, Iowa. We were traveling together, so of course I left with him. Racing doesn't lend itself to normal situations—like keeping jobs for extended periods of time. We were two very determined drivers. Had Jimmy and I carried business cards, they would have read, "Have desire, will race—anywhere, anytime."

When we got to Oskaloosa I started looking for a ride, but there were no vacancies in the cars that day. I watched Jimmy race that night. I was happy for him, but I was pretty down that I wasn't out there racing, too.

The next race was in La Crosse, Wisconsin, on August 24. Jimmy had secured a ride with the same owner and the same sprint car, and once again I was looking for a ride. Finances were getting tight. I was running out of money, and there was a payment due on my new Chevrolet Bel-Air two-door, which was parked in my parents' garage back in Fort Worth. If I couldn't secure a ride in La Crosse, I had just enough money to buy a bus ticket back to Texas from wherever Jimmy could drop me off. Once in Fort Worth, I would again look for a job and try to earn enough money to pay my debts and get back to racing the following season.

For the moment, we were in La Crosse. I went to the pit gate, walked up to the registrar, and asked him if there were any open cars. Jimmy had signed in ahead of me. Because he'd had a good run in Oskaloosa, everyone was congratulating him. The registrar looked at me like I was the last person he wanted to see, and said, "Yeah, there's two cars without drivers. The owners are here. Go talk to them."

He told me the car numbers and the names of the owners, and I told him that if I could get a ride with one of them I'd come back to buy my license. He gave me a skeptical look as I went through the pit gate. I found both cars and eventually picked the car I thought would be best. It wasn't any raving beauty and didn't have a lot of chrome on it—it was just a basic race car. But that was all I needed.

An older gentleman was polishing the car when I approached him. I said, "I understand you don't have a driver." He looked at me and said, "Well, I don't know. My driver said he might not make it today, but he also said he might. So I'm kind of waitin' to see if he shows up."

"Well, if he doesn't," I asked, "can I drive your car? Let me warm it up."

He studied me for a moment and then asked, "Did you ever drive one of these things before?"

Without missing a beat I said, "Yeah."

"Whereabouts?"

"Down in Texas."

He clearly knew there wasn't a lot of sprint car racing in Texas. But he said, "Okay, if my driver doesn't show up when it's warm-up time, I'll let you warm the thing up. By the way, my name's Merle Heath."

"Nice to meet you. My name's Johnny Rutherford."

We shook hands and I left the pit to sign in with the registrar. When I signed in, the registrar checked my driver's license. I was twenty-two at the time and looked very young. Before the race, even the officials seemed to be casting a wary eye on me. It was making me a little nervous. Sure enough, later that afternoon just before warm-ups, the race organizer came up to me and asked, "You sure you're twenty-one?"

"Yes, sir, I am," I said.

"Uh-huh. Well, tell you what. I'm gonna send you out in this first group and we're gonna watch you. I'll let you know whether you can run or not after I see you warm up."

A sprint car is a lightweight, high horse-powered vehicle that explodes when you mash the throttle. Driving a sprint car is like slapping a mountain lion on the behind with a handful of cockleburs—you just better be ready.

To the casual observer of that era, sprint cars resembled Indy cars with their open wheels, open cockpits, front engines, and single seats. But don't let that fool you into believing that sprint cars were second-class citizens in the world of auto racing. Or that sprints were any less challenging to drive. The sprint cars that we raced were pound for pound and inch for inch the most powerful race cars at the time. They were designed for racing on dirt and paved oval tracks that were usually a half-mile long, sometimes five-eighths of a mile. Those sprint cars were *fast*. In the early 1960s, for example, the Offy or Chevy engines that powered the sprints could work up to a horsepower of almost three hundred. We could get a sprint car that weighed fifteen hundred to eighteen hundred pounds well past 100 miles an hour on those short straightaways—in the 110–115 mph range, in fact.

If you've never seen a sprint car race, close your eyes and picture this: Dozens of sprint cars are flying around a half-mile dirt track at more than a hundred miles an hour. The drivers are standing on the power practically the whole time—lap after noisy lap—and this causes the cars' tails to whip out into hard slides that send dirt cascading all over the place. That's sprint car racing, and in my first warm-up I discovered firsthand what it was all about.

Though I'd never even driven a sprint car before, I did know how to start one, and I knew how to get it in gear. Having driven super-modifieds, which were similar to sprint cars, and having attended many sprint car races, I wasn't completely unprepared as I slid behind the wheel of Merle Heath's sprint car.

As I drove around the track, I thought to myself, *Boy, this is a helluva car*. Sprint cars don't weigh much and they don't have flywheels on the engines, so they wrap up fast. This car had a Chevrolet V-8 engine in a Dryer chassis—it was built by the legendary "Pop" Dryer—and it was exhilarating. I wore a leather mask that hung down under my goggles to protect my face from the rocks, dirt, and other flying objects. When I was driving super-modifieds it wasn't necessary to anchor the mask at the base of the goggles, so I had no inclination to do so before I got behind the wheel of the sprint car. When I gave that little tiger a pitch and slid into the first turn, my leather mask flipped up over my goggles so I couldn't see anything. I jerked my goggles and mask down and managed to finish the warm-ups without them. By the end of the warm-up my face was covered with dust and dirt.

After the warm-up, Frank Winkley, the International Motor Contest Association promoter, came over and nodded to Merle. I raced the car for the rest of the day, though it was almost a very short day.

In my first race, the heat race, I nearly crashed.

The racetrack was built on the side of a hill, and to make the back straightaway the grounds crew had pushed the dirt from the infield back. Then they brought in more dirt. The crew hadn't put much water on the track, so it was pretty dusty.

I was starting in the back, and when the green flag was dropped and we pitched it into the first turn, I suddenly couldn't see through all the dust. I was just hanging on as I tried to peer through the dust and dirt, but I couldn't see anything other than a glint of chrome off the car in front of me. I could only *hear* what was going on, and even then I could only make out growling engines and exhaust.

I managed to get out of the throttle and coast, hoping to see something. All of a sudden the dust cleared just as I was cresting the edge of the backstretch. It was a fairly steep grade off the back of the track down to the normal terrain level, and there was no guardrail. There was nothing to stop me. I started to turn back but the right rear dropped off and I knew that if I tried to get back onto the track I'd high-center the car and maybe even roll it. So I simply turned and went down the hill. I bounced toward the third turn—outside the racetrack. My plan was to find a place where I could try to drive back up onto the track.

But the hill was covered in weeds and grass, and the weeds kept getting taller and the dust kept getting thicker, and by then I had reached the third turn. I could see there was no place for me to reenter the track. I yanked it out of gear, shut the fuel off, and killed the engine.

It was real quiet down there. I sat for a moment before I got out and started climbing up the bank. When I reached the top, I looked over toward turn 2, where I'd gone off the track, and it seemed like World War III had erupted. The wreckers and ambulances had their lights flashing, and all the people from the pits were running full tilt to the spot where I had disappeared. They must have thought I had sailed off into the blue. They probably expected to find me lying down there, injured or dead.

Just as I reached the edge of the track, two of the drivers, A. J. Shepherd and Leroy Neumeyer, saw me at the same time and pointed over their windshields. I stood there a little embarrassed because my car was sitting down at the base of the hill. They had to winch the car out, pull it back up the hill, and restart me in the race.

Frank Winkley later said, "Well, kid, last year Pete Folse, the National IMCA Champion, went off there and did the same thing. You're not the first one."

Hearing that, I felt a little better about my own mishap. Despite my misfortune, I had raced in my first sprint car, and it was electrifying.

I raced well, all things considered. I finished fifth in the feature that after-noon and either seventh or eighth in the night race. I earned $180 for my part, and in 1960 that wasn't too bad for a day's work. I made enough for my car payment and did not have to take the bus back to Fort Worth.

I just whistled and thought, *How long has this been going on?*

Merle liked the way I drove his car, so he let me run it at Cedar Rapids the following week. We had some success that summer; we made some money. And that was the name of the game.

It is interesting to note that in the weeks leading up to the 1999 Indianapolis 500, Duke Hindahl, who was supposed to drive the sprint car I ended up driving that night in La Crosse, looked me up at the Speedway. I couldn't believe it. He was the guy who inadvertently gave me my first oppor-tunity to drive a sprint car.

Jimmy McElreath and I shared many adventures in those days. We traveled from town to town in his 1951 Ford pickup. Boy, that truck was strong. With its 1950 Oldsmobile V-8 engine it had a lot of poke, even with a camper on the back that housed two bunks, a propane stove, and room for our gear.

After Jimmy had been driving for a while it would be my turn to take the wheel, and vice versa. I recall one incident when we were driving through Iowa, and I can tell you this: Iowa is not, as some poorly informed folks would have you believe, flat.

The roads undulate. There are turns. There are some fairly steep hills. There are blind spots on the secondary roads. In the evenings the farmers drive their pickups only about as fast as they're used to driving their tractors—five miles an hour, at best.

One night I was driving while Jimmy was asleep in the camper. When I crested one of those hills, a guy in his pickup, going way too slow, was right in front of me. I slammed on the brakes, and I heard McElreath go thump-thump-blump as he rolled to the front of the bunk and hit his head on the end of the camper.

I was in the cab of the pickup, but I could hear him in there, cussing at me. "Rutherford! What the hell do you think you're doin'?!"

Many a time we'd bathe in a lake, river, or creek somewhere off the road, because we carried only enough water to drink and to wash our hands and faces. We learned to be quite inventive about our bathing practices. One time we parked the truck and started down toward the water in our bathing trunks. Each of us had a washrag and Jimmy was carrying the bar of soap. We got to the edge of the water and Jimmy picked up a two-by-four about sixteen inches long. I asked him, "What are you going to do with that?"

"You'll see," he replied.

We waded into the calm water up to our chests. Jimmy floated the board on the water and set the soap on top of it. He soaked his washrag, grabbed the soap, lathered it up, and then set the soap back down on the board.

"Okay. It's your turn," he said.

I started cracking up. American ingenuity in the form of a floating soap dish.

Road food was somewhat limited compared with what travelers can choose from today, and we weren't exactly raking in the big bucks at the time, so we usually bought groceries at a mom-and-pop store and made our own sandwiches along the way. We would buy a half-pound of baloney, a loaf or two of bread, and some mayonnaise and mustard. That was it—baloney sandwiches for breakfast, lunch, and dinner.

Jimmy and I consumed more baloney sandwiches than the human body should ingest in a lifetime, much less over a period of a couple of years. Later, when we started making a little more money, White Castle hamburgers were the order of the day. If you ever want to test your constitution, buy a bag of those burgers day in and day out. I get heartburn even now just thinking about the stuff we lived on back in those days. A typical racer's breakfast was a cheeseburger and a Coke. How we survived those years on so little nourishment is beyond me. But McElreath and I did it. All the racers did.

A whole book could be written on the history of the International Motor Contest Association or IMCA. The organization was a holdover from the 1930s and 1940s, before World War II. Most of the cars that we raced in IMCA had no roll bars, and none of them had cages. Some of the older cars even had wire wheels and four-cylinder Model A-type engines. I think of them as the last gasp of a dying breed of race cars. Still, it was good racing and a great training ground, with a lot of fun mixed in. I learned a great deal from my experiences in IMCA, not only about racing, but about people.

IMCA prided itself on the fact that its drivers hailed from all over the country. The organization boasted drivers from California, Minnesota, Massachusetts, Florida, and the Southwest. It was just a carnival atmosphere—literally.

We raced on tracks in front of the grandstands at carnivals and fairs, where the IMCA-sanctioned races were always set up. Before the races were to start, some drivers and mechanics would walk up and down the midway to play "carny" games or go to girlie shows. We met many people who were members of the fairs, carnivals, and shows because we traveled the same roads and played the same events as they did. The racers and their cars were part of the entertainment package being offered to the public.

After we had been to enough of these fairs and carnivals, we felt like part of the family, and began to understand the lingo and ways of the "barkers."

Anyone who has attended a fair or a carnival knows that barkers are the men and women who stand out in front of a booth or tent and try to persuade people to throw the ball at the pins or pick up a gun and hit moving targets. After months of being verbally accosted, we grew tired of the barkers. Finally, one old-timer told us that all we had to do when we walked down the midway was say, "I'm with it." He said that then the barker would holler down the line at the other folks walking by and would leave you alone. In fact, no one would ever bother you again.

It worked. The next time I walked down the midway at a carnival, one of the barkers looked at me and yelled, "Hey, there, Ace, step right up here and fire this ball at the pins! Win a bear for your sweetie!"

I yelled back, "I'm with it." The barker simply turned and yelled to another guy in the crowd, "Hey, there, young man! You look like you've got a strong pitchin' arm! Step right up and show the world that soup bone of yours! Win a bear for your sweetie!"

Armed with that knowledge, we racers were no longer bothered by the barkers. Of course, sometimes we'd want to show off our arms or our coordination or our strength, especially if one of us had a date that night. However, although we had plenty of opportunities, dating wasn't a big priority for many of us, because we were always on the move and racing all the time. As drivers, we were, to some extent, celebrities. But we weren't filled with ourselves. This was the late 1950s, early 1960s, and professional race car drivers weren't in the public eye as much as they are today. We loved what we were doing and, especially for those of us still new to the professional side of the sport, our lives were pretty much "eat, breathe, sleep racing."

We sometimes even took an active role in promoting the races. We'd go into a town a day or two before the race and work with the promoter to get area residents excited about coming to the races. Occasionally we would be interviewed by an announcer at the local radio station, or by a reporter at the local newspaper. In doing that, we started building up our names throughout the Midwest.

I met some of the thrill show drivers at those Midwest fairs and carnivals. The Lucky Teeter thrill shows and the Joey Chitwood thrill shows, as well as some of the lesser-known shows, occasionally played the same date as the racers played. We'd race in the afternoon and they'd put on their show at night under the lights in front of the grandstand. To drum up excitement for their shows, they'd sometimes put on a demonstration during a break between our heat races that day.

In the 1960s, thrill show drivers—in their stock cars and at speed—would perform ramp-to-ramp jumps or sail through rings of fire. Another crowd-pleaser was the "high skis," in which the driver tipped his car up on two wheels and drove around the track.

Although the subject jokingly came up now and then, thankfully we never traded places. The thrill car drivers did reveal some of their trade secrets to us, however, including how to perform the high skis. In fact, I met Al Swanson, the guy who invented that technique. I even recall performing that feat in a few sprint car races, though unintentionally. If I drove into a corner too hard and hooked a rut, the car would "bicycle"—go up on two wheels—for several yards. Of course, you don't win sprint car races by getting behind the wheel of a car with a souped-up Chevy engine and driving it around a dirt track on only two wheels.

The carnies, the thrill show drivers, and the rest were a colorful lot. Sometimes we'd pass one another on the highway and they'd motion for me to follow them to the next exit. We'd turn off and go have coffee together and shoot the breeze for a while. The coffee would fortify us for the next three hundred miles or so. We were a happy group during those times, and we all enjoyed the racing, the thrills, and the camaraderie.

IMCA incorporated two groups: Auto Racing, Inc. and International Speedways, Inc. Auto Racing, Inc. was headed up by the promoter Frank Winkley, who had his own group of IMCA cars and drivers. Al Sweeney was the other head honcho. At some point, Sweeney and Winkley divided between themselves the county and state fair races around the Midwest.

At that time you could run with both organizations, so even if you pledged allegiance to one group, you could still run a race for the other if yours wasn't running on a given night. Winkley had the races at the Minnesota State Fair and Sweeney had those at the Iowa State Fair in Des Moines. The races at both fairs ran fairly close to each other, allowing the racers to run for both groups. We used to run an afternoon race at the Minnesota State Fair for Winkley and then drive down to Des Moines and race at the Iowa State Fair for Sweeney. Then we'd drive back to Minnesota and race there. We traveled a lot, but in doing so we had more opportunities to race and to pick up some winnings.

Years before Winkley and Sweeney, other promoters pretty much set the tone for IMCA, particularly Alex Sloan. In the 1930s, Sloan essentially owned all the cars. He would hire a train and load all his race cars on it and go from town to town. The train would pull into a station, where he would fire up all his cars and make a lot of noise to gain attention for an upcoming race.

Then the drivers Sloan had hired would drive off the flatcars and motor through the town to stir up interest among the townsfolk. He'd mount a speaker on his truck so he could announce his races to anyone within earshot. "Races at the fairgrounds tonight at seven! Come on out and enjoy all the speed and thrills of professional auto racing! Bring the whole family!"

If one of Sloan's drivers couldn't make it to a certain town because of work or because his wife was having a baby, Sloan would hire a local driver. Some of the drivers of that era actually got their start that way and then began moving up the ranks of racing.

It was a real carny operation. Nowadays people have more diversions to keep themselves occupied in their free time, but back then it was a big deal when the circus or IMCA came to town.

I wouldn't trade those days for anything. And yet, quiet moments were hard to come by. I would run a night race in Oskaloosa, Iowa, for example, and then drive to Austin, Minnesota, for a race the next night. In fact, when I was racing cars in the Midwest I must have raced at almost every county fair, state fair, and free fair of note that you'd care to mention. Having focused my attention on sprint cars, I generally raced only on weekends.

In those days, if a driver raced a midget car, he could run virtually nonstop. Midget car drivers could travel to towns within a two hundred-mile radius of home and, because the tracks and promoters staggered their dates, they could run every night of the week.

For a time, I raced either sprint cars or midget cars three or four nights a week. Eventually that schedule proved to be a bit much, so for the most part I limited my racing to the weekends. Even though I usually raced sprints and midgets, I occasionally ran the early-model stock cars such as the '37 and '39 Fords and sometimes the modified or super-modified stocks. I kept busy, learned my trade, and made a little money here and there. I traveled and raced a lot.

Sometimes in traveling between races I would grow tired and would have to pull down into the grassy area between the highway and the cornfield. I'd open both back doors of the car and stretch out across the backseat. On a nice warm summer evening, if there's no breeze, you can actually hear the corn grow. It wheezes and snaps and crackles. At first I thought I was just hearing things, but later I asked a farmer about it and he said, "Oh, yeah, you can hear corn grow if it's a still night. Corn makes a lot of noise."

It was a peaceful respite in my hectic schedule. At least for a few hours I could get away from the din in my ears and the dust in my eyes and the smoke in my throat. I'd just close my eyes and let nature lull me to sleep.

In fact, fatigue was probably my biggest enemy during my IMCA days. In those days, the interstate system had yet to take hold in our country, and people still pretty much traveled from place to place on two-lane blacktops or four-lane, limited-access roads. I was either driving those roads or the racetracks. Traveling so much made staying awake a real challenge. Thus it was a good idea to pair up with another driver so you could share driving duties.

During that period of my life, I tried to get home to Fort Worth whenever my chaotic racing schedule allowed it. For example, I would be racing at Shreveport, Louisiana, toward the end of the season. Then I could go home to Fort Worth and catch up with my family and friends. My sister and my brother were starting school, and sometimes I was sad that I wasn't around more to see them grow up and to share in their experiences. However, it was fun for us to catch up on all they had done and accomplished since the last time I was home.

The only trouble was, my visits couldn't last too long. That was especially true by late 1961. As the IMCA season came to a close, the winter racing season in California would be about ready to start. I would leave for Los Angeles or El Centro, down near the U.S.-Mexico border, and run sprint cars for the California Racing Association in half a dozen events. Although it was truly a vagabond's life, it was also a way to make some extra money. It wasn't for everybody, but it was what I chose to do—and secretly, I enjoyed it all.

My little brother, Wayne, was enamored with my racing. In fact, he raced some midgets and sprints when he was in his early twenties. Our dad bought a modified sprint car and he and Wayne raced it in Dallas at the Devil's Bowl Speedway. My brother is still quite a racing enthusiast.

Another such enthusiast, and a real character, was a man by the name of Diz Wilson. He was one of the famous old IMCA car owners, and was based in Mitchell, Indiana.

I worked and drove for Diz in 1961. I drove one of his three cars, all of which had Offenhauser engines in them. My car was the old Pat Clancy six-wheeler from Indianapolis, a rather famous car. It had four rear-drive wheels and the two normal front wheels to steer it. It was a big old car that had been cut down to a two-axle, but it handled pretty nicely because it was long-wheel based and had a powerful 270 Offy.

For the most part I kept it up myself. I would take the engine out after a race and Diz would sharpen it up. I cleaned up the car and changed all the tires. I learned what the car needed to help us win races. Diz would say, "We're goin' to Kansas City, so we'll need this tire and that tire and those parts," and I would do the work on the car. Maintaining that car and learning what made it tick was probably the single biggest learning experience of my racing career. Diz was a great teacher.

Since the other two drivers often weren't around because they had full-time jobs, Diz would assign me the task of practice running the finished cars out on a country road. This allowed us to get the cars hot enough to leak oil if they were going to, and check for anything else that might be wrong with them before we actually ran them in races. It was perhaps a primitive testing method, but it worked.

Diz would nudge the push truck against the rear bumper of the race car to drive me down the street, across the highway, and onto a blacktop country road. When we got to the road, Diz would slow down, and I'd lock the rear tires up, jam the car in gear, start the thing up, and take off down the road. I bet you I ran 120 miles an hour down that country road. The car would bounce all around, and it didn't even have pavement tires on it—just dirt tires.

I would spin the car around at a big intersection and head it back the other way. Diz would be waiting for me, and he'd get behind me with the push truck and drive me back across the highway and up the street to his shop.

I get cold chills thinking about that now. The first time we did it I didn't even fasten my seat belt. I never even wore a helmet. The only protection I remember wearing was a pair of goggles that Diz told me to grab because the bugs might hit me in the eyes.

After that first time, I at least remembered to fasten my lap belt. But other than that, I was just "Mr. Hard-charger" in my jeans, a T-shirt, and goggles, flying down a country blacktop at 120 mph. There were so many things that could have gone wrong, but I didn't think about that. I just did it.

In 1961 the format of the annual Marine Corps summer camp had changed from two weeks to six weeks. Ordinarily I wouldn't have minded, but because I had begun to rely on racing for my living, losing six weeks out of the summer would have been devastating to my racing career, not to mention my budget.

When I received the summer camp notice in the mail, I immediately sat down and composed a letter to the Eighth Naval District in New Orleans, requesting that I be allowed to do some other program in place of the six-week summer camp. In the letter, I explained that I was a professional race car driver pursuing a career and that I couldn't possibly attend the six-week summer camp and still maintain my career goals.

Not long after that, I received a package from the Eighth Naval District, New Orleans, United States Marine Corps. It contained my honorable discharge and a letter from the commandant that read, "We understand the hardship that this change in the duration of the summer camp might impose on you. You have served the Corps and your country well." I was surprised and relieved at the same time.

When I was discharged in 1961 my Marine Corps rank was lance corporal. Had I stayed in the service, I would have been promoted to sergeant. I had served six years in the Reserve and it was decided that I had completed my tour of duty.

In 1962 I had an opportunity to run in the Little 500, the grueling sprint car race I first experienced as a spectator in 1960 just prior to seeing my first Indy 500.

The Little 500, like the Indy 500, fields thirty-three cars—eleven rows of cars—three abreast. The drivers and their race cars are really put to the test because the race consists of five hundred laps around a quarter-mile, high-banked, paved racetrack, and drivers must stop to refuel. Over the years, there have been some spectacular fires resulting from dumped fuel on hot exhausts.

It was my first time running the Little 500, but I set a new track record during qualifying to earn the pole position. Actor Vince Edwards, who was starring as Dr. Ben Casey on television at the time, served as the grand marshal at the race. He presented me with the trophy for fast time, then rode in the pace car for the start of the event.

I had a mix-up with another car on the opening lap, which bent the front radius rods of my car enough that it didn't handle properly for the rest of the race. The radius rods hold the proper caster, and with the angle of the caster now considerably bent up, steering the car became much more difficult and physically draining. I drove the car for about four hundred laps before having to request a relief driver because I was so exhausted from maneuvering the stiff steering. A friend of mine from Wichita, Kansas, Harold Leep, got into the car and finished the race. We ended up in fifth, so it wasn't a total loss.

In 1962 I began driving for Dave Beatson, an IMCA owner who also owned a plumbing business in St. Paul, Minnesota. I was leading in the points championship and Beatson had been bragging about me at the local track—the North Star Speedway just outside of Minneapolis-St. Paul. Races were held there every Saturday night and the track had its own champions. That particular year, the champion was very good and seldom ever lost at his track. Beatson, at a pub with his racing fan buddies, had bragged about me so much that he was willing to bet them that I could beat the track champion on his own track. I was not privy to this conversation, and was totally in the dark about his claim that I could beat the champion.

Leading up to the race, Don Shepherd, my mechanic, had prepared the car thoroughly, as he always did. He even fabricated and bolted a roll cage into the car.

Saturday night came and, still unbeknownst to either Don or me, Beatson had made a few side bets that we could "wax 'em on their home track."

In the qualifying race we did all right. But in the preliminary race—the heat race—I finished second or third. If Beatson bet on that race, he lost some money. He finally went to Don and confessed what he'd done.

Don was furious. He didn't appreciate being put in that defensive position, and he didn't want me in that position either. And he let Beatson know it. Then he came over and explained it to me: "We're behind the eight ball here, partner. Beatson's bet a lot of money on us winning the damn race. We had better try to win this feature or both of us may be looking for new jobs."

"Well, I wish I'd known that earlier," I retorted. "I might have tried a little harder to win the heat race."

The rest of the drivers and I lined up for the feature. I think I may have started back in the second or third row for either a twenty- or thirty-lap feature. Their track champion was on the pole, of course.

They dropped the green and the race began. I worked up to the reigning champion fairly quickly, but it was tough; his car had a good engine and it was working well. As we ran through traffic, there were no opportunities for me to pass him. When I did try to make a move, there would be a slow car in the way. This continued lap after lap after lap.

Then, with two laps to go, as we came off the second turn down the back-stretch, two slower cars moved in front of the champion. I was directly behind the champion, so whichever way the two slower cars decided to go would determine the outcome of the evening's race.

As it happened, one of the drivers pulled over and blocked the champion, and the second slow car was just fast enough to pass them. I just jumped right in behind the passing car and sailed by the leader to win the race on the last lap.

Beatson, of course, was thrilled, and best of all, Don and I saved our jobs. But that might not have been the case if we hadn't been able to trap the lead driver in the slower traffic.

During that 1962 season, when I was leading in points in the IMCA, there were two other drivers who were "dicing" for the championship. One was Johnny White from Warren, Michigan, who later was named the 1964 Rookie of the Year at Indianapolis. Johnny was a tremendous pavement driver, but he ran the dirt hard, too, which made him a good all-around driver. Johnny was driving a car for Diz Wilson, for whom I had driven in 1961.

The other driver vying for the championship was perennial champion Pete Folse, in Hector Honore's Bardahl Deuce black car no. 2. Hector, who owned his own shop in Pana, Illinois, was quite a builder and mechanic. Folse, who was from Tampa, Florida, had driven for Hector for two or three years, and had won the championship for him during that time.

My good friend and travel buddy, Jimmy McElreath, had by this time joined the USAC and had gone on to race at Indy and other USAC-sanctioned races for the 1962 season, so Johnny White and I occasionally traveled together and became pretty close friends. One time, we stopped in a small town on the way to our next race for some R 'n' R. On Main Street was a saddle shop that carried twelve-foot-long, rotating-handle bullwhips.

I'm not sure what prompted us to do this, but we each bought one. Maybe it was boredom. Being on the road as much as we were, we needed something to fill the time.

We practiced and learned how to crack those bullwhips. If you use the right technique when you crack those bullwhips, they can sound louder than a shotgun. We eventually became pretty good at it; I could even cut a potato in two from several feet away. Soon John and I were putting on demonstrations for friends and racers at the tracks where we raced.

Days before the bullwhip-buying spree, John and I had stopped off at a roadside stand that sold gifts and trinkets. We found some leather moccasin kits that allowed you to sew your own moccasins. Traveling to the next race, one of us would be driving and the other one would be sewing a moccasin.

Then we bought those bullwhips. We were mastering our new art, but we needed a "popper"—a strong, foot-long piece of nylon cord or something like it that we could fasten to the end of the bullwhip—to make them really come to life . . . loudly.

One of us had the bright idea as we were heading down the road one day that the lacing cord we used to sew the moccasins would make the perfect popper for the bullwhips. As it turns out, neither of us finished that second moccasin. But we both had a loud-cracking bullwhip!

During the off-season I worked any number of odd jobs back in Fort Worth to support myself and prepare for the next season of IMCA racing.

One of my dad's best friends was John Pittman, whose family owned Ben E. Keith Co., a big produce firm in Fort Worth. Mr. Pittman had a friend in Weatherford, Texas, twenty miles west of Fort Worth, who owned a small fleet of trucks. The trucks hauled bananas from the banana boats in Corpus Christi to the Ben E. Keith warehouse. Through these connections, I nailed down a job driving a banana truck, a big eighteen-wheeler. It had bunkers in the front of the trailer where we would place heaters when the weather was cold or ice when it was hot. I was instructed to be careful when I got the bananas off the boat; I couldn't let them get below fifty-four degrees or they would freeze, and I couldn't let them get above seventy-four degrees or they would start "gassing" and ripen.

I drove the banana truck for a couple of winters in Fort Worth. Once, somebody working on one of the trucks in the shop stuffed a red shop towel into the top of the gas tank because he'd evidently lost the gas cap. I was driving that particular truck to Corpus that night and, unbeknownst to me, the towel had worked its way down into the gas tank.

As I got closer to town, the engine kept wanting to stall. I'd back off the gas and the truck would run better, but then it would start stalling on me again when I stepped on the accelerator. It got worse and worse until finally the engine just quit. I was stranded out in the middle of nowhere on Highway 6 near College Station. It was early in the morning, about two or three, so I had to wake somebody up at the warehouse and tell him I had a problem with the truck. He told me to watch the temperature in the bunker until he could get someone out to help me.

Someone eventually came and towed the truck to the nearest garage. We had to wait until somebody arrived to open the garage for business that morning.

By then I was getting frantic because I was starting to lose my load of bananas. After looking things over in the truck, the mechanics finally found the red shop towel in the fuel tank. We determined that the towel had been floating in the tank and covering the pickup, but when I backed off the gas, the change in pressure blew the towel away from the fuel line before eventually working its way back and plugging the line again. Finally, it simply lodged itself in there and shut off the fuel. Once the mechanic fished the towel out of the tank, I loaded up the truck with fuel and everything was fine for the remainder of the trip.

Throughout those lean years, my folks remained supportive of me even though my mom had made it clear that I'd be better off doing something else with my life.

I myself never once gave any thought to quitting. I loved driving race cars. Most of the drivers from that era would have driven for nothing—figuratively speaking. We loved racing so much that the money was almost secondary. It was fine with me when I had a good day and made forty percent of five hundred dollars. I'd put that money into my pocket so I'd have food to eat and gas for my car, enabling me to get to the next town, the next race.

That's the way life was. It was the end of one era and the beginning of the next. I feel very fortunate to have been a part of that transitional time—to have experienced the thrills and chills of the "old days" and be able to embrace the birth of the present age of auto racing. There are very few of us who made it through that time. I came from the dirt track—the dirt-under-the-fingernails, T-shirted, beer-drinkin', flat-out racin', after-the-race-fight fraternity of race car drivers. It may have been an unsophisticated time, but for me, it was an unforgettable and profound education. Driving a sprint car may not have taught me how to drive an Indy car, but it sure did teach me how to race.

The unfortunate part of that period of racing was that most drivers didn't live past thirty if they stayed in the game. If you ran hard enough to win some races, sooner or later your number might come up. It was the nature of the business. The drivers only wore seat belts—they did not wear shoulder harnesses. They had no rollover protection. It wasn't that it was more macho to drive like that, it's just that up until that time no one had thought to put a roll bar on a race car. Safety just was not a priority. Finally, in the 1950s, some people in the profession got wise and said, Hey, if a roll bar is placed back here over the tail, behind the driver, maybe it'll hold the car up off of him.

It worked. But not everyone started jumping on the safety bandwagon all at once. And even with a roll bar, there were no guarantees that the driver would survive a serious accident. There are just too many variables in professional racing.

The roll bar evolved into the roll cage, which was a tubular framework that fit over the driver and was welded to the frame of the race car. It protected the driver in the case of a rollover. Sprint car racing, per mile, was the fastest racing going in the '50s and '60s, and thus was also the most dangerous. We ran those cars around half-mile, high-banked tracks in twenty seconds—plenty fast for a car with six-inch-wide tires, no shoulder harness, and no roll bar.

When I got involved in racing it was at the tail end of "the sportsman" era of auto racing. I actually experienced the transformation from front-engine to rear-engine Indy cars. All drivers were affected by the change to the rear-engine, independent-suspension, turbo-charged skyrockets that roared around the track at Indianapolis, without lifting, at 200 to 235 miles an hour. Some adapted, others just faded away.

I was fortunate. I survived a pretty good stretch of American racing history.

Eventually I reached a point in my racing career when I wanted to graduate to the next level, the top of the heap in racing organizations. That was the United States Auto Club, or USAC. I was becoming impatient to race in the series that included the Indianapolis 500. One of the reasons Jimmy McElreath and I moved on to the Midwest in the first place was to have that opportunity.

Most car owners of that era, particularly the ones who needed drivers, watched the results of the dirt races. The drivers whose names appeared regularly in the standings would be the ones the owners would track down and try to hire.

That was McElreath's situation. He applied himself well and did a good job on the dirt tracks. In 1962 he was given an opportunity to drive a "championship car," another name for the Indy car, and he didn't hesitate. He parlayed that opportunity by taking a test at the Indianapolis Motor Speedway and moving on to USAC. A year later, I was also given an opportunity to move up the ladder, and I seized it. This was the usual avenue to Indy. It seemed that the drivers of my era graduated from a different level of racing to get to Indianapolis than has been the norm in recent years.

To be in a position to run with USAC was quite an accomplishment. That was the big time, where all the money was. I could still run midgets and sprint cars—although not as often as I did in the outlaw midget circuits or in the IMCA—but more important, in USAC I could finally run Indy cars.

However, when the time came for me to consider making the move from IMCA to USAC in 1962, I did have some second thoughts. At the time, I was leading in points by a slim margin over Johnny White. He and I were really hammer and tongs for the championship, and I probably had a good shot at winning the title. Then I was given the opportunity to join USAC and race in the Hoosier Hundred. It was decision time. USAC beckoned, and I went for it.

A lot of people said, "Hoo, boy, you shouldn't have done that."

By "that" they meant foregoing my chance at winning the 1962 IMCA Championship.

Looking back on it nearly forty years later, I sometimes wish that I had stayed with IMCA—at least for that one season. It would be great to look at my dossier and see an IMCA Championship listed among my accomplishments. However, I chose to go to USAC and I don't regret my decision, although I do regret not finishing the battle for Don Shepherd and Dave Beatson. Despite my leaving with half a dozen races left in the season, I placed fifth in points for 1962. Johnny White went on to win the championship that year.

Had I stuck with IMCA, I might have been seriously injured or worse in my final push to win the title, and would never have had the chance to race at Daytona, Indianapolis, or at any of the other places at which I competed over the years. Things always happen for a reason. Second-guessing has never been one of my traits. I just decide, live with the decision, and move forward.

I was so eager to race at the Indianapolis Motor Speedway that it was all I could see on the horizon. My decision put me in Indy in near record time—four years—and it's one I definitely can live with.

☆ CHAPTER 6 ☆

Brickyard Bound

I was fortunate to have Jimmy McElreath as a friend and rival. He looked out for me and helped me gain the knowledge I needed to decide where I wanted to go and what I wanted to do—and sometimes even how to do it. He was a true mentor and our friendship was one the best things that happened to me during my early years in racing.

When Jimmy moved up from our dirt track circuit to Indianapolis in 1962, he made a clean transition to racing championship cars and was named Rookie of the Year. We were no longer traveling buddies, yet we always stayed in touch.

In fact, it was Jimmy who called me late in the summer of 1962 and told me that Buster Warke's car was open for the Hoosier Hundred, and that the owner was planning to ask me to race it.

I was ready and eager. The Hoosier Hundred was a dirt race run at the Indiana State Fair in September. By running this race I'd be taking my first step toward my goal of testing for—and racing in—the Indy 500.

I drove for car owner Fred Sclavi, who owned Bell Lines Trucking out of Charleston, West Virginia. The car was fairly new. It had a Meskowski chassis and the suspension was created with torsion bars, one for each corner. The car was known as a four-bar car—the torsion bars ran crossways to the chassis rather than parallel to it. It was a good car, but because its engine—an Offenhauser—had been run in a race previous to the Hoosier Hundred, the engine had a lot of dust and dirt in it, the rings were pretty much shot, and the valves weren't very sharp. It wasn't fresh or strong, and that's what ultimately gave us major trouble in the race.

Coming from IMCA, I was familiar with every kind of dirt track there was. The guys I was now racing against in USAC were also quite experienced, because they had either come from IMCA, the California Racing Association, or some other organization that granted them a lot of seat time. Not surprisingly, many of the guys racing at the USAC-sanctioned Hoosier Hundred were Indianapolis 500 veterans. Indy car teams also raced dirt cars because dirt race points counted toward the USAC national championship.

It had rained a day or two prior to the event, so the racetrack was quite heavy. Fortunately, the track officials let the rookies practice on their own for about five or six laps. The car was handling well, and I felt good about it. I was the quickest of the rookies during that practice session, and I qualified for the race with a whopping ninety-seven-miles-per-hour qualifying time. In the race itself, my first attempt at running "the big cars" in the United States Auto Club, I was forced to drop out just past the halfway point because the engine started missing and giving up. At least, however, I qualified for the race as a rookie.

The prize payoff was very good. All eighteen starters won prize money. I received as much money as I made in four or five IMCA races. For me, though, the money was not as significant as the fact that I had taken that first big step toward racing at the Indianapolis Motor Speedway.

I still had many steps to take before I would reach Indy. I was always looking for my next ride in a sprint car or a midget car. Some opportunities came my way and I was able to make a pretty good living—especially since the money was so much better in USAC. I had been living hand-to-mouth for five or six years while I raced in IMCA, so the increase in pay was nice.

I started running more Indy car races at the end of the 1962 season. From the Hoosier Hundred I went to Trenton, New Jersey, to race at the New Jersey State Fairgrounds' Trenton Speedway. Back then, the track was a mile-long paved oval. Years later, it was completely reconfigured to a 1⅛-mile tri-oval with a right-handed dogleg in the backstretch, which went into big sweeping third and fourth turns.

The car I drove in the Hoosier Hundred had been sold to George Walther, and an owner who had seen me race that day offered me a car for the next race in Trenton. Interestingly, George Walther would later give me a car for my rookie driving test at Indianapolis the next spring.

I raced on the paved track at Trenton in the Federal Engineering Special dirt car. It was a championship car, and an old one at that. It had a long wheel base, the same type you'd find on a dirt track car, but we put pavement tires on it to race at Trenton. Years later, in 1971 or 1972, I drove that same car, the Federal Engineering Special. It had been cut down, shortened up, and made into a sprint car and was powered by a Chevrolet engine instead of the Offenhauser engine we used at the Trenton race in '62. The Federal Engineering Special, so called for the company that once owned it, had been racing out in California for several years. At that time, Don Peabody owned the car, and he hired me to drive for him during the fall West Coast races. I had no idea his car was the old Federal Engineering Special, and when I arrived at Altamont Speedway in Altamont, California, you could have knocked me over with a feather. I got behind the wheel and set a new track record with the car I had run years ago in my second USAC race.

If cars are still in service as they get older, they retain their names. Traditionally, racers maintain an oral history about the cars: "Yeah, this is the old such-and-such dirt car from the Midwest," or "This car was the one that so-and-so won Milwaukee with back in '60." Thus, even if the car receives a new paint job or undergoes some modifications, real racers know the car's history.

From Trenton we went to Phoenix and raced the mile-long dirt track at the Arizona State Fairgrounds, which is now long gone. I was driving yet another car, my third in three consecutive races. It had a Kuzma chassis, named for one of the top-of-the-line car builders at the time. A good, steady race car, it was owned by Ollie Prather, a business owner and racing enthusiast from California who loved to work on his cars. He had some guys helping him out, but he got his hands plenty dirty. Ollie took care of that car—he spent money to keep the engine fresh and to put new tires and wheels on it as was needed. Jimmy McElreath's first ride at Indianapolis was in Prather's Indy car, a roadster.

The 1962 season turned out to be a busy one for me. Between IMCA and USAC, I ran seventy-three races that summer. I was considered a charger. I raced hard and I could go into a turn as fast as anybody. That was my style. A lot of people would wish me a merry Christmas in July, because as hard as I drove, I wasn't going to be around at Christmas.

The Indianapolis 500. I had dreamed of racing in that grand event from the time I first learned what it was.

In the late 1940s, after the race made a comeback from its hiatus during World War II, and in the early 1950s, my folks and I would listen to radio coverage of the race every Memorial Day. I remember that Mauri Rose and Bill Holland, who were teammates for a time, finished 1-2 in '47 and '48, and that Holland came back to win it in '49 when Rose's car developed a magneto problem with eight laps to go.

As I got a little older I realized how significant the Indianapolis 500 was to a race car driver. First I dreamed of simply witnessing the spectacle. In 1960, when I saw my first Indy 500, a fire was lit in me. I had been developing my racing career, climbing the auto-racing ladder by running a lot of sprint and midget cars. Then I began racing NASCAR and stock cars, which were fledgling and somewhat removed because they were based for the most part in the deep southeastern United States. On the other hand, Indianapolis, or "championship," cars ran all over the United States. By developing my career the way I did, I gained both experience and self-confidence along the way, and started seriously thinking that I could race at Indianapolis.

Jim Rathmann and Rodger Ward were two of the names I heard as I was making my way up the ranks. Of course, many of the headliners back then were household names among those of us who were attempting to race cars for a living. Tony Bettenhausen, Troy Ruttman, Eddie Sachs, Lloyd Ruby—they were all well known to us. They were the guys you watched if you were a devoted racing fan.

But I didn't look at them and think, *Man, I wish I could make the kind of money they're making.* My feeling was then, as it has always been, that you'll be more successful if you do something because you love it than if you do it because you want to make money. If you're doing something because you love it, the money will come. Most of the drivers from my era—no, all of them—would tell you that they race cars for the love of the sport. How fortunate we are to make a living in a profession we love.

I never thought about financial success; I was just enjoying the moment. I simply loved to race cars. I lived for each race. I didn't once stop to count my money or ponder my future. I never looked beyond my next race, my next ride. There wasn't a lot of money to be made in the late '50s and early '60s, but it was enough to perpetuate the lifestyle. I like to say that most of us from that era would have raced for nothing. And by today's standards, we did.

Every now and then I'd catch a glimpse of what the future might hold, like when I would observe another driver begin to enjoy some success of his own and then gain the opportunity to move onward and upward. I'd think, *Okay, so that's the way you do it.* For example, I watched and learned from my buddy, Jimmy, and did everything I could to follow the path I saw him taking.

Although I watched and learned from other drivers, I don't know that I ever really imitated any of them, except, perhaps, Tony Bettenhausen—Tony Sr. He had been my racing hero since I first watched him race sprints and midget cars in the Midwest in the early 1960s.

Tony always sat so straight in the cockpit. His head was erect and never flopped around. He just made it look easy, like he was out for a really smooth ride. He ran fast and he won races. I always thought his posture and form looked right, as though he truly knew what he was doing. I tried to emulate that posture. I combined what I learned from him and other drivers with my own natural abilities—a feel for the race car, its rhythms and moves, and how to anticipate, react, and make those rhythms work for me.

Unfortunately, today's driver is buried in the car so that all you can see is his helmet. At one time, fans would pick their favorite drivers by observing them and their own unique styles. Don Branson used to lean up over the steering wheel, which made him look like he was going fast whether he was sitting still or flying down the straightaway. Jim Hurtubise was another driver who leaned over the wheel and looked as though he was putting extra effort into it. A. J. Foyt sat very much like Bettenhausen—bolt upright, and always with the appearance of knowing where he was going and what he was doing. Parnelli Jones sat that way, too, but a little lower in the car. Troy Ruttman was so big that the windshield was taller than the car was high.

These were a few of the guys I watched as they traveled the path to success. I was experimenting with different styles and learning all the time. Soon I would be able to put it all to the test.

☆ CHAPTER 7 ☆

Daytona Was a Phone Call Away

☆   ☆   ☆

Someone was secretly watching me.

I didn't know how long it had been going on, but someone was studying me, judging me, making sure I was the right guy for the job.

By the end of 1962 I had raced the "fair circuit" for three years, and I'd come to intimately know just about every dirt track at every county and state fairground in the Midwest. The races I ran were dirt track races sanctioned by the IMCA; running a late-model stock car on a paved track was not yet on my résumé.

So I was completely taken by surprise when a friend of mine, Monk King, called me at the end of January in 1963, to tell me about a gentleman in Daytona Beach, Florida, who was interested in having me race his new car at the upcoming Daytona 500. Monk, a Pontiac dealer in Dallas, wouldn't tell me who this mystery man was, but he told me to come to his office so we could call him from there. I drove over from Fort Worth. We talked for a few minutes about my season that had just ended, and then he called the owner in Florida. After they talked for a few minutes, Monk said, "Yeah, he's here. Let me put him on."

He handed me the phone and said, "Here, Smokey Yunick wants to talk to you." My jaw dropped. Smokey Yunick was one of the premier stock car and engine builders of the period. At first I thought Monk was joking, but Smokey was in fact on the line. He wanted me to race his car at Daytona that year.

I was so dumbfounded that I could only say, "Well, that sounds good. Sure." But I was elated. Smokey Yunick wanted me? He asked me how soon I could get to Florida.

"Is tomorrow okay?" I asked.

The chance to drive for Smokey Yunick was the first big boost in my stock as a race car driver. I had never driven a late-model stock car in my life, but I knew how to watch and learn from other drivers. Racing is racing. The only thing you have to concentrate on is technique. It's mind over matter. The Daytona ride was something I wanted, and I was eager to get out there and race.

I drove to Daytona Beach about a week later in the new Bonneville sports coupe I'd bought from Monk. It had a 421-cubic-inch engine that I'm sure would have run 140 mph had I been allowed to open it up on the highways. But as excited as I was about meeting Smokey, I thought better of trying to race before I even got to the track.

I went straight to Smokey's shop when I pulled into Daytona Beach a little after dusk. A sign over his shop read "The Best Damn Garage in Town." Smokey was a GMC truck dealer; he sold trucks in the front of the building and had a shop in the back.

When I pulled in I noticed that the shop's windows were either painted or taped over with paper so passersby couldn't see in. As I walked toward the door I heard people inside hammering and welding, and voices calling out for this or that—there was a whole lot of activity going on behind those doors. I knocked a couple of times before some guy came to the door and said, "Yeah, what do you want?"

No red carpet for my arrival.

I said, "I'm Johnny Rutherford, and I'm here to see Smokey Yunick."

He gave me a hard look, then turned and yelled, "Hey! Smokey! Your driver's here!"

Smokey came to the door and introduced himself. He welcomed me in and took me over to meet all the guys. He had a real army in there. Most of them were crew members who were going to be working on the car on race day. They were still building the chassis, but Smokey had done all the dyno testing on the engine and was ready to put it into the car.

Dennis Bradley, a representative of Autolite Spark Plugs and one of the guys in the shop that night, had been assigned the job of fitting me into the car. I got in to see how it fit. It could have been lined with nails and I would have thought it was comfortable. The interior was gutted except for the driver's seat and the doors weren't even on it yet, but the car was beautiful.

The race cars of that period were quite primitive by today's standards. This car had a tubular sub-frame that made it strong, and attached to that was the roll cage, which formed the protective cockpit area for the driver. The car did not have protective window netting or many of today's safety features. The windows, in fact, were stock glass windows; the driver- and passenger-side windows, like passenger-car windows, were inset and could be rolled up and down. In today's race cars, the windows are flush against the edge of the body to make for cleaner aerodynamics.

While I sat inside the car, I was "fitted." The crew installed a shoulder pad for me to lean against, to help support me when I was at speed on the high-banked track. They adjusted the steering wheel and the seat and then locked, bolted, and welded everything into place.

By the time we were finished it was well into the next morning. Smokey had reserved a room for me at the Orange Grove Motel, and I did manage to get in a few hours of sleep before heading back to Smokey's shop later that morning. When I arrived at the shop the next morning it was nearly time to head to the track.

At the track, I went through credentialing and got all the passes I needed for access to the track, the garage, and the pits. Everyone at the track knew Smokey and his team, but I was an unknown. I felt as though everyone was eyeing me with suspicious looks, and from several people I got the sense that they wanted to ask, "What's this kid ever done?" No one could figure out why Smokey picked me.

I started feeling a little paranoid. I knew I was strictly an unknown, but I had raced sprint cars and had even had some success. This, however, was a vastly different arena for me. There was no comparing where I was coming from to the stock car racers, their crews, and the track officials. It may have been Smokey Yunick who picked me, but it was uncommon to go outside the southeastern United States to find a driver.

This was my first visit to Daytona and the fifth year of the Daytona 500. The race was something new and different for the fans—it took place on a high-banked super-speedway of 2½ miles that was constructed so that fans could see the entire racetrack at all times.

Many of the cars had the names of dealerships painted on the quarter panels. Strangely, we didn't even have a sponsor for the race. It was too bad that someone wasn't on board to take advantage of the forthcoming publicity.

Smokey and I both knew that the car I would be driving at the Daytona 500 in '63—an extremely modified Chevrolet Impala sport coupe—would react differently from what I had been driving in the world of sprints and midgets. I had driven early-model stock cars in Texas, but now I'd be going much faster on a big track in a new, late-model car. It would be a whole new ballgame for me.

Smokey casually said, "I've got somebody for you to talk to about going around this track." He left me by the car and came back with two guys in tow.

"Johnny, I want you to meet Fireball Roberts and Joe Weatherly. Fellas, this is Johnny Rutherford, my driver."

Once again, I was nearly speechless. Roberts and Weatherly were two of the top NASCAR drivers of all time. They were legends. The affable Smokey simply said, "Tell him what he needs to know about goin' around here, okay?"

I listened intently to what the two gentlemen had to say about their sport. Fireball talked with me about the car and how it might feel. He knew I was a sprint car racer, so he tried to give me some idea of what to watch out for. Weatherly—whom people called "Little Joe"—told me something I still recall quite clearly. He said, in his rich Southern drawl, "Kid, yew kin run this thin' 'roun' heer flat-footed if it's raht."

He didn't, however, tell me how superstitious he was.

Weatherly's race car was parked next to mine in the garage area at Daytona. That was okay except for one thing: my black and gold race car sported the number thirteen—considered by many, including Little Joe, to be unlucky.

A. J. Foyt used to delight in entering our area and touching my car, then reaching over and trying to touch Little Joe. Little Joe would jump clear over the hood of his race car to get away from Foyt. He would not let Foyt "contaminate" him, as it were, with the number thirteen.

Weatherly would occasionally forget about the mischievous nature of professional racing people. Somebody in the garage would "accidentally" give him a little shove into my number thirteen car, and when they did it was as if Little

Joe had come face to face with his own demise. It was fun to watch him go to great lengths to avoid coming into contact with my car, parked right next to his in the garage area. Eventually he would just remain on the other side of his car at all times.

Little Joe, although he was superstitious, imparted some good advice. I went out and drove just as he instructed. The car's setup was close to "raht," and I was able to race flat-footed. Since I was used to tearing around dirt tracks in sprint cars, the speed didn't bother me, even though I "felt" my way around the first few times.

Our quick time was about 166 miles an hour in practice. The track was so smooth that it was like driving on the interstate in my passenger car. This is not to say that it wasn't challenging, but after several years of running on dirt tracks, it felt good.

We practiced every day for three or four days prior to qualifying. We took the car out to the track and ran it every opportunity we had, making sure not to wear the car out. We were running quick. The car was doing just as well as Smokey had planned, and he must have been satisfied with my driving or he would have shared with me a few choice words. Sometimes silence is golden.

In the early 1960s we didn't have sophisticated computers to record everything the car was doing. Our method of evaluation was just two guys talking. I'd tell Smokey what the car did or didn't do when I had tried this or encountered that, and he'd rely on his years of experience and his knowledge of race cars to make adjustments to the car to ensure optimum performance for qualifying.

Smokey and I were not alone in preparing his new car for Daytona. We worked with an entire team of hardworking experts. Race teams and mechanics are such a dedicated lot that I've often said they work twenty-five hours a day, eight days a week. No matter if you're racing modified stocks, Indy cars, or sprints, the mechanics and the entire race team are always trying to improve on things. Whether it's overhauling or checking or changing, they examine that car from top to bottom. If they conclude that something is inadequate, they take the car to the next level to make it better, stronger, or bigger. If the car is not right, they're working on it. They want to be sure that the car will go the five hundred miles as well as withstand the rigors of day-to-day testing.

The crew chief calls the shots. He communicates with the driver, so it's important for you both to be on the same wavelength. It takes a little time to get in sync, which is one reason why you practice. After a run, the crew chief asks the driver what the car was doing and makes an assessment based on the answer. He then conveys that to the crew and the mechanics, and together they work on making things right. The driver then takes the car out a second time and goes through the whole process again. If the car is running worse, that tells the crew chief that they went in the wrong direction and that they need to try something different. The stopwatch, the real tattletale, also tells you if it's running better or worse. That's the way you sort out a car. The better the communication between the driver and crew, the more time saved in establishing a basic setup, allowing more qualified experimentation to reach the "edge" in competition.

Smokey was a good instructor because he was able to get his point across. He was opinionated, and I know he rubbed some people the wrong way, but we got along well. Smokey was not the average kind of individual. He had been a pilot in World War II and flew bombing missions in Europe, Africa, and the Pacific Islands. He had learned welding and some auto mechanics while he was a teenager, so when he got out of the service he eventually parlayed those skills into a career. He was instrumental in helping his team, often with Herb Thomas at the wheel and later with Fireball Roberts and other drivers, win many NASCAR races throughout the 1950s and early 1960s. He also won at Indy in 1960 with driver Jim Rathmann.

Stock cars seemed to be Smokey's forte, but I'm still not sure that his first love wasn't the Indianapolis 500. He was a mechanic for a couple of drivers at the Speedway, and he truly loved the track itself and the challenge the Memorial Day classic presented. Smokey loved to build engines as much as he loved racing.

Having said that, I have to add that Smokey hated dealing with people who threw their weight around, although I think he enjoyed butting heads with people sometimes, particularly those he thought interfered with his work. He sometimes interpreted the rules a little differently from the way the governing bodies did—particularly in NASCAR.

Once, for example, Smokey was running a race with a Camaro he'd been working on, and officials questioned the fuel his car was carrying. The car was supposed to have a twenty-two-gallon tank, but the officials suspected that he was running with a little more fuel than that. He had already been cited for other infractions, so the officials made Smokey remove the fuel tank from the Camaro. The rectangular metal box and the fuel cell were laid out on the floor.

Smokey was so furious over what he viewed as an insignificant oversight that he picked up the fuel cell, threw it into the trunk of his car, and sped off to his shop. Their suspicions were confirmed, I guess.

In the days leading up to the Daytona 500, Junior Johnson and I were competing for the pole position and, ultimately, the track record. He would take his car out and beat my time, and then I'd go out, run a few laps, and beat his time. The press loved exploiting the daily competition between the chicken farmer and the new kid on the block.

Junior was really making an effort to get that pole position, but I somehow managed to nail it down. I hoped that some of the people who had at first questioned my abilities were starting to believe that maybe Smokey had done the right thing by hiring me. I set a new track record and a new world record for a stock car on a closed course when I was officially clocked at 165.183 miles per hour in my black and gold no. 13 Chevrolet. The number thirteen isn't always bad luck.

I know there were a lot of surprised people at the track the day I won the one hundred-mile qualifying race at Daytona, my first NASCAR race. I'm one of six drivers in NASCAR history to win their first NASCAR race, and it's an accomplishment I truly cherish.

But I couldn't and didn't gloat about it. There was no time for that nonsense. The big race—the Daytona 500—was coming up. Unfortunately, my inexperience with stock cars coupled with some inexperience on the part of the crew probably kept us from winning the Daytona 500 that year.

Smokey, a real innovator, had come up with the idea for a fresh-air duct for the carburetor, which was located in the grating between the windshield and the hood. It was the first year this apparatus was used, and it was effective. However, it rained the morning of the race, at times fairly hard. The crew, who had never had to worry about carburetors before, forgot to tape up the fresh-air duct. The car was sitting out on the line all morning, and when the rain poured down on the windshield, it drained right into the fresh-air duct and the carburetor.

When we tried to fire the car up, it had a carburetor full of water and would not run. We wasted the battery trying to start the car. We were pulling our hair out. Only after we finally got it started and I pulled away from the line did Smokey realize what had happened.

The hard rain, however, also proved serendipitous for us at the start of the race. All the drivers ran their cars for about ten laps under the yellow caution flag to help dry the track. Those slow caution laps gave my engine a chance to clear itself of water and start running properly.

I had been forewarned by some of the veterans before the race that the crosswind at turn 2 could be tricky, even for an experienced stock car driver.

At that time, a double steel guardrail—called the Armco—was installed around the racetrack; today it has been replaced with a concrete wall. The airport runway was nearly parallel to the track's back straightaway and only half a mile away, creating a wide-open area for the wind to really move the cars around. About halfway through the race I came off turn 2 and the wind evidently caught me. I suddenly found myself brushing the Armco. I pulled the car down off the guardrail, and immediately the car sashayed to the middle of the track and slid a little to the right.

I gathered it up, but then the car started fishtailing. I caught the car going back to the left, toward the infield, and just locked the brakes up, turned the wheel, and spun the car. I didn't want it to hit that outside guardrail again, so I slid off into the grass and sand on the infield. It seemed like I spun forever. However, I didn't bounce hard or hit anything that would bend the car. I had it locked up, and of course the engine was dead when I slid to a stop. I started cranking the ignition, but my spinout had pumped the fuel backwards, up through the carburetor. I cranked it and cranked it to no avail. I didn't want to kill the battery, so I sat there for what seemed like an eternity to let it cool. Finally I got the engine to fire. I put it in gear and drove around the track and straight to the pits.

Because I had locked up the wheels, there was a good chance the tires needed changing. When you lock up the wheels on a race car at high speed, sliding sideways along the pavement, grinds the rubber off the tires. It's similar to getting a flat spot on the wheels of roller skates; the flat spots produce an unmistakable vibration.

Smokey's crew went right to work, but we'd lost a lot of time while I was sitting in the infield trying to get the car restarted after I spun out. The guy who changed the right rear tire had a little trouble getting it off, because I had mashed the quarter panel, or fender, down over the tire a bit when I scuffed the guardrail. This required them to manually pry open the space to remove the tire and replace it with a new one.

One of the crew members pulled the fender up and out just enough to get the wheel off. Then, as he was trying to put the fresh tire on, Smokey came over to see what was taking so long and angrily moved him out of the way. That cost us more precious time in the pits and four laps on the track.

Once they got the wheel on, I pulled back onto the track. The car chassis was okay; the bent sheet metal was the only problem. We managed to finish the race . . . in ninth position. If it weren't for all those things—my brush against the guardrail, the time spent restarting the car in the infield, the problems we had in the pit—we might have placed in the top five or top three at the 1963 Daytona 500. Who knows? We even might have won the thing. One can never be sure in racing.

Tiny Lund won the 1963 Daytona 500 for the Wood brothers, Leonard and Glen. Lund, who was a very successful driver, took over for Marvin Panch, the Wood brothers' No. 1 driver. In the weeks before the Daytona 500, Panch was involved in a fiery wreck when his tire blew while driving in a sports car race. The car crashed, flipped upside down, and caught on fire, pinning Panch underneath it. Lund and some other drivers were there at the track that day to watch, and when Panch's car wrecked, they ran over to him, picked up the car, and pulled him out. He was burned so badly that he couldn't race at Daytona. The Wood brothers needed a new driver, and Tiny Lund was their choice.

There was a stellar field of drivers that day, real stock car greats. NASCAR regulars included Junior Johnson; Ned Jarrett (who finished third); Fred Lorenzen (who finished second); Richard Petty (who finished sixth); Darel Dieringer; Ralph Earnhardt; David Pearson; Tiny Lund; and the two drivers who gave me tips before the race, Joe Weatherly and Fireball Roberts. United States Auto Club crossovers—Indy drivers—included A. J. Foyt, Troy Ruttman, Parnelli Jones, Jim Hurtubise, Len Sutton, and Paul Goldsmith.

Buck Baker, Cale Yarborough, and Rodger Ward were among the drivers who failed to qualify for the Daytona 500 but who ran in the one hundred-mile qualifying race I won.

The Daytona 500 clocked in at three hours, seventeen minutes, and fifty-six seconds, and 70,780 fans were there to see the race. Ford took the first five spots, and our Chevrolet was the first Chevrolet across the line.

As for Smokey, our crew, and me, we were disappointed that we didn't do better at Daytona that year. But Smokey understood that it was, after all, my first stock car race. We all talked things over after the race. I think the crew was glad to get a car back that wasn't banged up too badly, even though they would still need to do a lot of work on it.

The Daytona 500 was pretty much a stand-alone event in February, so the crew had enough time to prepare the car for the next race. That was on March 2 in Spartanburg, South Carolina, on a half-mile dirt track. Two weeks after Spartanburg we were off to the Super Speedway in Atlanta, a paved, 1½-mile track.

Smokey asked me if I wanted to stay in the South and run, but I had been offered a chance to take the test at the Speedway in an Indy car, and I told him

I really wanted to go to Indianapolis. Because the Indy 500 had been a lifelong dream, I just had to go.

Shortly after the Daytona 500, I applied for and received a United States Auto Club license. That meant I couldn't run any races outside USAC's sanctions without the organization's permission. USAC officials probably would have let me run stock cars, but I think that Smokey and Chevrolet wanted to hire somebody who could run full time for them. Since I couldn't commit to NASCAR and pursue my goal of racing Indy cars at the same time, I reluctantly parted company with Smokey's team.

I did run quite a few more NASCAR races over the years. But scheduling conflicts kept me from devoting more time to NASCAR racing. On those occasions when the NASCAR and Indy car schedules didn't conflict, I usually could head south and get a ride. Perhaps because of my accomplishments at Daytona in 1963—having set a new track record and having won a race—it was easier for me to pick up a ride if someone needed a driver for a second or third car. Through the years, everyone affiliated with NASCAR has been most friendly and helpful to me. My trial period prior to acceptance into the NASCAR ranks was relatively short—I always felt as if I belonged.

Smokey and I have remained friends over the years. In fact, many years after our experience at the Daytona 500, he and I were reunited at a function at the International Motor Sports Hall of Fame in Birmingham, Alabama. A bunch of us were standing around talking, and the subject of my racing for him came up. So I asked him why he picked me to drive his car at the 1963 Daytona 500.

I'll never forget his response: "I'd been to a couple of your races and watched you run those sprint cars. I liked what I saw and thought you might be the guy to do the job I wanted done."

It was as simple as that.

☆ CHAPTER 8 ☆

Betty

☆   ☆   ☆

It was a whirlwind romance. We met early in May, became engaged on June 2, and were married on July 7.

My wife Betty has been my rock, my soulmate, and my biggest fan since the day we met in 1963. I don't even want to think about what my life would have been like without her.

In 1963 I was a rookie at Indianapolis. I had completed the first three phases of my driver's test and was going out for the fourth and final phase of my test one afternoon in May. The crew was pushing my car from the garage area out to the pit apron. I went over to the car, gripped the roll bar, and leaned down to drop my helmet into the seat. When I looked up I saw two young women standing at the fence by the gate. My eyes met those of a cute little blonde, and I winked at her. To my surprise, she winked back.

Betty tells the story differently. She says she waved, but I know she winked. In any event, it was time for the test, and for the moment everything but the task at hand was forgotten. My crew and I went to the north end of the pits. I got into the car and we prepared to run the final laps of my test. The car was fired up; I drove out and started building up to speed.

On my second lap, going into turn 1, I got it in a little high. I wanted to get the car lower on the track, so I pinched it—turned it down—slightly. But when I did that, the back end whipped outward and I spun the car. I didn't hit anything, I just looped the car and spun it to a stop at the edge of the track near the infield.

No physical harm was done, but I was scared to death that Harlan Fengler, the chief steward at the Speedway, was going to tell me to go home and get some more experience. We got the car turned around and towed it back to the pits, where Harlan was waiting for me.

"Do you know what you did?" he asked me.

"Yes, sir, I think so," I said. "I got it in a little high, and I pinched it. Just tried to turn it down too fast, got the back end loose, and I spun."

I stood there expecting the worst, but I was relieved when he simply told me to sit out the rest of the day and think about what had happened. He said I could finish the test the next morning.

I watched the crew take the car back to the garage to change the tires, which were flat-spotted from my spin, and to check things over. When I turned the corner of the garage, I saw Betty standing in front of the First Aid station casually talking with some of her nursing friends. I nodded in her direction and she acknowledged me, so I walked over to her. The first words I ever said to her were "Haven't I seen you someplace before?"

I'll admit that it wasn't very original, but it did break the ice; we talked and I got her phone number. I asked her what she was doing that evening and she said she had plans. I said I would call her sometime. I walked back to the garage to check on my car.

The next night I called Betty and asked her if I could take her to dinner. She consented, but only because I agreed to take her friend JoAnn to dinner with us. At dinner we talked about our careers and the upcoming race. I learned that she was a registered nurse who was also a member of the volunteer medical team at the Speedway that May. Betty later told me that about halfway through the meal, she began to wish that she and JoAnn had arrived in separate cars.

They say when you find the right person, you know. I knew. In fact, I called my folks after our second or third date and asked them, "When are you going to come to Indy?" They told me they couldn't afford to make the trip up to Indianapolis to see the race. So I said, "I wish you'd come on up, because I want to introduce you to the gal I'm going to marry."

That was all I needed to say. They came to the race.

☆　☆　☆　☆　☆

The 1963 Indianapolis 500 was approaching when Betty's folks came to the Speedway to watch a practice run. They were seated up in the corner of the

Tower Terrace grandstands, right beside the entryway to the pits. Betty and I walked up there so I could meet her parents and her brothers and sister.

Unbeknownst to me, Betty's dad had asked her if I was married. Race car drivers were notorious for messing around behind their spouses' backs. Working at the Speedway, Betty and her nursing friends saw a lot of drivers, the drivers' wives, and the drivers' girlfriends—sometimes both in the same day. As a result, her perception of the racing fraternity was not too wonderful. Perhaps that's why her dad was somewhat suspicious when he found out that his daughter's new beau was a race car driver.

Betty, of course, had checked me out. She had read an article about me in the Indianapolis newspaper and I had told her on our first date that I was single. As far as she knew, I was a single man, and she told her father that. She had no intention of dating a race car driver if there was a chance that he might also be married. In fact, at one time she had even said to some friends that she would never marry a race car driver, because there wasn't any way to "tether 'em or trust 'em" that she could find.

Betty introduced us, and we were having some "get acquainted" conversation during a lull in the action on the track. Her dad was in midsentence when an announcement blared over the P.A. system from the garage area we were overlooking: "Johnny Rutherford! Please meet your wife and kids at the back gate of the garage area!"

The look on her dad's face was enough to strike me dead.

Betty looked at me with a red face, and everyone got quiet. I peered over the railing and spotted Chuck Hulse and Bobby Marshman, two driver friends of mine, practically rolling on the ground in laughter. It turns out that they had gone to the P.A. announcer and asked him to page me in that manner. Fortunately, Betty's dad quickly realized that it was a joke, and I was relieved when everyone broke out in nervous laughter.

As for Betty and me, we just clicked right away. Our dates were fun and filled with conversation, though we never discussed the dangers of race car driving. Betty never questioned my profession or asked me to quit during the entire time we were together and I was racing. She has been behind me one hundred percent all these years. She's been my sounding board, my partner, my teammate, and my best friend through the bad times as well as the good. Together we've experienced some incredible highs and some devastating lows—both personally and professionally. She helped me look beyond the next race.

Eventually everything worked out for us, but our relationship nearly ended before it began. Betty and her friend JoAnn were both registered nurses and had received their training at Methodist School of Nursing in Indianapolis. Betty, JoAnn, and another friend, Sue, had recently lined up jobs in Los Angeles at Cedars of Sinai Hospital. Betty was busy getting things organized for their move when she and I met.

I was supposed to attend a going-away party for the three friends, but I didn't show up until the very last minute. Betty told me later that had I not shown up, she would have never seen me again. I would have been out of her life forever. But, thankfully, I arrived just in time. For the rest of the month Betty and I saw each other every night.

When I proposed, Betty eagerly accepted, although she was still planning to go to California to begin her work at Cedars of Sinai. My feelings for Betty were so strong that I felt I had to talk her out of going to California—forcing her to give up her career. I didn't think it would be easy for us if I was racing all the time and she was working in another state. After much discussion, she consented. She virtually gave up her nursing career to marry a crazy race car driver.

As it turned out, Betty's knowledge of medicine and nursing came in handy whenever I had an accident or was placed in the care of doctors or other medical staff. She knew when they were not doing their job and would challenge them about it. In fact, she challenged them a lot over the years.

Betty has remained up to date in nursing advancements by attending continuing education courses, and still holds nursing licenses in Indiana, Texas, and California. She always says that she never regrets the decision she made on June 2, 1963.

My qualifying time for the 1963 Indianapolis 500 was a little better than 148 miles per hour, and I began the race in the twenty-sixth position in the thirty-three-car field. My team was sponsored by the U.S. Equipment Company.

As the start of the race drew near, I experienced the gamut of emotions: anxiety, anticipation, guarded optimism, humbling awe. I was twenty-five years old, and this day—Thursday, May 30, 1963—would be the realization of my longtime dream of running in auto racing's greatest event.

As soon as I was strapped into my Watson roadster and the Offenhauser engine was fired up, it was business as usual. I felt cool and calm. I experienced more butterflies when Betty and I were married five weeks later than I did in my first Indy 500.

I raced around the track for forty-three laps before the car developed transmission problems, forcing me to drop out of the race. I finished in twenty-ninth place. I was disappointed to be sure, but I was already looking forward to my next championship race, which was scheduled for June 9 in Milwaukee. I was still driving sprints and other race cars, too, and all that, plus my impending wedding to Betty, gave me much to think about—and a lot to be grateful for.

And, though it was a year away, I was also looking forward to my next shot at the Indianapolis 500. I had realized one dream, that of racing at the Speedway. Now I could attempt the realization of another dream—winning the legendary event.

Unfortunately, the 1964 Indy 500 would be a nightmare.

☆ CHAPTER 9 ☆

Fireball in My Face

I was running for the second time at Indy in 1964. As it turned out, I never made it past the second lap. One of the worst crashes in Indy history made sure of that.

I was driving for Ebb Rose, who owned a new Watson roadster that he had bought from A. J. Foyt. Herb Porter was my chief mechanic. We didn't have a sponsor's name on the car, but it was painted and covered with decals from accessory firms such as Champion Spark Plugs and Monroe Shock Absorbers. Applying these decals was the team's way of saying thanks and recognizing the companies' contributions.

I ran well in qualifying and earned the outside spot in the fifth row for the start of the race. It was a good starting spot and the team as a whole was confident. The car was comfortable; we were running on Firestone's new, low-profile, fifteen-inch tires, and the car handled and ran really well, thanks to Herb's engines, which always ran strong.

After the last weekend of qualifying, Ron Mussen, the publicity director for Bardahl, visited us in the garage. Bardahl was sponsoring a team, but neither of the Bardahl cars had qualified for the race. He offered to pay us to paint our car Bardahl colors and carry their name in the race. Both Ebb and Herb agreed. So the car's colors went from Fontana rose and black to Bardahl yellow, no. 86, with "Bardahl" painted across the hood, and our car became the "Bardahl Special."

On race day, everything was looking and feeling good. We had beautiful weather for the race—sunshine and moderate temperatures.

Dave MacDonald, a rookie who was driving Mickey Thompson's car, was beside me in the middle of the fifth row. Veteran Eddie Sachs, who had a loyal following at Indy and had nearly won the race a couple of years earlier, was right behind us in row 6.

I was thinking, *Eddie always goes to the front. He's a seasoned pro. If he gets by me somehow, I'll just fall in behind him and follow him, see if I can hang on, and go to the front.*

Sure enough, once the race started, Eddie charged ahead of me, and I let him in. I fell in line behind him, reminding myself that it was a long race.

Things settled down in the first lap and everything was looking good. We went into the first turn on the second lap, and out to the wall on the short chute. I was close behind Eddie, and as I started down the chute, a car came up on the inside of me. It was Dave MacDonald, and he was driving the wheels off his car. The car was bouncing and bounding. Davey dragged his left side in the grass and shot some grass and dirt out as he slid in front of me. Then he took off and eased past Eddie and a few other cars down the backstretch.

I thought, *Whoa, boy! He's either gonna win this thing or crash, because you just don't run like that this early in the race.* He was gone. We came around turn 2 and down the backstretch, through turn 3, across the short chute and into turn 4. I was closing in on Eddie's bumper.

As we came down around the corner on the line and just before we started letting it drift up, I noticed something off to my left and just ahead on the inside of the track. It was difficult to see clearly because the track was still dirty from the past week of inactivity and from all the cars running so close together. But in a split second I saw a flash of red.

A red car—Dave MacDonald's—went out of control two-thirds of the way around turn 4. I saw it out of the corner of my eye as it skidded sideways into the infield wall. Davey's car, fueled with gasoline, exploded into a huge, billowy, orange-and-black fireball as it slid down the wall and moved backwards across the track, into the path of the other cars.

Eddie was right in front of me as we came off the fourth turn. The top of Eddie's helmet was painted fluorescent orange so that his crew down in the pits could identify him. Drivers always did that kind of thing. They'd paint fluorescent colors on the front of their cars, around the grill openings, or on their helmets—anything to make it easier for the crew and the fans to locate them.

I watched as the orange fluorescent paint on top of Eddie's helmet appeared on one side of the roll bar and then the other side as he glanced from side to side. With Eddie in front of me and about twenty drivers behind me, I was rapidly closing in on Davey's car.

I was hard on the brakes in a second—harder, I think, than I'd ever hit them. But at the speeds at which we were running, the brakes were like coaster brakes; they were just barely dragging and not doing much good. I was trying to keep my car straight while hitting the brakes hard. We were coming out to the wall as Davey's car was crossing our path and dragging the huge fireball with it. Sticking out of the fireball was Davey's left-rear tire and the tailpipes of his engine. His car probably slid to within three feet of the wall. That was my last vision of him.

I don't know if Eddie misjudged the speed of Davey's car as it slid across the track, or if he thought the car was in a different position because it was so consumed by the flames that he couldn't see it. Whatever the reason, Eddie turned left just as we came on the scene like he thought he could go under the mess, but instead he hit Davey's car dead-broadside. They were both using gasoline in their cars. Davey's car held about eighty gallons and Eddie's held seventy-five. That's a lot of gasoline to build a fire with.

When Eddie slammed into Davey, the back end of Eddie's car reared up in the air and I went under it. His right rear tire left a perfect tread mark about thirty-six inches long up the nose of my roadster. Then, most likely, my left front picked up the back of his car and punted it up and out of the way. This initial impact caused Eddie's car to burst into flames. All that gasoline—it was like jerking open the door on a blast furnace.

The impact threw me forward and whipped my head downward. Fuel rained down on me and flames seared the back of my neck, giving me second-degree burns. As I went under Eddie's car I also went over the back of Davey's car and ripped a couple of the injector horns off the left side of his engine. They became lodged in my left rear under-pan. Then my car rose up and scraped the top of the wall, where it left tire marks before dropping back onto the track.

The gasoline shooting through the air engulfed my car in flames. My two-speed transmission was in high gear, but my car had slowed down so much that it was starting to buck from going too slow for that gear ratio. I reached down and unlocked the transmission, and just as I was about to shove it into first gear I looked over and saw Bobby Unser heading for me in his Novi. His steering had been knocked out and his car was out of control. It slid sideways and he hit me broadside in the left rear tire. It was like a shot—*BANG!*—and it was over.

When Unser hit me, the force of the collision caused my car to lift up and slam into the outside wall on the front stretch. I had a wrap-around—also known as a granny—on the right side of my seat that held me up while I was driving. When Unser's car crashed into mine, the impact was so jarring that I slammed into the granny and bent it out over the edge of the cockpit. That's where it was when I finally stopped moving. My uniform was four layers, double-stitched, but the impact caused it to split open right at the center of the chest area. It looked like someone had grabbed my uniform at the sides and pulled it apart down the middle.

The Unser impact also ruptured my fuel tank, which was still full of fuel. But I was carrying methanol, and that is probably the only thing that kept my car from lighting up as well. The chain reaction involved several others: Ronnie Duman was also severely burned. Unser had hit him from behind, which is what had disabled Unser's steering. Duman's car then caught fire as he was trying to get out of it.

My car was still consumed in flames. I managed to get the clutch down and shift into first after Unser hit me. I jazzed the throttle and tried to pick up speed—I needed to extinguish the flames that were burning inside my car. We had placed a piece of carpet under the transmission on the cockpit floor to absorb oil, and flames flickered across it. Flames also swept along the side of my car and around the windshield, but I managed to pick up speed and the flames blew out.

I drove into the first turn, down low, staying out of the way. Of course, the yellow flag was out and everybody was slowed down under the caution. I got through the first turn and as I started across the short chute, whatever part of MacDonald's car I had collected beneath the left rear corner of my car became dislodged, and I ran over it. The object was large enough to elevate my car, which slammed down on the track with a hard bump. It wasn't until they found the car parts in the first turn that they realized my car had carried them from the site of the accident.

As I went across the short chute and into turn 2, another driver, Bob Veith, pulled up beside me and pointed to the infield—motioning for me to go off there. But my car felt okay and I didn't think anything was wrong with it. I nodded and moved over in that direction, but Bob stayed with me and again pointed to the infield, indicating that he wanted me to move off the track. This time I moved down and ran along the inside of the track. I still wasn't sure what, if anything, was wrong with my car. But as I pulled down to turn 3, I thought, *Maybe this thing is on fire.* Even though I had driven through the fireball moments earlier, I thought I had been able to clear away the flames.

A corner worker was standing in the third turn with a fire extinguisher. I pulled down to him and took my car out of gear while I kept my engine running. I motioned him over and yelled, "Is this thing on fire?" He looked at it and said, "I don't think so." I thanked him, put the car in gear, and took off, driving across the short chute at the north end and around turn 4. At this point the red flag was being waved—the signal that all drivers were to stop on the track.

There before me was the carnage. The fire, with Eddie and Davey inside it, was still blazing. Smoke was everywhere. Firefighters were hurriedly putting out the flames. Don Branson was standing outside by his car, and he motioned for me to stop. I stopped, shut off the fuel and the ignition, left the car in gear, and unhooked my seat belt.

When I stepped out of the car and turned around, I noticed that the fuel puddle under my car was growing bigger and bigger. That's why Bob Veith had asked me to get off the track and onto the infield. Just then, some firefighters with fire extinguishers came running over.

Branson looked at me and asked, "Are you okay?"

"Yeah," I said, "but my neck hurts."

He looked at it. "Yeah, you got some blisters there. It's got to be uncomfortable."

I just shrugged and started to walk toward the accident scene, but Don grabbed me and said, "You don't wanna go up there."

He led me over to the side of the track, where I got into one of the ambulances and was taken to the infield hospital. The doctor examined me, treated the burns on my neck, and sent me back to the garages.

Betty was in the stands that day. We were in just our first year of marriage. She always kept track of where I was in the race, so she noted that I was the fourteenth car in line when I went by her the lap before the accident. She had her radio tuned to the broadcast of the race, and while there was no mention of the accident at first, Betty could see that something was happening in turn 4. She was sitting close to the start/finish line.

Betty started counting cars, and when she got to fourteen, I wasn't there. Nobody was there. She did eventually see me come down the track, but she didn't know that I was on fire briefly or that my fuel tank had ruptured. Later she said it seemed like hours had passed for the accident to unfold, but in reality it lasted only seconds.

Eddie and Davey were both killed in the accident. In the hospital, I was on the stretcher next to Davey's. His burns were indescribable; I had never seen anything quite like that before. He died at about two o'clock that afternoon.

Davey had been a strong, healthy, blond-headed kid from California. He was a spectacular sports car driver and drove hard enough to broadside around corners. He had shown a lot of promise at Indy, and he had been convinced that he would win that year.

Eddie was like family. He was a close friend and one of the growing legends at the Speedway, having won the pole at Indy two years straight in '60 and '61. He was an extrovert—we called him "the Clown Prince." How sad that we lost them both.

Before the crew brought my car back to the garage they sucked out the remaining fuel to eliminate any hazard that could be caused by the ruptured fuel tank. They got my car back to the garage about the same time I arrived from the infield hospital. Herb Porter was there, and I gave my chief mechanic my perspective on all that had happened.

We walked over to the car, and Herb undid the hood restraints and lifted the hood next to the engine. There was a lot of trash in the engine—gravel, pieces of Plexiglas from windshields—all kinds of debris. Herb bent over the engine compartment and picked out a lemon that had a piece of string looped through it. One end had been cut off, exposing the fruit.

Later I asked around and discovered that Eddie Sachs always hung a lemon around his neck so that on the cautions, when he didn't need both hands on the wheel, he could squeeze and suck on the lemon to get a little moisture. Perhaps the tartness gave him a little boost.

Evidently, when Eddie slammed into Davey, the lemon flew off his neck and sailed through the air, and my car scooped it up.

That's close.

☆ CHAPTER 10 ☆

The Win at Atlanta

☆   ☆   ☆

Bob Wilke didn't want me driving his car. But A. J. Watson did.

Rodger Ward, who had won Indy for Wilke and Watson in '59 and '62, was no longer racing for the pair, and they were looking for a new driver. Even though I was only in my third year of Indy car competition, I knew I was ready to race for A. J.

I learned years later that A. J. supposedly called Bob and said he was going to put me in their car, and that Bob expressed doubt over my experience and abilities. A. J. said he thought I could handle it, but Bob gave him the names of a few other drivers to call. A. J. wanted me to drive the car, though, so he waited until Wilke, his cantankerous partner from Milwaukee, was out of the country before he hired me to race for them in the 1965 Atlanta 250.

Things work out in strange ways. The car turned out to be the one Rodger Ward had narrowly missed racing at Indianapolis earlier that year. He had completed a four-lap qualifying run, but it wasn't fast enough to bump Bill Cheesbourg, the slowest qualifier of the race.

The car was one of the first monocoque-constructed, independent-suspension, rear-engine cars of American manufacture. "Monocoque" is the term for a unitized auto-body frame structure with stressed sheet-metal panels.

Upon arriving in Atlanta, I had only one day to familiarize myself with the car, the crew, and the track before qualifying and racing. Because rear-engine cars in U.S. racing were still virtually unknown, no one really knew how to set one up for racing.

There was still much to be learned about a car with independent suspension, such as how the driver is supposed to steer with that steering rack. When the chassis on such a car runs through its ride mode—that is, when it lifts up and then comes down after hitting a bump—the sudden deflection of the suspension changes the steering direction. This is called "bump steer." When you hit a bump, it literally steers the front end, which can be unnerving. Unless the crew has figured that out, the driver could be in a world of trouble. If you're driving at high speed and you hit a bump, the car wants to go right or left. You really have to work hard to stay in command.

That car had a bad case of bump steer, but we didn't realize it until the next season, when we became aware of the concept. During practice at Atlanta one day, with the morning sun over my shoulder, I came off a turn and hit some bumps on the track. The Firestone tires we were using featured gold stripes that ran the circumference of the tires' side-walls. The car was undulating over the bumps, and I could see the gold stripes on my tires appear and disappear as the wheels toed in and toed out. That was definitely unnerving. We now know that adjustments in the geometry of the steering arms determine how the car steers. You adjust it so that when it moves up and down it doesn't toe in or out.

It was an evil-feeling race car. However, because I had no knowledge of rear-engine cars and no means of comparison at the time, I just drove the thing. Fortunately, I kept the car and myself out of jeopardy.

I started fifth in the Atlanta race, inside the third row. I was always a good qualifier and I really loved running on high-banked tracks. Atlanta was a 250-mile race—167 laps on a 1½ mile, high-banked track, one of the better high-banked racetrack venues where the fans can see the entire track. I enjoyed racing at Atlanta and won a few races there over the years.

The other A. J.—Foyt—and I dueled for a while in the 1965 race at Atlanta. Racing with A. J. was the highlight of the day for me. Anytime I raced with A. J. it was good. He's such a strong competitor, and he ran the rest of us so clean that it was fun to race him. I always enjoyed racing wheel to wheel and changing positions with guys like A. J.

A. J. and I ran a good race for a while before his car broke, spun, and hit the wall after eighty-seven laps. Fortunately, he didn't do himself any harm, but his car—a Lotus—was done for the day. There were other crashes during the race, including a few that were pretty wild, but I managed to stay clear of any real trouble until my own car nearly deserted me with just three laps to go. Something in the car's suspension broke and I almost spun in the first turn, so I had to cool it the rest of the way.

Yet, in the end, we won the race. I led Mario Andretti and Canadian Billy Foster to the checkered flag. Atlanta was my first victory in a championship race, and it was a thrill.

The car, as it turned out, was not all that bad once I got a feel for it. In fact, I even set a new track record with it when I averaged better than 141 miles per hour. And I certainly couldn't argue with the $17,450 I collected in prize money.

For most of the estimated twenty-seven thousand fans who attended the race, it was not the type of race they were used to seeing at that track. Atlanta was a major speedway on NASCAR's stock car circuit. Having Indy cars race there was something of a novelty, and we put on a good show.

I felt a great sense of accomplishment after my first Indy car victory, which secured my position with A. J. Watson for the rest of the 1965 season. He had a great dirt car, too, and the dirt series was still involved in the Indy car championship then. Running the dirt car and the rear-engine pavement car at different tracks, I found myself a part of one of the premier auto racing teams.

We could have really developed a great team beyond the '65 season, but in April of the following year I crashed at Eldora and broke both of my arms. Sidelined for the 1966 season, my ride with A. J. Watson's team was over.

☆ CHAPTER 11 ☆

Sprint to the Championship

I began the 1965 sprint car season driving for car owner and builder Steve Stapp. Steve's dad Babe Stapp raced at Indianapolis for many years and was a California Ascot Speedway sprint car and big car driver of note.

Steve's black no. 4 was a fast race car with state-of-the-art suspension—one of the better cars I had driven up to that point. My first race with Steve was at Raceway Park in Indianapolis, a five-eighths-of-a-mile paved track. Prior to the qualifying race, I was running "hot laps"—practicing with the rest of the drivers and their cars on the track—and I was *flying*. During qualifying, I was really leaning on it hard, pushing myself and the car to the edge. I was running pole speed—nearly track record speed—when the car slipped on me and just kissed the wall coming out of turn 4. That "kiss" bent the front axle and broke a wheel. We were out for the day.

Steve was furious. He had probably been counting his money already from what he thought would be a sure victory for us. We loaded the car onto the trailer. Seething, Steve came over to me and said, "I'm gonna talk to Foyt. I'm gonna hire him to drive my car."

"Fine, Steve," I said. "You're not gonna let me run it anymore?"

"No, I don't think so. You're fired."

"Well, okay, but you're making a mistake."

"What do you mean?"

"I'm gonna win the championship this year."

Stapp just laughed. "Yeah, right," he said. "Sure you are."

I turned and walked away.

A. J. Foyt was driving for Wally Meskowski at the time, but A. J. really liked Stapp's car. At least, that's what I think, because when Stapp told A. J. that he had fired me, A. J. took the ride in Stapp's car. I figured that since A. J. was going to take the ride with Stapp, Wally Meskowski would need a new driver. I decided to go talk to Meskowski about letting me race for him.

Wally agreed to put me in his ride for the next race on a trial basis. I went over to Wally's shop in Indianapolis and sat in the car. It fit like it was made for me.

The next race, and my first race in Meskowski's car, was at Eldora Speedway.

When we got to Eldora, I checked out the track. It was a high-banked dirt track—my kind of track—and when they watered it, gravity still prevailed; the water ran downhill to the bottom of the track. During the course of the evening, the cars would knock off the moisture; it wouldn't be dusty, but it wouldn't be tacky, either. Everyone would slip and slide because the track would become "hard slick." The race would be run at night, under the lights.

I walked down to the first turn to watch one of the heat races. I noticed that the part of the track around the bottom was still pretty moist because all the water had collected down there. I walked onto the track and dug my heel into it. I discovered that it wasn't soupy or muddy at the bottom, just moist. I thought, *I'll try that dirt in the feature.*

I started the orange-and-white no. 9 in the fifth spot in the feature. We came down for the green flag and everybody went into the turn on the banking. But I went around the track on the flat part at the bottom.

I had really stumbled onto something—I got a hold of that racetrack and it was just right. I'd never driven a race car that got that much forward and side bite at the same time. It was uncanny.

I was busy driving the car, and when I passed everyone ahead of me and came out on the backstretch, I suddenly realized I was in the lead. I looked for the yellow caution light, expecting that someone had wrecked behind me. Why else would it seem like everyone had gotten out of throttle? Boy, I was gone.

Wally had put a soft right rear-tire on the car for the feature. It was called a Firestone Lightning Drag, and was a drag racing tire for passenger cars. The tire was made of a softer rubber, and when it was grooved for dirt racing it ran really well on dirt tracks. Because those tires were so soft and we were running them so hard, they would not go thirty laps; they'd go twenty-seven laps and then go flat.

Sure enough, with two laps to go in the race and me leading by nearly a straightaway, the car got a flat tire. It was a wonder I didn't dump the car, but I managed to keep it under control and get it into the pits.

Wally seemed disgusted with himself. He said, "I'll never do that to you again. We'll never run another Lightning Drag except in a heat race."

He was true to his word; we never ran a Lightning Drag again unless it was in a heat race, which had a shorter duration.

I don't recall where exactly I finished in that race, fifth or sixth perhaps, but what a race car! It was as though it had been made especially for me. Regardless of the setback at Eldora, we set a new track record there and continued to have a great season. Wally's car was so tailored to my driving style that we won many races with it and finished well with it in others. We set track records at just about every track we raced. That season we won two races, including a one hundred-lap race, at Winchester—a tortuous, high-banked, half-mile, paved racetrack. At Winchester we were lapping the car in the eighteen-second bracket and the high seventeens, well over a 110- or 120-mph average. Today's drivers, with their sprint cars that use big tires, are now lapping there in fourteen seconds. It's incredible how fast they go. It's *too* fast. I raced cars for a living and even I know it's stupid to go that fast.

Another memorable race for me that season was held at the state fairgrounds in St. Paul, Minnesota. I had raced there many times when I was on the IMCA circuit. It was a dirt track then, but the track officials had it reconfigured and it was now a fast paved track.

I earned quick time both days, and my teammate and nemesis in championship car racing, Don Branson, had second quick time. It seemed that Don, A. J. Foyt, Roger McCluskey, Jim Hurtubise, Parnelli Jones, and I were always vying for pole position, dueling for the lead, or battling to win a race. That weekend I won both races, back to back, in my first time running on the pavement at St. Paul.

After my second win, Branson walked over to me and said, "That's it, kid."

"What are you talkin' about?" I asked.

"I'm not tellin' you anymore. You're on your own," he said. "You keep askin' me questions and I keep tellin' you how to do this or do that, but I'm not tellin' you anything anymore. You're startin' to beat me."

Having come from Don Branson, one of the all-time racing greats, this struck me as a compliment.

All season long I was in the hunt to win the 1965 USAC sprint car championship. Even with Wally's car I still was not a lock to win, especially since Greg Weld, my closest challenger, was a very good driver. We raced each other one tough race after another. In the end, though, Wally, the crew, and I won the championship by two and a half points—it was that close.

I saw Steve Stapp at the last race of the season at Ascot after I won the championship, and said, "I told you." All he could say was: "I should have listened to you."

I've seen Steve on more than one occasion since then—and I even drove for him years later—and every time I have reminded him of my prediction that I would win the 1965 championship. He just sighs and says, "Yeah, I know."

Over the course of my racing career, there wasn't one specific moment that really crystallized for me that feeling of having "made it." There was always so much more to do—records to set, races to win. But winning the sprint car championship in 1965, along with the fact that I was winning races and making money, did inspire in me a huge sense of accomplishment.

Winning races and winning championships was what I had intended for myself all along. I didn't do it to get my name in the papers; trophies, plaques, and rings were nice, but I tried to remain humble and stick to my credo of always keeping my eyes on the future. For me, focus was the key. More or less, that's how I'd like to be remembered as a race car driver.

I had watched A. J. Foyt, Parnelli Jones, and Jim Hurtubise win races and championships and earn success. To join that elite group—to be considered a real racer by the fans and my peers—was the ultimate reward.

Long ago I took to heart the wise advice of Herb Porter: "If you read your press notices, pretty soon you'll start believin' 'em."

I never tried to pump myself up by reading my press notices—I did that by driving a race car. Winning: that's what it was all about anyway . . . though I did always hope they'd at least spell my name right.

☆ CHAPTER 12 ☆

My Comeback after Eldora

Little did I know that I wouldn't be doing much winning—or much racing, for that matter—when the 1966 racing season began. My accident at Eldora had sideswiped all my racing dreams for the moment, but I was still a part of the community that had become like a family to me over the years. In fact, I was graciously welcomed back by my racing friends.

Whenever I visited a track during the 1966 season, people were always encouraging me and inquiring about my recovery. But when they would ask how they could help me out, everyone would scatter, because my reply was so unpleasant: "Yeah, I really need to go to the bathroom."

It was like pulling the pin on a hand grenade and dropping it on the ground. I'd look around and find myself standing alone.

The situation was unpleasant, but on occasion it was a little funny, too. In midsummer of 1966, Dick Wallen, my longtime friend and a great racing photographer from California, consented to take me to Terre Haute, Indiana, where I was scheduled to do some promotional work for Don Smith, the promoter at the Viego County Fairgrounds "Action Track." Dick and I made a few stops at the local newspaper and radio stations. I may have had two broken arms, but I was the reigning sprint car champion with two broken arms, and interviews were part of my duties that season.

While we were in Terre Haute, Dick and I decided to have some lunch. With both my arms in casts, we decided that a chocolate milkshake would probably be my best option. That, and whatever scraps of solid food I could manage to eat without making a mess of myself. I must have been such a sight to behold!

Dick and I finished up our promotional tour after lunch. When we got into the car to head back to Indianapolis, I said to Dick, "Hey, Wallen, can you pull over? I really need to go to the bathroom."

I think we set a new land speed record that day. Dick would not stop anywhere for me to go to the bathroom. He just couldn't fathom having to help me with my duties, so he sped back to Indianapolis and deposited me at my apartment so Betty could take care of me. I've made the trip from Terra Haute to Indianapolis many a time, and that was by far the fastest I've ever done it.

Everyone was very supportive of me during my healing process. However, as I had my casts removed and began attending physical therapy to prepare myself for my return to the cockpit, there seemed to be a lot of raised eyebrows around the racing community.

It's not unusual for people to begin questioning a driver's abilities—or lack thereof—after he sustains serious injuries from a racing accident. His fellow racers want to know if he's lost the "right stuff," if he's really going to be able to do it again. Car owners wonder if they should invest the time and money to determine if he's still as good as he was before the accident.

It was frustrating—enormously frustrating—to feel the tension begin to build whenever I approached a car owner. No one was sure I could still cut it out there on the track. That was my endurance test in early 1967: the doubters. Not everyone doubted me, but enough did. I was starting my racing career from scratch—again.

I eventually hooked up with a new owner, Sid Weinberger from Jackson, Michigan. Sid hired me to drive his Ford Indy car with Wally Meskowski, my former sprint car owner and mechanic, as my crew chief. Wally often worked on both sprints and Indy cars throughout a racing season. In 1967 he parked his sprint car for the month of May and stayed in Indianapolis to concentrate on the Weinberger car.

Wally was probably the reason I was able to get a ride with the Weinberger Homes team for the 1967 Indy 500. As Weinberger's chief mechanic, he convinced Sid that I would make a good addition to the team.

Once I passed my usual spring physical and the USAC physical at the track hospital, I was deemed fit to drive a race car at Indy and my USAC license was reapproved. I was ready to show everyone I was capable of driving again.

Until the 1970s, the Indianapolis Motor Speedway track was open for practice every day from nine A.M. until six P.M. Those normal practice runs were the best therapy I could find to get myself back in shape after my yearlong layoff.

The first day I took the car onto the track was pure bliss. I was again doing what I loved to do after being away from it for so long. Any apprehension I had was normal, and it quickly gave way to elation.

It was the best I'd felt emotionally in a year.

Physically, though, it was another matter. I thought I was fit and okay, and although I felt somehow different, I really thought that I was performing reasonably well behind the wheel. I was healed and on top of the world, and the feel for driving was coming back to me—even after nine operations on my right arm, my coordination was still good. I did not yet realize what poor physical shape I had slipped into during the year of inactivity I endured after my crash at Eldora.

Although we had few if any problems qualifying for the race, I didn't immediately grasp that I wasn't at full strength yet. I eventually discovered that stamina doesn't return overnight. It was at least a year before I noticed how much better I felt compared with those first few months back in the game after my accident, especially at Indy in '67.

After my operations, I had to rebuild a lot of arm muscle mass because my arms had been in casts for so long that the muscles had atrophied. And, because of the injury to my elbow joint and the resulting scar tissue from inadequate physical therapy, my right arm would not extend past a seventy- to seventy-five-degree angle.

For a time it was difficult trying to drive with my right arm not being able to extend to a normal driving position, because it required me to reach out for the steering wheel.

The doctors told me my arm could be fixed, but that I would probably lose twenty percent of my arm strength and/or the ability to keep it from dislocating in the process. Hearing that, I just told them to leave it alone.

But I knew that something had to be done to compensate for that lack of mobility. Our first adjustment was to the steering wheel—we moved it back slightly so that I'd have more leverage and I could be a little more comfortable in an Indy car. Later, we discovered that one of the other drivers—it might have been Gary Bettenhausen—had placed a wedge under his steering wheel to cock it upwards. In my case, I needed the steering wheel cocked low on the left and high on the right. The guys on my team went to work. They formed a wedge out of aluminum that was then fitted into the steering system so that the bolts for the steering wheel itself went through the wedge.

The result was that the top of the steering wheel was a little farther away from me than the bottom was. When I turned the steering wheel, it didn't move away from me. This made it much easier for me to turn the car to the left, and even to the right. Rather than having to extend my arm to reach the top of the steering wheel, I could keep my arm in the position in which it was most comfortable since the top and the bottom of the wheel were the same distance from me in the cockpit.

This little adjustment helped me considerably in racing my car, but it wasn't able to help me finish the 1967 Indy 500.

Considering that this race was my first in more than a year, I was doing well. I was only a dozen cars behind the leader just before the halfway point in the race. And then there was an accident on lap 99. Cale Yarborough spun out at the north end of the track and a couple of other drivers, including veteran Lloyd Ruby, hit the wall trying to avoid Cale's spinning car. Right away the caution flag was raised.

At Indianapolis at that time, when the yellow caution flag was displayed you had to hold your position; you didn't "pack up" behind the leader. Even if you were alone on the backstretch, you had to hold your position, maintaining your speed as best you could. But because it was hard to maintain exact position under those conditions, you might lose time to the leader or gain time on the leader.

I was running with a group of cars when the caution flag was raised. After several laps under the yellow the track crews were finally able to clean up the debris, and it was time to go green. I was ready to go for it. However, Ronnie Duman, who was in front of me in the race, didn't go when the green came on.

Without two-way radios or spotters to alert the drivers about situations regarding the race, Ronnie was unaware that we had been given the signal to pick up speed. He simply was not moving. I was in a position to pull down to the bottom of the track and try to go under him to get by. But when I did, I got into the grit and dirt that collects at the bottom of the track. My car turned sideways and spun, and I just barely bumped the inside wall in the backstretch coming out of turn 2, which bent my suspension. My race day was over.

Once again I had been unable to finish the Indianapolis 500. I was really upset with Ronnie. Of course, some of my frustration about the '67 Indy was directed inward. I kept thinking that maybe the spinout was my fault because I cut under him. With Ronnie running so slow, if I had locked up the brakes I would have hit him. I had to dodge to miss him, and when I did, my car spun in the grit.

I had been running in the thirteenth spot—perhaps that number *is* unlucky— when I spun out. I ended up twenty-fifth. Ronnie eventually picked up speed and continued racing for another fifty laps before his engine blew. He finished a couple of spots ahead of me. It was just another one of those "racing accidents," a learning experience. Nevertheless, I was angry and disgusted about it.

A. J. Foyt took the checkered flag at the 1967 Indianapolis 500. He won when Parnelli Jones's transmission gave out with about three or four laps to go. Mario Andretti, who started on the pole position, had dropped out about a quarter of the way through the race when he lost a wheel in the first turn and spun out across the infield.

Even though we finished low that year at Indy, I was grateful for the opportunity to race again after my sprint car accident. The team ran together for the duration of the season, but we didn't meet with a lot of success due to some engine troubles and other assorted mechanical problems with various cars. Still, my toughest challenge as I continued my comeback in '67 was to build up my physical stamina. As I grew stronger over the next few months, I could sense that my reaction times and endurance were returning. I was becoming more productive out on the tracks.

I look back on that period as a part of my maturation as a race car driver. I became frustrated at times, even angry, at the way things were going for me, particularly at the Indianapolis Motor Speedway. Yet somehow I kept at it. I persevered.

Betty helped me stay on an even keel. She was always with me—she was my rock. My life would have been so chaotic without her.

I never experienced any doubts about my comeback as far as my abilities or my desire were concerned. Finding cars to drive was the hard thing. That, and trying to finish an Indy 500. Some of the larger and better-funded racing teams were running tests, but I mostly just got behind the wheel and raced on weekends. I didn't have the time or much of an opportunity for testing; I just needed to concentrate on getting back into racing. My only priority was finding a car in which I could race. I didn't need frills or extras—I would take what I could get. I was still on the comeback trail. It was as simple as that.

After I ran a few races in 1967, something started happening. I could see it in people's faces, hear it in their voices. I could even feel it when I went to the track. Any misgivings or doubts people had been harboring about my decision to return to racing after my accident were disappearing. The glimmer of hope was there. Even though I still had a ways to go, when people saw that my desire, my love of the sport, and my basic abilities were intact, they stopped looking at me with apprehension and treating me as though I were now somehow different.

People noticed something else about me, too—a new helmet. It was not new in the sense of safety features, but in that it sported a new design. The idea for my helmet's new paint scheme came to me during the latter part of the 1966 season, when I was still very much out of racing and recuperating from the Eldora crash.

In the late fall of 1966, Betty and I attended a sports car race at Nassau, the Bahamas. Goodyear Tire and Rubber Company had invited Betty and me to Nassau as their guests, to relax while helping Goodyear with some PR at the event. We were seated in the elevated pit boxes at the track, and when the cars came in they stopped right beneath us.

One of the drivers, Buck Fulp, was from Atlanta, Georgia. Buck was driving a Lola, and he'd had some success with it in that series. When he pitted during practice, I looked down and noticed that he had painted a Confederate flag on the top of his red helmet. It looked really slick, and I thought to myself, *I could do that to my helmet, only with the Texas flag.*

I've always been proud of my Texas heritage even though I was born in Kansas and spent part of my youth in Oklahoma. I've always identified myself as a Texan. Like the old saying goes, "I'm not a native Texan but I got here as fast as I could."

When Betty and I returned home, I got a new helmet shell from the manufacturer and used some eighth-of-an-inch masking tape to map out my idea on the helmet. I determined that the star had to be at the very front, with the stripes coming down the sides. I then took the helmet to a painter to have it done.

The helmet was first painted pearlescent white; I always had a pearl-white helmet. Then the painter sprayed the candy red and blue stripes. The star had been masked out with tape, and when the red and blue paint dried, he just peeled off the tape and we had our pearlescent-white star. To top it off, he hand-striped the black border around the star.

The new paint scheme marked the revival of my career and depicted the Texas heritage I so enjoyed. The helmet sort of became my trademark, and when people saw it coming down the track, they knew it was Lone Star J. R.

☆ CHAPTER 13 ☆

Heartbreak, Hope, and Hospital Food

Phoenix is named for the mythological bird that arose from its own ashes to live again, so it seems fitting that I survived my own fiery crash there on April 7, 1968.

I was driving for Jerry Eisert and the Harrison racing team. During the race, Al Unser's car blew its engine on the backstretch. I was the first one to reach the oil spill on the track, and when I did, I spun, hit the fence, and slid around the corner, stopping in turn 3. Roger McCluskey hit the spill next; he slid on the oil, too, but instead of hitting the fence, he hit me. Seconds later, Mario Andretti slid on the oil, spun around, struck the fence, and then hit McClusky. Upon impact, Andretti's car turned, slid backwards, and hit me broadside, rupturing my fuel tank with his exhaust pipes and thereby igniting the fuel in my tank.

Back then, we wore tight fitting, leather golf-type gloves that allowed us to get a good grip on the steering wheel. In order to push myself out of the cockpit after the crash, I had to place my leather-gloved hand into the gaping split in the now burning fuel tank. I jumped out of my car and ran away from it. My right-hand glove was so hot it began melting to my hand. I was desperate to pull it off, but when I jerked it down my skin went with it like it was attached to the glove. I pulled the glove off, and the skin on the back of my hand was turned inside out and was just hanging off my fingertips.

A. J. Foyt had already dropped out of the race and was standing at the end of the pits, not far from where the accident had unfolded moments before. He ran over and found Roger lying on a stretcher, dazed and woozy; he had most likely sustained a concussion. A fireman was walking me across the track as I held my grotesque, skinless right hand with my left. My feet were still hot because my black shoes had absorbed a lot of heat, so I was practically falling down with each step.

A. J. was standing there, looking over McCluskey, when I cried out, "A. J.! My feet are still burning! Is there something wrong?"

He ran over to me, dropped to his knees, and raked his fingers down both of my shoelaces. The laces had burned, and they just fell apart when he touched them. We got my shoes off and were relieved to find that my feet weren't burned. But when A. J. looked up and saw the skin hanging off my hand, he turned white.

A. J. turned around and gently picked McCluskey up off the stretcher, set him down on the ground, and then picked me up and laid me down on the stretcher. He looked at McCluskey and said, "Sorry, Roger, but you're not hurt bad enough. Look at Rutherford over there!"

I have a belly laugh every time I think about that. Good ol' A. J. He even went to the hospital with me. When we got there he told everybody that he was my brother so he could stay with me in my room. In fact, he angrily paced up and down the hallway, constantly checking the time while we waited for the doctor to finish mowing his lawn and get to the hospital to treat my hand.

Burns, I think, are perhaps the most painful injury a driver can suffer, because they kill the nerve endings. The medical staff shot me full of painkillers, soaked my hand in ice water to keep the swelling down, debrided it, and finally dressed it.

During the entire procedure, A. J. really took care of me; he sat with me and talked with the doctors and nurses about my condition. He even called Betty—who was pregnant and at home in Fort Worth—every half-hour to give her a progress report. I overheard A. J. talking on the phone with Betty; he spoke about the accident as though it wasn't as bad as it really was, so that Betty wouldn't get upset. I've always been indebted to him for that.

This is a side of A. J. that a lot of people never get to see. Later he took me back to the hotel, and on the way there I became nauseated and told A. J. to stop the car. He immediately pulled off to the side of the road, stopped the car, and got out. He ran around to the passenger side so he could hold my forehead while I threw up. Once he was convinced I was okay, he sped back to the hotel.

At the hotel, A. J. and his wife Lucy kept an eye on me overnight and took good care of me. He made arrangements for me to fly home to Fort Worth and put me on the plane the next day.

Back in Fort Worth, I wasn't able to relax too much because the Indianapolis 500 was coming up and I had to prepare for it. My desire to race again—especially at Indy—was so strong that it may have even helped me heal faster.

Although the doctors suggested that I should have a few skin grafts, I decided against it. They kept checking my condition regularly in the weeks after the accident, making sure that everything was healing cleanly. The affected area was debrided frequently—a very painful, though necessary, procedure.

When the skin started growing back, it grew in little islands that expanded and joined together, forming a new covering of skin on my hand. Sometimes I couldn't even bend my fingers to make a fist because the skin was so tight. I had to keep my hand lubricated so that the new skin would be soft and pliable.

My situation wasn't without humor. As Indy approached, I was still scheduled to drive for Alan Green. When practice began my hand was still very tender, so I had to overlubricate the skin and wear a white cotton glove under my leather racing glove. On my way out to the pits one day, Vic Holt, the president and CEO of Goodyear Tire and Rubber Company, walked over to me to talk shop.

I had known Mr. Holt for several years. He was a tall, big man, and quite friendly. He greeted me with a handshake, and my face turned white. My hand hurt so much from the pressure that, while we exchanged pleasantries, all I wanted to do was run out back and throw up.

When you look back through the history of motor sports, I'm just another example of a driver who has come back from an injury to race again. A. J., for example, broke his back at Riverside in a stock car. He recuperated over the winter and, against doctors' wishes, was back testing and running his race car in the spring. People always have stories like that about guys who came back from crash injuries as soon as they possibly could. I was one of many.

The car I drove in the 1968 Indy belonged to Alan Green, a car dealer from Seattle, Washington. In fact, the car was sponsored by the city of Seattle and was called the "City of Seattle Special." The car was first assembled in California, and then my crew chief, Jerry Eisert, and his crew took it to Seattle for a big celebration beneath the Space Needle. It was a rah-rah, go-get-'em kind of affair for the team, the Chamber of Commerce, and the citizens of Seattle. The car was painted in the colors of the Chamber of Commerce, yellow and purple.

The crew drove straight from Seattle to Indianapolis and I joined them there for the start of practice. When we arrived in May, a sadness lingered over the track. The month before, Jim Clark, who had won Indy in 1965, died in a Formula 2 race in Hockenheim, Germany. It was raining the day of the race, and Jimmy's race car went off the road and struck a tree. He was killed instantly. Sadly, Jimmy was not scheduled to race that day, but for some reason his car owner thought it would be good for them to run there.

Rain also created havoc at Indy qualifying that year, so officials announced that there would be an extra day of qualifying. In yet another unfortunate loss, rookie Bob Hurt, who was attempting to earn one of the remaining spots for the feature, crashed into the wall in the first turn and suffered a paralyzing spinal injury.

Joe Leonard, who had replaced Parnelli Jones on the Granatelli team, won the pole position for the race. Parnelli had done well with the no. 40 STP turbine car the year before, but was unhappy with the new air inlet restrictions imposed by the USAC, which reduced its size by a third. Parnelli didn't think his car had much of a chance to compete, so he withdrew from the race.

Our qualifying time was only good enough to put us in the middle of the grid for the start of the race. We never really were a serious contender that day, but we gave it everything we had. After running about two-thirds of the race, I was hit from behind by—of all people—Jimmy McElreath, and I crashed. My race was over. Although it was not the outcome our team had worked toward, I was at least grateful for the opportunity to race at Indy so soon after the incident at Phoenix.

In the days following the Indy 500, I did some film work at the Speedway and then attended a business meeting in Akron with Goodyear Tire and Rubber Company. From Akron I flew to Milwaukee on Saturday, June 8, to attempt to qualify for the Indy car race there the next day. When I arrived in Milwaukee, I was told to call Dr. Strickland at Community Hospital in Indianapolis immediately.

Betty had given birth to our first child, a son. But the little guy was two months premature, so Betty and I felt both elated and concerned. In the years leading up to our son's birth, we had lost three babies due to premature births. Betty was extremely depressed after the loss of our third child, and recovery was difficult for her. It was a rough period in our lives, but it probably brought us closer together in the end. Only parents who have faced that heartbreak can understand what we went through. Even now I don't like to talk about it. But this time, God smiled on us. Now we had to wait and pray he would survive.

Unfortunately, because I was committed to the race the next day, I couldn't leave Milwaukee. Before we had children, Betty and I had agreed that if I were scheduled to race, I would race no matter what. As an independent woman, Betty was comfortable with this scenario.

On race day, my mind was in two places—on my newborn baby boy and the task at hand. I was able to focus on my job well enough to qualify for the race on Saturday and finish fourth in the race on Sunday.

After the race I hotfooted it back to Indianapolis to see Betty and the baby. Because of his low birth weight, he remained in the hospital nearly a month before Betty and I were allowed to take him home—all five pounds of him.

I always tell people that Betty beat me to the registrar. We hadn't really discussed names for the baby, because after losing three, we were just hoping for a healthy child. I recalled how much of a hassle it was for my dad, granddad, and me to share the same name, but Betty said she wasn't about to be the one to depart from family tradition. Therefore, John S. Rutherford IV was it. John was born prematurely, but he was a tough little kid, and he made it.

From 1963 through 1968, Betty and I lived in an apartment in Indianapolis during the summer and in Fort Worth during the off-season. One late summer evening, we were having a get-together with some racers from the neighborhood on the lawn near our apartment. Suddenly, A. J. said to me, "I'm going to give your kid his first taste of beer," and he stuck his finger into a glass of beer and put it into John's mouth. John was about four months old at the time.

The two have forged a special bond over the years. A. J. was John's favorite racer . . . well, maybe his second favorite. When John was three years old, I bought him a real motorcycle, a "mini-Indian" with training wheels. John and I went to Houston to pick it up at the dealership, and while we were there, we stopped in to see Jack Starnes, one of A. J.'s mechanics, and his wife Betsy. A. J. happened to show up and said that he had a helmet that would fit John.

The helmet belonged to A. J.'s son, who had worn it when he raced quarter midgets. A. J. helped John strap it on and then we helped John get on the motorcycle and start it. A. J. ran alongside the bike as John drove, operating the throttle. But A. J. turned the throttle a little too much and the bike got away from him. John was holding on for dear life. Jack yelled to A. J., "What are you tryin' to do, kill Rutherford's kid?"

Fortunately, John and A. J. survived that first ride and became lifelong friends.

☆ ☆ ☆ ☆ ☆

Because of all the problems Betty and I had encountered in trying to have children, it was necessary for Betty to have a hysterectomy. She was unable to have anymore children, but Betty and I wanted a little girl to complete our family. So in the spring of 1970 we contacted the Edna Gladney Center, an adoption agency in Fort Worth, and began the process. Eight months later, in January of 1971, we received a call from the agency—we had been selected to be the parents of a thirteen-day-old beautiful baby girl born on January 13. We named her Angela Ann.

As they grew up, Betty and I quickly grasped how different our children's personalities were: John was calculating—he wanted to know about everything and how things worked; Angela, on the other hand, was our daredevil.

Our little girl was absolutely fearless. One time we took the kids to Six Flags over Texas, between Fort Worth and Dallas. Angela rode all the wild rides with me in tow until I nearly got sick. She'd just laugh and pull me by the hand to the next ride, saying, "Let's go, Daddy! This is fun!"

As a young girl, Angela struggled at school. Some of her teachers would say, "We just don't think she wants to learn," or "She shows very little interest in her studies." Some teachers felt she just could not learn.

We knew this was not true, and we were determined to find out what could be troubling our daughter at school. It took a while to figure out what was wrong, as not many people were educated in the field of educational differences, and even fewer studies had been done on it. After many tests, we were told that Angela had auditory perception disability and ADD, attention deficit disorder, which made learning by conventional methods difficult for her. Angela really suffered. She was a bright, loving child who was eager to learn, but the schools in Fort Worth just were not equipped with the knowledge or expertise to help her. When Angela was three or four, her speech was difficult to understand and John was the only one who could comprehend her most of the time. But she was learning, and by the age of five we were trying to keep her quiet.

Betty started looking for schools that could teach Angela the way she needed to be taught. There were only about four schools in the country that focused special attention on learning differences. Finally, we enrolled Angela in a northeastern boarding school for her remaining high school years. The teachers and administrators there understood learning differences and knew how to help our daughter. She excelled at her extracurricular activities, winning several state medals and local trophies in swimming and many awards at her summer sailing camp. Angela graduated from high school in June of 1990 and attended both Schreiner College in Kerrville, Texas, and Tarrant County College. She earned her degree in early childhood development.

Angela married Craig Price, an attorney, in 1994, and they bought a home about twenty minutes away from where Betty and I live. We are so proud of our daughter, who is a wonderful woman, wife, and mother. Angela and Craig have three beautiful children: Conner, Evan, and Grant. Betty and I love having grandkids. We are typical grandparents, putting everything else on hold when our grandsons visit. We enjoy the opportunity to watch them grow up, and just hope they're not growing up too fast.

Watching our grandsons grow up reminds me often of my own son's childhood. John, like his father, participated in many activities, but would soon realize that his true passion was for auto racing. At Fort Worth Country Day School, John played football, baseball, golf, tennis, and soccer, on which he ultimately chose to focus. During the summers he attended a six-week-long aviation camp at Culver Military Academy, and eventually earned his pilot's license when he was seventeen. Upon graduating from the Culver summer program, John was awarded the Carpenter Award as the Outstanding Aviator for 1985.

After graduating from high school, John attended Westminster College on a soccer scholarship. During the summer after his freshman year at college, John worked for Goodyear's Racing Division and traveled the same circuit that I did. Then, during his sophomore year, John, who had always denied wanting to pursue a career as a race car driver, shocked Betty and I by announcing that he had decided he wanted to race. He began in earnest to prepare for a racing career by attending the Skip Barber Racing School, working at Jim Hall's Karting School, attending SCCA's Formula Ford School and Licensing, and the Winfield Racing School at the Paul Ricard racetrack in France.

Once John graduated from college with a degree in Art and Design, he entered go-cart racing. He built and maintained his cart while earning several victories during the next two years. Since I was often racing myself whenever John raced, Betty attended all his races and served as John's "pit mom." John soon moved into the highly competitive USAC F-2000 pro series. He finished sixth in point standings among more than thirty drivers and narrowly missed rookie of the year honors.

In 1996, John entered sports car racing. He had respectable runs at 24 Hours of Daytona and Sebring, and earned a class victory in the SCCA 24

Hours of Moroso. In 1997 and '98, John moved up to the Toyota Atlantic Championship, where he had respectable runs and was poised to run a third year when sponsorship was withdrawn too late for him to find another sponsor. John is running again in 2000, in the Grand Am and Motorola Cup races. He has great talent, and I hope he can persevere and become a great champion.

When not racing, John is a high-performance driving instructor, a demonstration driver, and a product-training specialist for several automobile manufacturers.

Betty and I had decided early in our marriage that she would attend my races whenever she could. And for the most part, she did. She would sit in the stands and time all the drivers with her stopwatch. It was her way of coping with my career; she couldn't have just sat at home or gone out to lunch with the girls. She had to be there so she could offer support and encouragement, and know what was going on when I was on the track. Then she only worried when there was something to worry about.

Betty was not the type of person to sit at home. She decided that if she had to give up her nursing career—which she did reluctantly because she and the nursing profession couldn't come to a working agreement—she was going to be a true partner in my travels. While it wasn't easy for her to give up something she had worked so long and hard to achieve, she felt she was trading it for something that was equally as good, or better.

Betty and I agreed that even if we had to eat beans because of the extra costs of her accompanying me to the races, we would. She probably only missed a total of four races in my career, and that was because she was pregnant and under doctor's orders to stay home.

When Betty and I were home, our children received one hundred percent of our attention and time. We know that the time we spent with them during their childhood was good quality time. And when we were gone, we spoke with them every single day. In fact, we still do, incredibly, even though our children are now both adults.

Betty and I were very lucky to have had such wonderful people to count on to take care of John and Angela while we traveled. In Fort Worth, a grandmotherly woman named Orene Eagle, who lived down the street from us, took care of the children. And, of course, we could always rely on my parents.

Whenever we were in Indianapolis, either a young woman named Judy or Betty's family watched over John and Angela.

When the children were able to attend the races, they did. In fact, every summer we traveled as a family from race to race. Only during the school year did they have to stay home and focus on education, friends, and interests. They needed that continuity in their lives as well as the appropriate degree of supervision and discipline. Betty and I always made it a priority to be there for our children's important occasions. I don't think we missed a single one. Not long ago, Betty asked John if he felt that he had been neglected when he was growing up because his parents were gone so much. He told her no, that it was perfectly all right and that he had accepted early on that this was the way his family lived.

Through all of our personal and professional ups and downs in the mid- to late 1960s, Betty still managed to attend virtually all of my races. So in late 1968, when John was just four months old, he made the trip with Betty and me across the United States to the West Coast, where as usual I would finish my racing season.

The '68 season had not been a good one. My teammates and I had encountered numerous car problems, and I ended up with only five top-ten finishes. But I didn't put any extra pressure on myself just because my family was growing. My desire and drive to win was always there, and I knew success would come.

Still, there was a brief period in the spring of 1968 when I immersed myself in winning with a capital "w."

Vince Edwards, a.k.a. "Dr. Ben Casey" (middle of front row) and me at the Little 500 in Anderson, Indiana, 1962.

First big car USAC race: 1962 Hoosier 100 at the Indiana State Fairgrounds.

*One of my favorite photos of me in the dirt: the 1965
Sacramento 100 with A. J. Watson as my chief mechanic.*

Betty and I were wed on July 7, 1963, in Napoleon, Indiana.

My rookie year at Indy, 1963.

Winner of the one-hundred-mile qualifying race at Daytona Beach, Florida (left to right: Smokey Yunick, me, and Smokey Yunick Jr.).

I set my first world record in this stock car, Smokey Yunick's black and gold Chevy, number 13, at Daytona International Speedway, February 1963.

Getting fitted to Smokey's car at Daytona, Brad Dennis assisting, February 1963.

On my way to victory at the 1965 Atlanta 250, my first win in championship car racing.

The day I put Steve Stapp's sprint car against the wall at Raceway Park in Indianapolis and was fired. I drove for Wally Meskowski for the remainder of the season and, as I had promised Stapp, won the 1965 championship.

Buckling up to win the 1965 National Sprint Car Championship at Ascot Raceway in Los Angeles, California.

On my way to the National Sprint Car 1965 Championship in Winchester, Indiana.

1965 USAC National Sprint Car Champion.

Racing definitely runs in the family: my brother Wayne in a midget race car in 1974.

☆ CHAPTER 14 ☆

Winning Was Everything —For a Few Weeks

☆ ☆ ☆

Movie critic Leonard Maltin gave it three stars. I've noticed, though, that he didn't comment on my performance in the film.

Yes, I was in a major motion picture. In 1968, Paul Newman, his wife Joanne Woodward, and Robert Wagner came to Indianapolis to shoot a film called *Winning.* I was hired to be the "driving double" for both Newman and Wagner. I would simply change uniforms, gloves, helmets, and goggles—and, of course, cars—to shoot scenes as the double for the two drivers.

Paul Newman's car in the film was painted to resemble Bobby Unser's 1968 Indy-winning car. The directors also used actual footage from that race: when you see Paul crossing the finish line in the film it's actually Bobby.

There were other drivers in the film as well, including my longtime buddy Jimmy McElreath, who drove Wagner's car in a few scenes. Newman and Wagner did some close-up work in the cars when Jimmy and I weren't driving for them.

In addition to driving, I also had a couple of cameo appearances in the movie. One was right before the start of the race, when a group of drivers who are heading to their cars to get strapped in stop by Newman's car to wish him good luck. If you watch closely, you may recognize the crewcut kid.

The film crew shot on location at the Speedway for nearly three weeks. In one scene, the filmmakers staged a reenactment of the front straightaway accident of 1966 to spice up Hollywood's fictional 1968 race. In '66, there was a huge pileup just as the race went green, and though no one was seriously injured, eleven cars were wrecked, including every car in rows 6 and 11.

The crew recreated the accident with actual race cars. The director had the props department make foam rubber tires, which looked just like real racing wheels. The foam tires were compressed, stuffed into an air cannon, and fired fifty to seventy-five feet into the air. When the tire was shot out of the cannon, it immediately expanded to its normal size and looked like a real tire flying through the air. Several of those air cannons were set up in strategic places around the accident site to create the scene, and smoke machines equipped with large fans blew smoke around the area. Real race cars wove in and out of the debris, just like it happened on race day.

The crew did a great job recreating that front-stretch incident with all the props and effects. It was fascinating to see it all come together.

The whole filming experience was enjoyable and enlightening. I have always welcomed the challenges of trying different things, and the added benefit to my work in *Winning* was that I got to know Paul Newman. Evenings after shooting, the racers would all go to Paul's trailer, relax with a beer, and tell racing stories. In preparation for his role, Paul was always studying the drivers and their actions to learn how we thought and talked and carried ourselves.

Soon after filming began, we realized that Paul was getting hooked on racing. Each time the director shot a slow scene of Paul and Wagner or another driver racing around the track, Paul was allowed to actually drive the race car because the speed was kept to sixty miles an hour. When Paul finished the scene—somehow always on the front straightaway—he would pass the camera car, leg it across the short chute and around turn 2, and then peel out. We could hear him all the way down the backstretch, flat on the throttle. He was truly enjoying himself.

After the film was released in 1969, Paul eventually started racing sports cars, and then moved into Trans Am racing—full-bodied sports car racing. He won a number of races and has been involved with various winning racing operations. He was one of the best amateur drivers I have ever seen. Paul now is an owner in CART and Michael Andretti and Christian Fittipaldi drives for his team.

Newman concentrated intently on his acting, and he understood what was required of him for this film. As he is in all his films, he was terrific in *Winning*. Paul's a hell of a guy and a great talent. Everyone involved had a lot of fun working on that film.

Now go rent the movie.

☆ CHAPTER 15 ☆

A Step Closer to Victory

In the 1969 Indy 500, I was part of the Michner team, driving for Walt and his sons, Joe and Jim. I was in the middle of the pack, at seventeenth, when the green flag was waved. That's the good news.

The bad news is that, after about twenty-four laps, I received the black flag, which means "Come in to the pits for consultation on a problem." My car was leaking oil.

When I pitted, we checked out the oil cooler and all the lines. Everything looked normal, so I went back out on the track. The car, however, was still blowing oil. I had to return to the pits and was forced to drop out of the race.

My old sprint car teammate, Mario Andretti, won the Indy that year for Andy Granatelli's STP team. He ran the entire race on one set of tires.

We brought the car back to the garage, and the mechanics took it apart to try to locate the source of the leak. They searched everywhere, but nothing appeared to be wrong with the area near the right-front corner of the car, where the oil had appeared. That particular car's oil tank was in front with the radiator, and had no side pods. We checked the oil cooler, the lines, the hoses—nothing was leaking. Everything was tight. The car was dry. But the oil had to be coming from somewhere.

The mechanics started cleaning up the car and preparing it for the next race. That's when they saw something in the engine. It was the three-quarter-inch pipe plug that threads into the gear case of the engine, but had not been safetied and had come loose during the race. They were pondering the mystery of the plug's appearance in the engine when suddenly the light came on. They determined that the plug had fallen out of the engine, and that the car's air stream—the way the air traveled through the car and pressurized portions of it—caused the oil that was coming out of the engine to be pulled up inside the car, to the front, and then out down the side of the car.

For the price of a twenty-cent piece of safety wire for that plug, we might have at least finished the race. Over the years, drivers, mechanics, and owners have talked about the six-dollar bearing or the three-dollar piece of hose. But those things happen. There's always some story like that after a success or a failure at the Indianapolis 500.

In qualifying for the 1970 Indy, I very nearly sat on the pole with a three-year-old car—a '67 Eagle-Offy.

Mike Devin, the chief mechanic on the car, and I collaborated on a wedge-shaped body design. We borrowed the idea from the wedge-shaped turbine cars that Colin Chapman at Lotus had brought over to the United States from England. Mike and I could see that the car's design, which featured a large, flat top that sloped down toward the nose of the car, gave it downforce and added stability.

However, when we brought the car to Indianapolis for practice runs and qualifying, we discovered something about the car that we didn't like: the front end had an understeer, or push, so when I turned the steering wheel, the car didn't respond as it should have. It wanted to push instead of turn and thus kept me from going fast.

We made some changes, but nothing seemed to work. Then, on a Thursday night after practice, we added a chin spoiler—a small, flat piece of metal that wraps around the bottom edge of the car's nose to give the front of the car downforce similar to the downforce on the back of the car. This spoiler was the forerunner to the more effective front wings on today's Indy cars.

That was it. Once that spoiler was on the car, everything came into focus. By Friday evening, the night before the qualifying draw, we were running as quick as Al Unser, who had dominated for the past few days. Parnelli Jones owned the car Al drove, and he was the only one who noticed my car's increase in speed. He stopped by our garage and asked us what we had found.

We were coy. We said we didn't know what had caused the difference in speed. We told Parnelli that we had simply changed the car's setup, that we had rethought our approach to the design. I'm surprised any of us could keep a straight face.

He just shrugged and said, "Well, you're goin' good," and as he walked off I knew he was thinking that his team might have some competition for the pole.

During morning practice the next day, we were quick. At eleven o'clock the cars were lined up to begin qualifying. My first qualifying lap was as quick as Unser's had been, and suddenly everyone in the pits and stands knew what my team and I had known for a few days: we were a pole position contender. The Unser team had some anxious moments, aware that they might be upset by a team they had not even been watching.

As it turned out, I was second quick time after Al Unser. The difference in Al's and my time during qualifying was one-thousandths of a second—the closest pole position run in the history of the Indianapolis Motor Speedway. As a statistician at the Speedway later explained it to me, if Al and I had started our run side by side, run our four laps (ten miles), and crossed the line to take the checkered flag, Al would have been two and a half feet ahead of me. That's all, and that's averaging more than 170 miles per hour.

I started the race in the Patrick Petroleum no. 18 car between Al, who had edged me out for the pole position, and A. J., who was on the outside of row 1.

I got off to a fairly good start. An accident occurred during the pace lap when the rear suspension broke on Jim Malloy's car. When the green flag finally came down, I shot past Al into the lead, and led going into the first turn and down the backstretch. But Al's car was so much stronger than mine that he passed me at the end of the back straightaway. We ran 1-2 like that for much of the race.

After 138 laps, my car sustained a broken header and I finished eighteenth, which tied my best previous finish at Indy in 1968. Al won the thing pretty handily, leading for 190 of the 200 laps. He ran a great race—consistent and steady the whole time.

The car I drove in the 1970 Indy was named "Geraldine." At the time, Geraldine was a popular character on comedian Flip Wilson's television show. Wilson came up with the famous catchphrase, "The devil made me do it." Once, somebody called our car "Geraldine," maybe because the devil made her "do it"—run so fast, that is—or maybe because the car was acting up for a brief spell. Anyway, the name stuck.

Our back-up car, because it was old and reliable and always ready whenever we needed it, was named "Old Shep." Other than the car I later had with McLaren, the M24, which we named "Moneymaker," Old Shep and Geraldine are the only cars I can recall having christened. Now, there were a few cars that I *called* names. But that's something altogether different.

At the end of the 1970 racing season, I toured several bases in Vietnam with USAC drivers Larry Dickson, Roger McCluskey, and Gary Gablich, who had just set the world land speed record. We were flown out of California's Travis Air Force Base to Wake Island, in the middle of the Pacific Ocean. We refueled there and went on to Tan Son Nhut Air Base in Saigon. Ray Marquette, the press officer for the USAC, was our liaison.

We took racing films and projectors with us, and when we flew into an area we would go to the NCO or officers club, set up a projector, show the films, and talk with the guys. It was quite an eye-opening trip for us. We'd never been to the Far East, and we realized right away that the people of that region of the world thought very differently from the way we did. Locals who had been hired to run the bar or bus tables in the clubs watched the racing films, too, and they must have thought that car crashes were the funniest things they had ever seen. Every time a race car crashed or hit the wall, they would absolutely crack up laughing.

We all participated in a lot of autograph signing in Vietnam. We even toured some firebases out in the bush, where the soldiers were in the most intense situations imaginable: living in tents, patrolling enemy territory, fighting off nightly Vietcong attacks.

Because they never had visitors, they would ask us who we were. When our guides would introduce us, the soldiers, most of whom turned out to be big racing fans, would excitedly greet us.

Traveling to Vietnam was an educational trip for me. I was able to view, first-hand, the war and the ravages of it. I met many wounded GIs who were in hospitals, recovering from injuries ranging from missing limbs to bullet wounds. In one camp we visited, a shirtless soldier was sitting in his bed, looking at a magazine. Bruises and cuts covered his body.

We learned that he and his fellow servicemen had been running a PT boat down in the delta and had found a cache of Vietcong munitions. They had loaded all the ammo onto the bow of the boat and were pulling away from the bank when the Vietcong discovered them and fired a round into their boat, setting the ammo off. In the attack, the soldier had been hit by shrapnel. He lost his hearing when his eardrums ruptured from the explosion.

Because he didn't hear us when we came in, one of the orderlies or nurses touched his shoulder and he looked up. We were introduced while my fellow drivers talked with some of the other wounded soldiers.

My new acquaintance was very confused. He didn't say much; he just nodded and smiled. Roger McCluskey walked over and asked the soldier what his name was. He told Roger his name, smiled, and simply went back to his magazine. Roger signed a picture of himself and laid it down on the bed next to the soldier. As we turned to walk to another wounded soldier, a booming voice from behind us said, "*Roger McCluskey!*"

The soldier reading the magazine, whose damaged hearing caused him to talk loudly, had just realized who Roger was. He said, "I'm from Tucson, too!" The two men started talking as best they could. It was a great feeling to see wounded soldiers excited and happy, some for the first time in weeks, to hear news about back home.

We had a chance to meet a lot of really nice people while we were in Vietnam, and see much of the country. During our visit we went up north to Na Trang to visit the 5th Special Forces, the Green Beret outfit. We landed just at dark, so we went straight to the officers club. There we were introduced and gave our little spiels on auto racing. Then the soldiers ushered us over to tables where they bought us drink after drink after drink. We could only try to catch up. Our hosts sure knew how to drink.

Our trip to Vietnam was amazing, to say the least. We received incoming fire at one of the bases and watched villagers and troops patch up some buildings and huts that had been hit by VC mortar rounds the night before. We came to realize that it wasn't really worth fighting for, but that our guys were there, doing their best to defend the U.S. decision to be involved.

Because of testing commitments in the United States, I had to leave early. I flew in a helicopter to Saigon, where I picked up a flight to Guam. It was on that flight that I met and befriended the pilot, Jim Ellis, a Continental Airlines captain.

Jim, a racing fan and an off-road racer himself, asked the stewardess to escort me to the cockpit when he heard I was aboard the plane. I went up and sat in the jump seat behind him as we flew across the Pacific, talking with him about racing.

Jim was from Lake Arrowhead, California, where he lived with his wife, Raeanna. During our conversation, I told him that I had to leave the tour of Vietnam early because I was scheduled to test with my team at the racetrack in Ontario, California. Since he didn't live that far from Ontario, I told Jim to give me a call or just come out to the track while I was there.

Jim didn't show up at the track the next day, so I called him that evening and jokingly asked where he had been. It turned out that Raeanna had told him that I was just being polite and that I didn't really mean for him to come out to the track.

I assured Jim that my invitation had been sincere, and we set up a time to meet at the track the next morning. As I showed him around, we just picked up right where we left off on the flight back from Guam, and have been best friends ever since. In fact, he held my signboard for twelve or thirteen years of my racing career.

Now Jim supplies timing and scoring equipment for the Indy Racing Northern Light Series. He has always been somebody I could talk with and depend on. I guess that's what friends are for.

We returned from our tour of Vietnam in late 1970, and spent the next few months preparing for the '71 season and yet another trip to a far-off land. In late February of 1971, I went to Argentina to race Indy cars for Rolla Vollstedt. About twenty-five drivers made the trip. We were housed in hotel rooms in the historic city of Santa Fe, located on the east bank of the Salado River in central Argentina.

We ran two races on Sunday, February 28, at the hastily made Grand Prix of Rafaela near the city of Rafaela, northwest of Santa Fe. I finished seventh in the first race and twentieth in the second race.

Then it was back to the states to prepare for the 1971 Indy 500. I was driving Pat Patrick's no. 18, and again finished eighteenth. The remainder of the season was average, with the team only managing to earn three top-ten finishes with that car.

For the 1972 Indy, we added a Brabham chassis to the no. 18. The chassis was built by Australian race car driver and builder Sir Jack Brabham, who won the Formula 1 championship three times in the late '50s and early '60s and now owned a company that built cars and engines.

Brabham had had some success at Indy, so Pat Patrick purchased one of his chassis and had his crew do some aerodynamic work on it. Looking back, I realize the approach was all wrong, but at the time we thought it was the latest and the greatest. The car was very stable but it had too much drag. If we'd had more knowledge of aerodynamics, we might have been able to make the car cleaner, and thus, faster.

We suffered an early exit when we broke a connecting rod after running about a quarter of the race. We ended up well back in the twenty-seventh position.

I was starting to sense a pattern. At every Indy from my comeback after Eldora in 1967 through 1972, I'd experienced either a mechanical failure with the car or a mishap on the track. I began to question whether I would ever finish an Indy 500, much less win the thing.

The worst news during the 1972 Indy was that we had lost Jim Malloy, the same driver who had crashed during the pace lap two years earlier. Jim had been running some blistering laps during the first week of practice, 180 to 181 mph. He was driving for Fred Gerhardt and was a definite pole position candidate.

But during a morning practice run about two weeks before the race, he was driving down the backstretch at about 188 miles an hour when he lost control of his Eagle in turn 3 and rammed into the wall. He died in the hospital a few days later.

As professional race car drivers, we're aware of what can happen and we respect the dangers involved, but it's never easy to lose a member of the racing fraternity. Especially when it's a great guy like Jim.

The Patrick racing team turned out to be my path to greater success, though I didn't realize it at the time.

After the 1972 Indy, Pat Patrick decided to close down his operation and begin reorganizing for the following year. Driver Gordon Johncock, a Michigan native like Pat, was rumored to be Pat's choice to drive for the newly reorganized Patrick Racing Team in 1973. Pat also wanted a top-of-the-line chief mechanic, so he decided to hire George Bignotti, who was with Parnelli Jones at the time and had been A. J. Foyt's mechanic for a number of years. George was Foyt's mechanic when Foyt took his first win at Indy, and was considered one of the best Indy mechanics.

As a result of Pat's restructuring, several members of the team found themselves looking for new jobs, including me. Due to Jim Malloy's death before the 1972 Indy 500, Fred Gerhardt needed a driver, so I went to work for the Gerhardt team, with Phil Casey as my crew chief, for the remainder of the '72 season.

Milwaukee was the next race after Indy and my first with the Gerhardt team. The team didn't have their new Eagle replacement car yet, which was still being built in California. However, Fred had an older car that he had built, and the team prepared it to run at Milwaukee's Wisconsin State Fairgrounds. No one on the team was happy about running the old car, but we had no alternatives.

The car was known as a "locker." When the driver accelerated, the car's locker, or open differential, locked up and caused both drive wheels to pull in the same direction down the straightaways. The theory was that the locker made it easier for the car to make the turns.

We were running fairly well when something broke in the car's differential on the backstretch. Only the right-rear wheel was driving the car. I was still flat-footed on the throttle when this happened, and the car gained rpm because it lost traction on the left-rear wheel. The right-rear tire, still driving, broke loose and turned the car to the left, forcing it across the track and then across the infield grass toward the steel infield guardrail.

The car hit the guardrail nose-first. Part of the car went under the rail and turned so violently that the fuel tank ruptured. The fuel caps popped open and fuel shot up into the air, immediately catching fire. The last thing I saw before my visor completely frosted over from the intense heat was a pool of methanol on the floor of the car. That fuel lit up and things got real hot, real quick.

The impact with the guardrail sent the car spinning back across the track and toward the outside wall going into turn 3. The car was still at speed and sliding as it burned. Blindly, I unhooked my seat belts while the car was still moving. I knew I had to get out—the intense heat was excruciating.

Just as I was getting out of the car, it hit the outside wall. It jolted me so hard that I was propelled from my seat, but my thigh struck the steering wheel, causing it to break off the column, and I was slammed back down into the fiery car. I was able to jump out and I ran down over the nose of the car to get as far away as I could. My feet and calves were badly burned; when I ran it felt like somebody had cut my feet off at the ankles and I was running on the stumps. It was an incredibly awkward and painful sensation.

I ran for several yards and leaned against the wall. Firemen were rushing over to put out the flames. I grabbed a fireman as he ran by me and yelled at him to spray my feet with his fire extinguisher. He seemed confused and distracted by the burning car, so I yelled again, "Just spray my feet and my legs!"

He sprayed a few blasts on my feet and legs and then ran over to the car. The ambulance pulled up within seconds and found me somewhat dazed. My uniform was charred, and my nose and cheeks were burned from where the bandanna I wore under my helmet left my face exposed. I also suffered burns to my sinuses and throat from inhaling that superheated air.

I'm still amazed that, with my seat belts unfastened, I wasn't killed on that second impact.

That mishap inspired me to help design a new face protector that would cover the end of my nose. I asked Bill Simpson, manufacturer of Simpson helmets, uniforms, and other safety equipment, to sew a protective tab on my mask to cover my nose and to make special face pieces that could be Velcroed in place over my mouth to prevent burns like those I suffered at Milwaukee. A former race car driver himself, Bill is an innovator when it comes to driver safety, and over the years he and I have worked together on my helmets and many other projects.

Though I never experienced an accident like that again, I felt better having the added protection.

With Phil Casey as my crew chief at Gerhardt Racing, I enjoyed the best season I'd had up to that point in my career, finishing seventh in points. I would have "no. 7" painted on my car for the 1973 season, the first single-digit number I had ever earned in championship Indy car racing. The first twelve numbers in the championship point system are protected numbers; only if a driver has earned one of those numbers can he have it painted on his car the following year.

Abruptly, the team began to fall apart. Phil Casey decided to leave the team and auto racing to pursue a new life path. The news devastated me. Phil had been the glue that held that team together, and his departure would leave a huge void in the Gerhardt team. I simply didn't want to be racing there if we didn't have all the key people, because I understood the importance of their presence to the overall success of the team.

I needed some sound advice, so I went to see Herb Porter, one of my former car owners and mechanics, at his shop in the Speedway garage area. Herb was one of the premier mechanics, and had been a good friend, confidant, and mentor to me over the years.

I told Herb that Casey was leaving the team and that I had found myself in a hell of a spot. Indy was only six months away and I wasn't sure what was going to happen. I asked him if he had any ideas.

Herb told me that Team McLaren, a British outfit, was looking for a new no. 1 driver because Pat Patrick had hired McLaren's Gordie Johncock. Herb got on the phone and called the McLaren people in Detroit. As luck would have it, Teddy Mayer, the managing director of Formula 1 for McLaren in England, was in the country.

Herb told Teddy that he should come to Indy and work something out with me. I also think Herb told him that I was on the verge of winning Indy despite my history at the Speedway. Teddy was familiar with my racing and knew about the problems with my current team. There aren't many secrets among the racing community.

It was fall of 1972, and Teddy flew to Indianapolis to meet with me. I was at the track, tire testing for Goodyear with the Gerhardt car. Teddy and I had breakfast together at the Holiday Inn not far from the track. He outlined the deal, I agreed to it, and that was that. He told me I was hired and that he would send me the contracts the next day.

I was signed as the driver for the "works" Indy team at McLaren. My car, unlike those McLaren built and developed for customers, had all the latest innovations—the "works." Our sponsor was Gulf Oil, a substantial sponsor. We started testing the car at the Speedway in March of 1973. Practicing that early was a first for me, and I liked it.

I could tell right away that I had found the magic. McLaren Racing was a business. It was not a hobby.

In my early days with McLaren, two gentlemen—Bill Smith and Gary Knutson—owned the McLaren engine shop in Livonia, Michigan. There they maintained the British-made cars and did a substantial amount of research work for Ford, Chevrolet, and any manufacturer that wanted to develop secret projects.

Everyone McLaren employed in the states worked at this race shop. Roger "Boost" Bailey, the director of CART's Indy Lights Racing Series, was the engine man at the time. Everybody at McLaren had a nickname. We had "Chicken Lips," "Tulip," "Abo," "Trellis," "Hanger," and a slew of others.

The job of organizing the most important aspect of professional auto racing, the line of communications, was largely left up to Tyler Alexander, who headed up the team and served as team manager. He was one of the best racing professionals I have ever worked with.

Team McLaren was first organized by Bruce McLaren, a race car driver from New Zealand. McLaren began building his own cars in the mid-1960s. He first built Can-Am cars, which he raced successfully with Denny Hulme in the Canadian-American Road Race series. He also built and drove Formula 1 race cars.

In the late 1960s, Team McLaren took on the Indianapolis 500. The McLaren cars caused quite a stir because their design was a radical departure from the norm as far as Indy cars went. The M16 had a wedge-shaped nose, front wings, and a larger wing in the back. In the '71 Indy, Peter Revson took second in a McLaren car. After that, everybody started copying their design.

Sadly, in 1970 Bruce McLaren died in an accident while testing his race car in England and never got to see any of his company's M16s race at the Brickyard. Teddy Mayer was the company's business manager at the time of Bruce's death, and he took over the operation.

I always told Betty that if I ever found a team that loved racing as much as I did, I'd be a winner. In the ten years prior to my first victory at Indianapolis, I had not finished the race once. I had not gone the distance.

My frustration at never even finishing the great race was beginning to wear on me. Yet every spring I was back at Indy, hoping to qualify, hoping to finish, and most important, hoping to win.

When the 1973 Indy 500 rolled around, I was thirty-five years old. I was happily married to a wonderful, supportive woman and we had two small children who were all too aware of their father's frequent absences.

But it was not yet time to consider retiring or moving on to something else. I was thrilled to be a part of Team McLaren, and to have another chance to grab for the brass ring.

I sensed that we were very close to taking the checkered flag. And though I didn't know it at the time, my best years were just around the next turn.

★ CHAPTER 16 ★

New Start for
an Old Hand

Imagine yourself speeding down a stretch of racetrack at two hundred miles an hour in a car that's equipped with a big rear wing.

When you try to turn, the wing is creating such strong downforce on the back of the car that it wants the car to go straight. Now imagine that there's a concrete wall up ahead. You're trying to turn your car to avoid hitting that wall and meeting your maker. But you can't.

That was my reality in early spring of 1973.

McLaren's people had made some adjustments on their M16 for the 1973 Indianapolis 500. When Gordon Johncock had driven the car in the '72 race, it had a short bell housing and a long nose. In a manual transmission car, the bell housing is a bell-shaped enclosure for the flywheel and clutch. The new design on the M16 had a shorter nose and longer bell housing. The McLaren crew and I had been testing the newly redesigned car for nearly a week at the Speedway, trying to find a way to achieve both speed and handling.

However, in 1972 USAC had passed a rule that established larger rear wings for Indy cars. Larger wings meant greater downforce, which in turn meant faster speeds in the turns. All of sudden, Indy drivers were posting practice laps of 190 to 195 miles an hour.

The rule was still in effect for the 1973 season, but the larger wing was overpowering the rest of our car. Because of the downforce, or pressure, on the back of the car, the rear wheels were achieving better traction than the front wheels, which caused the car to push.

"Pushing" is what happens when the front end of the car tends to slide, or push, toward the outside of a turn. The slip angles—the difference between the direction the tire tread is pointing and the direction the tire is truly moving—of the front tires were greater than the slip angles of the back tires. We just couldn't get the car to stop pushing. And at those speeds, you don't want that to happen.

We tried to come up with a design that would work, but after a week of testing we were stymied. So we went back to the shorter bell housing of 1972, which moved the gear box closer to the engine. Then we put the longer nose back on so that the car would meet USAC's length requirement of sixteen feet, which was the total length allowable.

The bigger nose gave the car the extra downforce we needed in the front, and thus better balance. Roger "Boost" Bailey, the engine builder for McLaren at the time, built the engine that would help us qualify, and it was strong. Bailey could really make an engine run. The team was confident.

Confidence or no, 1973 was a terrible year at Indianapolis. It began on Pole Day, the first day of qualifying and the day that determines the race's pole position, when Art Pollard, a close personal friend and fellow USAC racer from Oregon, crashed into the outside wall off turn 1 and was killed on impact. About two hundred thousand people were in the stands that day and witnessed the horrible accident. Art's death cast a pall over the Speedway. But I knew I had to keep going, and I focused on the task at hand.

We lined up for qualifying and I was raring to go. I had already been around the track that month flat-footed, so I knew I could do it. On several occasions during the past month of practicing, I had unofficially reached speeds of up to two hundred miles per hour, and had even run two or three two hundred-mile-an-hour laps in a row. However strong my practice runs had been, the conditions on that first Saturday of qualifying didn't allow me to do quite so well.

Even so, we had a hell of a qualifying run, averaging better than 198 miles an hour to set a new track record and earn the pole position. Our best lap was just under two hundred miles an hour. I drove flat-footed around the track, and people in the stands went crazy. I had a lot of fun, too.

Tyler Alexander and I were on the two-way radio during my entire run, and he would tell me how we were doing on each lap. As I came off 4 on the final lap and headed for the checkered flag, I started singing "Everything Is Beautiful" into the two-way radio. Tyler turned to the other guys in the pit and said, "You're not gonna believe this."

"What?!" they asked.

"He's singing."

The guys all gave him puzzled looks.

" 'Everything Is Beautiful.' The song."

Bobby Unser came close to beating me out for the pole position, but fell just short. He ended up next to me in row 1 at the start of the race, and Mark Donohue, who had won Indy the year before, took the outside of the row. Overall, the starters averaged qualifying speeds that were almost ten miles an hour faster than those recorded in 1972. That's quite a jump.

So was trading in my racing uniform for a white necktie and tails. After I won the pole position, I was asked to be the guest conductor for the Indianapolis Symphony Orchestra in an evening extravaganza called "From Bach to Bacharach." I led the orchestra in a very swinging version of "Back Home Again in Indiana." It was the first and only time I ever wore a white tie and tails.

One of the things I always did prior to the Indianapolis 500 was read the newspapers. Once qualifying is over and the field is set, the newspapers in Indianapolis print a lineup with each driver's picture, his qualifying speed, and in some cases, a picture of his car. To mimic the starting grid at Indy, the drivers are pictured in eleven rows of three.

I would study that three-column presentation after qualifying, mentally reviewing the styles and idiosyncrasies of each and every driver. It was a way for me to recall what I'd seen a driver do over the years, or if it was a rookie driver, what he had done during practice or qualifying. But be it a veteran or a rookie, I'd look at each picture and set up hypothetical situations. I'd create a scenario in my mind and think to myself, *Okay, if this guy does this, and that guy's tendency is to do that, then what would happen if . . .*

I would run through all the possibilities for several days leading up to the Indy 500 until I had developed a pretty solid game plan. I knew what I would do at the start of the race and what moves I would make based on past experiences with the drivers who were starting around me. I did that every year I ran at Indy, beginning in 1963.

Sometimes my game plan helped and sometimes it didn't. The best example of it not working out was in the 1964 Indy, when I was caught in the middle of the horrific Sachs-MacDonald crash. There was no way I could have prepared myself for that. Looking at the 1964 lineup every day for the rest of my life wouldn't have changed a thing. Still, performing my pre-race ritual of cutting the lineup out of the paper and setting up scenarios helped me more often than not.

The 1973 Indy 500 was scheduled for Monday, May 28, Memorial Day. Weather was everyone's rival that day. Heavy rain delayed the start of the race for about four hours.

When we were finally able to start the race, one of the drivers, Salt Walther, crashed into the wall as he was making his way along the outside of the front straightaway—a result of a chain-reaction that began in the back of the starting field. His car flipped over and burst into flames. He was severely burned and suffered numerous internal injuries as well. About a dozen spectators were also hurt, and several other drivers got tangled up in the accident and resulting fire on the track.

The red flag came out before we ever really started. Then it began to rain again, and eventually USAC officials postponed the race until the next day.

Tuesday wasn't a whole lot better as far as the weather was concerned. It rained in the morning, right before the race. We got underway around midmorning, but as the pace car was pulling into the pits the skies opened up and it started pouring again. By early afternoon we still hadn't started the race, so USAC officials announced that it would be postponed until Wednesday.

Two days lost to rain. It was the first time in Indy history that the race had to be pushed back two days in a row.

It rained again on the third day but we finally got going at around two in the afternoon. Bobby Unser shot past me to take the lead, but it was a long race, so I wasn't too concerned about it. Then Peter Revson, the other Team McLaren driver, spun in the fourth turn after we'd gone just a handful of laps. He hit the inside wall and wrecked his car, leaving only me to represent McLaren.

A little more than a quarter of the way through the race, Swede Savage, Gordie Johncock's teammate with Patrick Racing, grazed the wall in turn 4. He just barely touched it, but at those speeds it doesn't take much to knock a driver off balance. Swede's car slid across the track sideways and hit the inside wall. The car burst into flames and burning fuel spewed across the pavement. Swede suffered horrible burns, as well as multiple fractures of his legs and pelvis, and died in the hospital about a month later.

Then, in another horrible turn of events, the driver of the safety truck that took off for the crash site went the wrong way up Pit Lane and struck and killed a crewman. The crewman, Armando Teran, was a member of Andy Granatelli's STP team.

That whole series of events was a terrible tragedy. With the injuries stemming from Salt Walther's mishap two days earlier and Art Pollard's death on the first day of qualifying, the 1973 Indianapolis 500 would have been gloomy even without all the rain.

After waving the yellow caution flag at lap 129 due to heavy rain, the officials decided that enough was enough, and the checkered flag came down at lap 133 with Gordon Johncock in the lead. I was one of about a dozen drivers still driving when the flag was dropped. We took ninth, and at the time we felt lucky to have at least survived the day.

Of course, I was once again a bridesmaid. After the race, when I had time to reflect on all that had happened, the only thing that made any sense was to prepare for the next race.

☆ CHAPTER 17 ☆

My First Swig of Milk

While USAC officials spent the 1973 postseason addressing safety issues and fuel economy, the McLaren Racing team was addressing how to win the Indy 500.

Swede Savage's fatal crash at Indianapolis in May forced a reduction in the maximum size of the rear wing by about fifteen percent. This ensured that cars would take the turns more slowly. The USAC also set the maximum fuel capacity at forty gallons, a big difference from the seventy-five gallons many of us were carrying when Swede's car burst into flames. In addition to these new restrictions, there was a new limit placed on the amount of horsepower allowed for turbo-charged engines.

USAC also made safety changes to the track itself. For one thing, the pit lane was extended farther north so that drivers could use turn 4 to exit the racetrack rather than having to make a tight, left-hand jog off the front straightaway. The height of the retaining walls was increased to nearly three feet, and some additional safety fencing was also installed.

The McLaren team came back to Indy that fall and tested with the new, smaller wing configuration, the longer bell housing, and the short nose, and . . . voila! We had our combination. The smaller rear wing balanced the car perfectly and it was quick. Even without the horsepower we had in 1973 when I set the record, the better handling set us up for what would be a big year in 1974.

We had a great deal of confidence going into the race. It seemed that every-thing had started to come into focus, and the entire team, myself included, felt an eagerness that was hard to hide. But because I had missed the brass ring so many times over the previous ten years, the idea of actually winning the Indy 500 never occurred to me. I was so intent on simply doing the best job I could and letting the chips fall where they may that a victory at the Speedway was still only a dream. Racing there for ten years and not even finishing had built up a callus.

I didn't know what to expect if things actually went according to plan. My experience at Indy in the past had always involved a mishap with the car or an incident on the track, and never finishing. But I wasn't bitter; I was just world weary. I loved my job and I was doing the best I could. Winning at Indy was still my dream, but I wasn't going to let myself get too pumped up every spring, just to be disappointed in the end. I'd simply say, "Let's give it a go and hope for the best." I had become somewhat philosophical about the whole thing.

But as the 1974 Indy approached, things felt different. Because we had tested a great deal for Goodyear and had done all the evaluation work, our car was already set for the tires they would supply that year. Other factors that seemed to lend themselves to our team's success were engine builder Boost Bailey's continued involvement with the team and the recent USAC safety changes.

Practices were going well for us. The car felt good. Then, on the first day of qualifying, we went out to practice and hadn't even gotten up to speed when the engine blew. The guys rushed the car back to the garage to change engines, and did it in record time: fifty-eight minutes. It was then, as we were preparing to return to the track, that the most bizarre set of circumstances unfolded.

Harlan Fengler had been the chief steward at the Indianapolis Motor Speedway for many years. He was in his early seventies when he retired some months before the 1974 Indy, and Tom Binford, who was about twenty-five years Harlan's junior, was named to succeed him.

It was soon apparent that the two men interpreted track rules very differently. Binford was conservative in his reading of the rule that stated if you were not in the qualifying line when practice was over at eleven A.M., you lost your position. Harlan had always said that as long as you were there to present yourself when it was your turn to go through tech inspection before qualifying, you were okay. Because we returned to the line after eleven, we were shuffled to the back of the line and lost our chance to go for the pole position. It was upsetting to all of us to have to adhere to a new interpretation of the rule after so many years.

The next bizarre circumstance was a result of the unprecedented "energy crunch" in 1974. Gas stations closed early, and when they were open there were long lines to the pumps. Everybody was doing what he or she could to conserve fuel and not pollute the atmosphere. Speedway officials decided to do their part by consolidating four days of qualifying into two, so fans wouldn't burn so much of their gasoline coming out for two weekends in a row.

This unnerving scenario topped off an already unusual qualifying process. Qualifying for the pole at Indy only occurs on the first day of qualifying. Everyone else who qualifies on the first day lines up, in order of qualifying speed, behind the pole position. The second-day qualifiers line up according to the speeds run the second day, but they all start behind the first-day qualifiers, regardless of their speeds. The same routine follows for the third and fourth days during the second weekend of qualifying.

Bumping into the field begins after thirty-three cars have qualified. The car attempting to bump into the field must go faster than the slowest speed in the field regardless of its original qualified position. Once the car is bumped, all the cars behind that spot move up to fill the vacated position. The "bumped" car is eliminated, but its driver may requalify in another car.

We knew that we had to qualify on the first day or we would be placed in the back of the field. Al Unser was in the same boat because he had also lost an engine that morning.

By the time we got back in line and set up, we were in the third day's qualifying, which really upset us. Al Unser and I both went to Binford to protest. It was only fair that, as the Speedway's chief steward, his word was final. But he should have told everyone at the meetings prior to qualifying what his interpretation of the rule would be. We didn't learn of this new interpretation until my crew brought the car back to the pits after their unbelievable fifty-eight-minute engine change. They went berserk. They couldn't believe that they had just knocked themselves out to get ready to qualify, and now wouldn't even be able to run until the third qualifying race.

Al and I were upset, too. We had such a hot discussion with Binford that it's a wonder he didn't throw us out of the place and ban us from the Indianapolis Motor Speedway. We argued and argued. All was for naught, as Binford stood his ground.

His decision completely changed our strategy. The McLaren team said, "If we can't go for the pole, we're not going to make an exerted effort and take a chance with the car by trying to grab the fastest speed. We'll just put together a good, solid, qualifying run, get into the race, and give it all we've got when it counts."

As ticked off as I was about the whole thing, McLaren's response was perfect. It was another reason why I liked McLaren. I always appreciated their philosophy and steady attitude. They just said, "Let's not go too far out on a limb;

somebody's liable to saw it off." They always had a good plan, and the 1974 Indy bore that out. At McLaren we always ran our race, not someone else's.

We took our qualifying laps and ended up with the second fastest time in the field, but because it was considered the third day of qualifying, we started pole in the ninth row—the twenty-fifth starting spot. It was exasperating for me to have what could have been the fastest car out there and be stuck that far back in the field. Al was right beside me in the twenty-sixth starting spot. A. J. had the pole position.

It would be a pretty daunting task to move up to the lead from where I was. Starting in the twenty-fifth position meant I was virtually giving up three-quarters of a lap. Very few drivers had ever won the race from that far back. But I kept thinking, *I've got a good car, so we'll see.*

Make that a great car. They dropped the green flag and in twelve laps I was running third. The car was flying. I could pass every car I came upon. I then knew it was just a matter of being able to go two hundred laps (five hundred miles) and stay out of trouble.

Wally Dallenbach had started next to A. J. in the second position. He surged ahead of A. J. when they dropped the green, and on lap 2 he ran the fastest lap of the day at better than 191 miles per hour. But in the third or fourth lap, Wally pitted with a burned piston and was done for the day.

A. J. took the lead for about twenty laps. When A. J. made his first pit stop, Bobby Unser took the lead and stayed there for a couple of laps until A. J. caught up with him. I was running in third place until our first pit stop. Bobby and A. J. switched places again on lap 49 when A. J. pitted a second time. But again, A. J. got out of the pits, caught Bobby, and passed him. Only this time, when A. J. took the lead, I was right on his tail.

A. J. and I dueled throughout the middle stages of the race. His car, with its four-cam V-8 engine, was a little stronger down the straightaways than my car was. When we were racing each other, it was always A. J. in the lead and me trying to get by him. I just didn't have quite enough power to pass him when we came down the straightaways, and because A. J. was wily and experienced in running traffic, he could work the other cars to his advantage. He made it very difficult for me to get by him.

However, I was all over him in the turns because my car handled so much better than his. If I had been able to get up beside him going into the turns, that would have been it. I would have been through the turns so fast that I would have just kept adding to the lead.

Yet I knew that if I continued to put on the pressure, I could make A. J. run hard enough to either blow his engine or blister his right-rear tire. Then I could get by him and move ahead. I knew A. J.'s team had been having problems with the car's right-rear tires during practice.

It was a real standoff. He'd pit, and I'd take the lead. I'd pit and he'd regain the lead. On lap 138 he caught me on the front straightaway and got underneath me in the first turn to take the lead. The crowd was on its feet to see A. J. and me duke it out. But then, on lap 139, A. J. was black-flagged.

His engine was blowing oil. I was so close behind him that the oil just covered my car. I had to back off about a hundred yards in order to stay away from it. I also had to watch the track to make sure I didn't get into something that would make me slip and hit the wall. In fact, with all the oil on the track, it was a wonder we didn't both spin out.

When A. J. pulled into the pits, I retook the lead. His crew wiped off his car and looked it over, and I guess they didn't really find anything, because A. J. pulled back onto the track and went after me. Almost immediately, he was black-flagged again. This time he made the hard left turn off Pit Lane into Gasoline Alley, which signified that he was out of the race.

After A. J. dropped out, I led for much of the race until Bobby Unser took the lead when I made my final pit stop with about twenty-five laps to go. The McLaren pit crew led by Tyler Alexander was so good at what they did that I feared taking a drink of water when I pitted. I didn't want to upset their timing. When they finished with the fuel and tires, I wanted to be ready to go. Usually, by the time I settled down, checked everything over, and mentally prepared myself to return to the racetrack, it was time to go.

Back on the track, I overtook Bobby in no time. But I wasn't home free yet.

Soon I had just fifteen laps to go. Then ten. Then five. Those last five laps were like hours to me. I had witnessed plenty of drivers run out of fuel on the last lap, or have their engines go. If you're running down the backstretch and the car breaks, you're not going to make it to the finish line. Racing can be a real heartbreaker like that. I've seen it happen.

In the latter stages of a race, most often you're by yourself or at least with "strung-out" traffic. You don't have to be wary of a field full of cars running together, fighting for positions. What you do have to be wary of is that one guy on your tail who wants your position.

If you're by yourself, it's a matter of watching the car closely: the temperature, the gauges, the tires. The old saying that a race car driver can hear all sorts of weird noises in his car during that last lap is partially true. You start imagining things. *What's that noise? Is that the gearbox?* You're trying to nurse the race car to the finish line whether it needs nursing or not. And the whole time you're hearing noises or smelling something burning or feeling a grinding vibration.

In truth, those cars were making noises all the time. If the driver realizes this, he starts to wonder, *Has this thing been doing that since the start of the race? Have I been so intent on driving through traffic and as hard as I can that I'm just now beginning to hear it?* But if you're racing somebody to the wire, all that worry flies out the window. You forget about noises. You concentrate on driving "flat-chat" around the track to get to that checkered flag.

Before I knew it I was coming across the short chute before turn 4, ready to zoom down the straightaway to get the win. I started wondering, *If this thing up and quits, can I get the clutch down and put it in neutral so that it'll roll far enough to get the checkered flag?* It became a game of mental calculation.

But I had no need to worry. The car made it across the short chute and through turn 4, and I had plenty of power left to get to the flag. I was home free.

I saw glimpses of the fans waving their programs, clapping, and yelling. One of the track officials held up the board with my number three on it, and the flagman leaned out over the railing, waving the two checkered flags. That was the prettiest sight in the world. I finished twenty-two seconds ahead of Bobby Unser.

I crossed the finish line knowing that I had won the greatest race in the world after failing to finish the race ten times. I don't think words will ever do justice to what I felt in those moments.

Tyler called me on the two-way radio and told me to go an extra lap in case the scoring was screwed up. So I ran one more hard lap, and then I slowed down. At that point I couldn't hear the fans because my ears were ringing from the constant drone of the engine, but I saw them—thousands of them—leaning out over the railing and waving at me.

Some of the fans got a little too carried away in the emotion of the moment. As I was heading down the backstretch, they climbed over the fence in turn 3 and came running across the grass to the apron next to the racetrack. I wasn't able to see around the turn and I was terrified when I saw them pour onto the track. I prayed that no one would slip or accidentally be pushed into the path of my car, because I had very little room to maneuver in. I actually saw people run onto the racetrack and slap my car as I went by them.

If I had stopped I'm sure they would have stripped the car clean. But I didn't care about that. Seconds after I had experienced my greatest thrill in racing, I was probably more scared than I'd ever been during the race. *They can have the car*, I thought, *but please, God, don't let me hit anybody.*

I made it around the turn, across the short chute, through turn 4, and into the pits. Once inside, we got up on the victory podium. They pulled my car up onto a riser that was covered in black and white checkered carpet. They draped the victory wreath over me and set the Borg-Warner Trophy on the back of the car. All the photographers, camera people, track officials, and reporters were there. It was chaos, but it was sweet.

Betty and the rest of my team were there too, waiting for me. Betty was the first one to greet me, and she planted a big kiss on my face. As an official member of our racing team, she was in the pit doing the timing and scoring for us during the race.

Someone then handed me the traditional bottle of milk. I took my first swig as an Indy 500 champion. To some, another beverage might seem easier to swallow after such a grueling race, but I had no problem with it at all. I loved the tradition and finally being a part of it.

When it came time to move the car off the riser and take it in for its post-race tech inspection, I got in the passenger car that was waiting to take us around the track for the victory lap. However, we barely got through because the fans were still out on the backstretch.

After we returned to Victory Lane to do another interview or two with the media, I looked over to where my car had been sitting. There, on the ground, was a perfect outline of my car in oil. It was the oil that A. J.'s car had sprayed on me right before he was black-flagged. Because my car was going around the track at such high speeds, the oil was kind of pinned, or suspended, against my car. When I finally slowed down at the end of the race, pulled into Victory Lane, and stopped, the oil simply ran off my car and onto the ground. You could make out the nose, the wings, the suspension—everything.

Through it all, I kept thinking about how much the guys on my crew had put into winning the race. I was the driver, a part of the team. From day one they had worked so hard to make that car the best that it could be. I was as proud of them as they were of me.

In addition to Tyler Alexander, we had Teddy Mayer, who kept things under control. He was an organizer, the kind of guy who is constantly thinking of a better way to do things. The rest of the guys on the team—Denis, Jim, Sid, Michael, Roger, Gary, Don, Lance, and Charlie—were just superb at what they did. I don't recall us ever having a bad pit stop. They could unwind with the best of them when the race was over, but they were all business at the track. We led for 122 of the 200 laps in what was, at the time, the world's only million-dollar auto race.

Along with the rest of the guys on the McLaren crew in the pits that day was my favorite teammate—Betty. Beginning in 1973, Betty did the timing and scoring for me, and would continue to do it for more than twenty years. The 1974 Indy was the first time she was in the pit at Indy. Betty always maintained that serving on the team in that capacity did more for her sanity than it did for the team. It also made her feel like she was a more valuable part of the team. Working with me in the pit, she felt a stronger connection to what I was doing.

Although she was doing the timing and scoring for my team, Betty said she never had any trouble concentrating in the pit. If there was an accident in turn 4, she wouldn't let it distract her from what she was doing. She knew she had to make sure that her stopwatch stopped when I went by, because if she missed a lap there was a good possibility that they could call me in for fuel at the wrong time. Betty's participation in the pits also opened the door for others. Women were being treated as equals at the tracks, and even some of the well-known chauvinists on the Indy car circuit finally caved in and accepted—if not welcomed with open arms—women into the pits. In less than two years, most of the drivers' wives were helping with timing for their husbands' teams. Some chose to simply stand at the back of the pits and offer moral support. And that was okay, too.

Because Betty was at the track timing every day in the weeks leading up to the race, she had the opportunity to study and become familiar with the cars. She could recognize the cars when they came off the fourth turn by their paint jobs and the subtle differences in their chassis. Even when they were running 205 miles an hour, she said it wasn't that difficult to distinguish them, unless two or three cars on the same team were painted so much alike and she couldn't see the numbers. Betty also enlisted help from Jim's wife, Raeanna, her "bestest" friend, to help her memorize the drivers' helmets.

Betty's arrangement—a large keyboard and printer, set up on a card table across Pit Lane by the scoring tower—was primitive by today's standards, but it was just the beginning of the electronic age in auto racing. Today teams can program their own systems on laptop computers. Now, in fact, there really is no reason to even have someone timing and scoring in one's pit because the computerized timing and scoring done in the towers comes straight to the pit monitors. Big changes occurred in twenty-five years, but each one represents a challenge.

After the 1973 Indy disaster, with all the rain delays and accidents and tragic losses of lives, the 1974 race was magical. The month of May at Indy and the race itself had redeemed its old charm. Betty likes to say, "The knight on his white horse rode in to save the day."

Looking back on the 1974 Indianapolis 500 a quarter of a century later, I still remember the names that played such an integral part in my first win at the Speedway. Bill Vukovich came in third after myself and Bobby Unser. Gordon Johncock was fourth. My McLaren teammate, David Hobbs, was fifth. My old buddy from the IMCA sprint car days, Jimmy McElreath, was sixth.

Jimmy was involved in the one big scare of the race. He always raced hard—it didn't matter if he was ten laps down or going for the lead, he ran just the same all the time. That's why he won races.

At one point when I was leading the race, Jimmy was getting the "move over" flag but wouldn't let me by. I could see that he and I were going to catch Pancho Carter, a very good rookie driver, in the first turn. I decided to use Pancho to get by Jimmy. I would to try get Jimmy to run into the corner groove where Pancho was, and then I would dive under him and pass under the line.

I went by McElreath on the inside and pulled up by Pancho, and it almost worked, but Pancho either didn't see me or saw me too late and felt like he wasn't giving me enough room. I'm still not sure. But with Pancho on the line and me under it as we went into the first turn, things were getting a little too close. Cars were gaining on me, and I had to keep moving. So I slipped up a little bit, and Pancho moved abruptly to miss me. When he did this, it upset the balance in his car, starting what we call a "tank slapper," and he spun his car. Fortunately, that's all he did; I would have felt sick if I had put him in a position to hit the wall or another driver. I did apologize to Pancho later for sneaking up on him, but there is no doubt that I needed to get by McElreath to protect my lead. That incident could have ended it for all three of us.

Pancho was able to get his car restarted after he spun out. He was already a lap or two down when it happened. He wound up finishing seventh, and when you consider that he began the race in the twenty-first spot, later spun out, and still managed to finish in the top ten, you'd probably agree that Pancho was a very strong rookie driver.

I would have liked to have won the pole position that year, but perhaps the story and the win were much more fantastic the way it all played out. Only three other drivers in the history of the Indianapolis 500 had come from further behind to win the race. It was also the first Indy 500 I had finished. I guess that was all I had to do to win: finish. My payday was $98,000—forty percent of the team's winnings. I also got to take home the Hurst/Olds pace car and all the assorted personal gifts that go to the Indy champ.

To this day, I think that our 1974 McLaren was by far the best race car I ever ran at the Speedway. It was certainly the easiest car to drive. In fact, I later told Clarence Cagle, the superintendent of grounds who virtually rebuilt the Indianapolis Motor Speedway to what it is today, "Clarence, if you had put a lawnmower on my car, I could have cut the infield grass for you during the race and still won!" The car was that good.

Despite my victory, I felt a sense of irony at the Speedway that day. I had finally won the Indianapolis 500, but the man who years earlier had been so supportive of my decision to become a professional race car driver wasn't in the stands to cheer me on. Dad was watching the race from his easy chair back home with Mom in Fort Worth. He'd been fighting prostate cancer for about two years. By the time it was diagnosed, it had already begun to spread through his system, and during the 1974 Indy 500, he was in a lot of pain.

I believe that was the first Indy 500 my dad had not attended since I started racing at the Speedway in 1963. Mom later told me that Dad had eagerly watched the race and was very happy when I took the checkered flag. As soon as the race was over, he went to bed. He never got out of bed again.

During an interview after the race, I said, "I'd like to dedicate this race to my dad back in Fort Worth, who is critically ill."

I went home to visit my folks a few days after the race. Even though I had been back frequently during Dad's long battle with cancer, it was tough seeing him so ill. He had been such a vigorous, energetic man. As we talked about the race, it was clear that he was thrilled for me. Dad knew what winning the

Indianapolis 500 meant to me, and I got a sense of what it meant to him. He said he had seen my various TV appearances following the race, and that he was very proud of me.

Dad was taken to the hospital shortly after I left Fort Worth to resume the racing season. Betty and I received word after the Michigan race on July 21 that Dad was failing. We made the trip home to be there with him and Mom. He was failing quickly, and could only communicate to me by squeezing my hand. I talked to him about the family's future and his two grandchildren. I struggled so much, seeing him in that condition. I sat there watching as the man who took me to see my first race when I was nine, played catch with me, let me sit inside his midget racer and crawl around his P-51s—the man who was my hero—slipped away from me and into a coma.

Dad passed away on July 25. He was sixty years old. I've always been grateful that he was able to see me win my first Indy 500, and sad that he couldn't be around to see me collect the next two. Dad was on my mind a lot during the races I ran after he died. In fact, I felt that he was always with me in spirit over the course of my career, and still is.

☆ CHAPTER 18 ☆

After "the 500"

My win at the 1974 Indianapolis 500 uncorked a wild year.

After the race we had a brief team celebration before Betty and I flew to New York to appear on *The Today Show* early the next morning. Then we flew back to Indianapolis for the winner's photo shoot and the victory banquet that night.

Soon, agents started calling. Endorsement offers were coming at us from all sides. Companies wanted me to appear in their commercials or print ads to promote their products. Reporters from what seemed like every major newspaper and magazine in the country were calling me, wanting an interview, photographs, an exclusive.

In 1974, auto racing didn't enjoy the mass popularity it enjoys today. But the Indianapolis 500 was a different story—as an internationally recognized race, its winner was, and still is, the only professional race car driver to receive any significant notice or acclaim. Team McLaren won "the 500" and I happened to be their driver, so for a while life was crazy for Betty and me.

The publicity was somewhat of a double-edged sword, because while it afforded me some wonderful opportunities to "make hay while the sun shines," it also became overwhelming in the weeks and months following the race. We still had a racing season ahead of us. I had to concentrate on my responsibilities to the McLaren Racing Team and still find time to accept and honor various commercial offers and speaking engagements. Betty really stepped in at that point and helped me make sense of it all, choosing wisely which endorsements and public appearances we would take. She essentially became my agent as well as my buffer.

My life within the racing community had changed too, though it was a subtle change. I had long ago earned the respect of my peers, but until 1974 I had never even finished an Indy 500. Now that I had finally won the race, I found myself accepted into the fraternity of Indy winners. Though the media was in a frenzy over this thirty-six-year-old new kid on the block, I wasn't expecting a lot of backslapping and congratulations, particularly from the guys who had won Indy before me. Their support came in the form of a look, or a certain tone in their voices when they spoke to me, that said, *You're now a member of the club.* It was a good feeling. Those guys more than anyone else understood the importance of my accomplishment and what I had endured to accomplish it.

Of course, I did get a chilly reception from some of the other drivers, those who were so competitive and selfish that they didn't care or understand what it was like to be in the limelight at that level. I encountered very few of them, but certainly racing doesn't have a lock on this type of individual. Most of the drivers, whether they had won Indy in the past or were still looking for that first drive into Victory Lane, felt a combination of envy and elation over my 1974 win. I know, because that was how I felt every year I saw someone else take the checkered. But generally, I sensed that people within the racing community were happy for me.

After the win on May 26 at Indy, the McLaren team geared up for the next race, which was in Milwaukee on June 9. It was the twenty-fifth running of the Rex Mays Classic, a 150-mile race in suburban West Allis. Having spent the past month practicing at Indy on a 2½ mile track and racing five hundred miles, the Classic, which took place on a mile-long track and required just three days to prepare and run, was a real change for the drivers and the teams as a whole. The teams had to set up their cars differently and adapt a whole new mind-set. The Milwaukee course required different strategies, different techniques.

After qualifying for the 500, some teams would go to Milwaukee with a skeleton crew and do a day of testing there to see if their car's setup needed any adjustments. But for most teams, including McLaren, the preparation for Milwaukee simply involved cleaning up the car after Indy.

The Milwaukee race took place at the Wisconsin State Fairgrounds. The track fielded twenty-four cars; I started in the no. 2 position in the grid and A. J. was the pole-sitter. I spun out on the eighth lap, but didn't crash. When he heard someone lament that my spinout had finished my chances to win, my son John, who was celebrating his sixth birthday at the race, said, "If he can start twenty-fifth at Indy and win, I bet he can do it here, too!" I got back in the race and kept at it. I took the lead for good on lap 124, but I still had to beat out Gary Bettenhausen and outlast the rain to win by thirty-one seconds. Happy birthday, son!

By that point in the season, I was beginning to attract some unwanted attention. I remember thinking to myself that if I ever wrote a book, I would title it *Suddenly My Friend*, because all of a sudden I started getting calls from people I hadn't heard from in years. I was getting calls from people I didn't even know, who inevitably wanted me to join them in some supposed money-making scheme. One of the oddest calls I received was from a man in Colorado who wanted me to invest in a gold mine. How the guy got my number I don't know, but I laughed so hard my eyes started to water. I soon realized that calls like this were just another consequence of being an Indy 500 champ.

The next race of the season was a five-hundred-mile race on June 29 in Pocono. The team arrived well before the actual race so that we could put the car through a two-day test. While we were there, the media was still trying to catch up with me in that post-Indy flurry of attention.

Evidently, word had gotten out that we were going to be testing there, and the press, particularly reporters from the East Coast near Pocono, started calling the racetrack to talk with me. I'd make my test run, pull in and stop, and talk things over with Tyler about how the car felt and whether we needed to change anything. Then I'd have to run over to the office in the garage area and answer several phone calls or meet with someone who was waiting to talk with me. (My "buffer" had returned home for a few days.) After about three or four trips to the office, I finally said, "That's it. This is too distracting. I'm here to race, not be a media star."

At that moment I made a promise to myself that as long as I was dealing with the race car, I wasn't going to do anything else. I told the staff at the track to take messages and tell people that I'd call them back later in the evening or the next morning. And I kept my word. I was sincere in my efforts to return phone calls, grant interviews, answer every single piece of fan mail, and be as accessible as I could. But I was not going to be distracted from my job by all this media business when it was the race car and my profession that put me there in the first place.

I was adamant about my policy on dealing with the media away from the racetrack, and as a result we did well in qualifying at Pocono. We started in the middle of the second row. The car ran great, and the crew did a terrific job despite a long pit stop early in the race that put us a lap down.

The race itself was a nail-biter. A half-dozen drivers were involved in about twenty lead changes that day. Wally Dallenbach was in the lead as the race was winding down, but when his engine blew with about eleven laps to go, I grabbed the lead from him and won the race.

I thought the media attention was a bit much after our win at the Indianapolis Motor Speedway, but after we'd won three straight Indy car races it really intensified. The foreign press and television reporters were in the hunt now, and the requests for my time would have been overwhelming if it weren't for my ground rules. I was grateful that so many people were interested in me, in Betty and me, and in the McLaren team, but I was there to race cars. I had to stay focused.

In early July, before my next race, I accepted a Formula 5000 ride with Hogan Racing in Watkins Glen, New York. I wanted a diversion from Indy car racing and the ride with Carl Hogan's team seemed to be the best way to achieve that.

Formula 5000 cars were similar in design to Indy cars, but they were smaller and lighter. They also had Chevrolet V-8 engines and ran extremely quick on road courses.

Because I had to fulfill some previous commitments, I was late arriving at the Watkins Glen track. David Hobbs, my teammate with Hogan Racing, had taken the car—a Lola—out for some shakedown runs before I arrived. When I got to the track, David told me the car was in good shape. I took it out to see for myself, and aside from a minor problem that the crew fixed, I agreed. I decided to go back out on the track to run a few more laps.

The car really wasn't up to speed yet when I looked in my mirror and I saw faster cars approaching me. I moved closer to the inside of the track to give them room to pass me. Suddenly, I hooked one of the front tires on the new curbing that ran along the "S" turns on the backside of the track. I was carrying just enough speed that the car turned sideways and slammed into the guardrail with such force that it ripped the whole front end off the car.

I was dazed but able to get out of the car. My adrenaline pumping, I walked across the track, all the while thinking how bad I hurt. Eventually I had to lie down on the grass to wait for the ambulance. They rushed me to a hospital in nearby Montour Falls, took X-rays, and evaluated my condition. I had a broken left leg.

The medical staff put my leg in a knee-high plaster cast that they said I would have to wear for several weeks. They also told me I couldn't race during that time.

Fat chance, I thought.

The next race for me on the championship circuit was about two weeks later on July 21 in Michigan, on the fast, high-banked, two-mile track. I wanted to run. McLaren wanted me to run. So I had to prove to USAC officials that I could get out of the car with no problem in the event of an emergency—specifically a fire. They timed me exiting the car, and once they were satisfied that I could get out in a reasonable amount of time, they let me race with a broken leg.

During practice runs, we quickly learned that the cast was so heavy that my left leg kept sliding onto my right leg and foot, the throttle foot. Finally, one of the guys in the crew brought over a bungee cord with hooks on either end. We used the bungee cord to hook my leg to the inside of the car so that it wouldn't fall against my right leg while I was racing. It worked. We finished fourth, but perhaps running a two-hundred-mile race with a broken left leg *and* finishing fourth wasn't so bad after all.

Perhaps due in part to my physical health after the Watkins Glen incident, a season that had begun so promisingly for us changed directions during the second half of the season. We were on a roll with that car until the Michigan race three weeks later. Three weeks after that, we slipped to fifth place at Milwaukee. Back at Michigan for a race in mid-September, we fell to ninth. The best we could get was a fourth-place finish in the first of twin races on September 22 at Trenton.

Overall, though, the season was a stellar one. With wins at both Indy and Pocono, I became the first driver to win two 500s in one year. Plus, with our wins at Ontario prior to Indy and in the Milwaukee 150 after Indy, we took four checkereds in 1974. Even with our poorer showings in the latter half of the season, I finished second in the point standings for 1974. We were disappointed that we didn't finish first in points, especially since the driver who wins Indy usually wins the championship if he has a decent season. But when you're racing against drivers named Andretti, Foyt, Johncock, and Unser, you've got your work cut out for you. They kept the points close, and it was never easy to beat any one of them.

As disappointed as we were after the 1974 season, we felt we had done everything in our power to nail down the championship. It just slipped out of our grasp, and no one was to blame.

As I learned early on with the team, there was never any finger pointing with McLaren. Tyler Alexander was probably the most diplomatic team manager I ever had. Our first race together was in Trenton, New Jersey, in 1973. During the race I spun the car and backed it into a fence. It wasn't a serious crash, but the crew still had to put the car back together and prepare it for the next race.

I was devastated. Here I was with my brand new team, and the first race out of the box I ran their car into the fence. I respect all the hard work the crew puts into preparing a race car, and anybody who knows me would tell you that I'd rather fight King Kong than wreck a car.

I felt sick at heart after the wreck at Trenton. I called Tyler and the crew together and said, "Guys, I want to apologize for what I did out there. I really am sorry for crashing your race car. It wasn't intentional. I guarantee you that, if it's at all within my power, it'll never happen again."

Tyler looked me right in the eye and said, "John, if you won't keep score, we won't either."

That set the tone for the way we did business at the track. My situation with McLaren was very comfortable, productive, and successful thanks to that initial statement from Tyler. There were disagreements among us over some things, but we had been together for several years and had experienced so much together that we didn't let those things stand in the way of our work.

The team was like a family, and a culturally diverse family at that. McLaren was composed of Americans, Brits, New Zealanders, and Australians. When we socialized together after a race, usually at our motor home—they loved Betty's meatloaf and chocolate chip cookies—or after a test run, I learned about British humor, history, and philosophies. And the Americans on the team would share their stories, ideals, and history with their British counterparts. It was like a cultural exchange program.

All the guys on the McLaren team were hard workers. Racing was their business as well as their passion. That fit my persona to a T.

In the summer of 1974, during a rare break from our busy racing schedule, I was invited to participate in a celebrity golf tournament put together by the International Management Group in Turnberry, Scotland. Turnberry was a beautiful setting, even though the weather at that time of year alternated between rainy, cold, and blustery and sunny and warm.

The format of the tournament pitted the United States against the United Kingdom. Each team consisted of entertainers, sports celebrities, and one professional golfer—Tom Weiskopf for the U.S. team and Peter Usterhaus for the U.K. team. The American team also included actors Fred MacMurray, Robert Stack, and Telly Savalas; comedian George Kirby; singer Johnny Mathis; and myself as the reigning Indianapolis 500 champion.

During the event, each celebrity played nine rounds of golf with the pro on his respective team for the BBC television cameras. At first I was hitting terribly, but once I started bearing down and concentrating on what I was doing, I began hitting the ball better.

Every now and then I'd hit the ball into a sand trap. One such trap bowled down and then turned upwards, forming a lip of tufted grass almost like a thatched roof where it met the side of the green. Only a seasoned pro could knock a golf ball out of there comfortably and still put it near the hole.

Tom assessed the situation and told me to hit the sand trap about an inch and a half behind the ball. I thought about this for a moment, drew my club back, swung through, and struck the sand about two inches behind the ball. The ball lifted on the sand blast and cleared the lip of grass, went up in the air, and landed two feet from the cup.

Cheers and applause rose from the gallery. Just as it died down, I heard a Scottish voice say, "Aye, he's a ringer."

Tom and I both cracked up.

According to Tom, it was my round that won the tournament for the United States. To have been in that position was a great thrill. After the tournament concluded, we had a victory party. They served haggis, a traditional Scottish dish of the liver, lungs, and heart of a sheep or calf minced with onions, potatoes, turnips, and seasonings, and then boiled in the animal's stomach. The servers brought it and a dagger over to our team captain, Fred MacMurray. Fred stabbed it with the dagger to break the covering, according to tradition, and the food was served. We all enjoyed the food, the wine, and hospitality of the Scots at the party.

Betty and I had a chance to do some sightseeing while we were in Scotland, and we enjoyed ourselves thoroughly. We also enjoyed meeting and socializing with celebrities from both sides of the Atlantic Ocean.

During the 1974 off-season, I was honored with the Jerry Titus Memorial Award from the Auto Racing Writers and Broadcasters Association as their "Driver of the Year." The award was named after an auto-racing writer and accomplished driver who was killed in a racing accident at Road America in Elkhart Lake, Wisconsin.

The next year, 1975, was a mixed bag for Team McLaren. We opened the season with a second-place finish at Ontario in early March, followed by a seventeenth-place finish a week later at the same track when a burned piston knocked us out after eighty-six laps. The following week we ran the 150-lap race at Phoenix and won, and then in early April we raced at Trenton and took second place. Despite our initial slow start, it seemed that we were headed in the right direction again as May and the Indianapolis 500 approached.

That year, incidentally, was the first year in which the car wasn't painted its usual McLaren orange. We had a major sponsor that year in Gatorade, a product made by an Indianapolis company, Stokely-Van Kamp, so the car was painted Gatorade colors—white and green. Bill Stokely was our backer.

Now, Bill was a great guy, the company was a terrific sponsor, and we appreciated their involvement. But I was of the old school mind-set that green is a "hoodoo" color on a race car. In fact, we called green race cars "hoodoo wagons." Though I wasn't sure how the superstition began, I knew that green was bad luck. The first time I ever drove a green race car was in Phoenix in 1968, when I burned my hand. I hadn't driven a green car since then until my affiliation with Bill Stokely's company began. But then, those of us on the McLaren team simply chose to ignore old superstitions and just keep plugging away.

At Indy qualifying that year, our time was good enough to earn us a seventh-position starting place on race day. We were feeling pretty good about our chances of winning despite the usual mix of seasoned veterans and promising young rookies competing against us. One of those veterans was Lloyd Ruby, who happened to be my teammate on the McLaren team that year.

Lloyd was one of those drivers who had experienced success in just about any kind of race car you can name, from sports cars to midgets to stocks, and he'd done all right in Indy cars, too—at other tracks. But winning at Indy always eluded him. A lot of fans thought 1975 might be Lloyd's year, especially since he started on the outside of row 2. But his car burned a piston after six or seven laps, and he was done racing for the day.

A number of racers—such as Wally Dallenbach, Pancho Carter, Roger McCluskey, Bill Vukovich, and Bill Puterbaugh—hung in there lap after lap. But when Dallenbach, who had led for much of the race, was forced to pit with less than forty laps to go because of a burned piston, the race basically boiled down to a battle between A. J. Foyt, Bobby Unser, and me.

My final pit stop before the end of the race was a good one; the McLaren team had me in and out in no time. I had pitted for enough fuel to race the last laps, which meant that when Bobby and A. J. made their pit stops, I would be back in the lead and there wouldn't be any way they could catch me. I had been running extremely well all day. With Bobby, me, and A. J. running 1-2-3 after my pit stop, the final eighth of the race was about to begin, and both Bobby and A. J. still had to make their last scheduled pit stops.

It started drizzling with fewer than thirty laps to go, and the yellow caution flag came out. The drizzle soon became a downpour. I slowed down immediately and put the car in first gear, something Denny Hulme, an Indy rival of mine during the 1960s, had told me to do to keep from spinning out on a wet track. A driver can't go very fast in first gear because he'll wind the engine too tight. Still, it was treacherous driving out there, because not only was the pavement wet, there was about an inch of standing water on the track in some places. We were all driving on smooth (slick) tires, and we were in real danger of hydroplaning and spinning out. On lap 174 the officials brought out the red flag to stop the race. Bobby drove down the front straightaway to take the red flag and ultimately the last lap of the race. I was right behind him. A. J. was about a lap behind us.

A bunch of cars had some trouble with that wet pavement just as the race ended. There were a couple of spinouts, several cars collided with one another, and at least one car smashed into the wall. It was a wild conclusion to the 1975 Indy 500, but all the drivers escaped serious injury.

I wish that race had gone the full two hundred laps. We were right there; we had a chance to win. But coming in second at Indy after winning the race the year before showed that our win wasn't a fluke. McLaren meant business.

The next scheduled race after Indy was the 150-mile event at Milwaukee two weeks later, in which we finished third. Then we had back-to-back sixth-place finishes at Pocono and Michigan in June and July. At Milwaukee in August, we ended up well back at thirteenth when a broken scavenger pump knocked us out of the race after about 160 laps.

We regrouped for a return to Michigan in mid-September, placed second, and followed that up with a third-place finish at Trenton a week later. The last championship race we ran that year was at Phoenix in early November. A broken piston resulted in our eleventh-place finish.

As I said, it was a mixed bag for the McLaren team that year, but we did well enough to finish second in the point standings behind A. J. That gave us some positive reinforcement to take into the 1976 racing season. But considering the way that season opened for us, it's a wonder that our confidence and positive attitude didn't quickly sour.

☆ CHAPTER 19 ☆

Walking to Victory Lane

Finishing eighteenth is not how you want to start out a brand new racing season, but that's exactly what happened to us in 1976.

We were racing at Phoenix in mid-March, having started in the sixth position, and the engine died on us after fifty laps. We earned no points toward the championship and received a very small purse. After finishing eleventh at Phoenix four months earlier, we were looking forward to racing on a different track.

For the 1976 season we had obtained a new sponsor. Although we'd had a strong season in 1975 with Stokely-Van Kamp as our sponsor, Bill Stokely decided he wasn't going to carry on his sponsorship of the McLaren team for the 1976 season. I told him, "You're gonna regret this, Bill, because we're gonna win Indy."

"Well, John, I hope you do," he said. "I mean that. It's just that the company is headed in a different direction."

Bill eventually sold the company to Quaker Oats, and Gatorade hooked up with NASCAR. We hated to lose them, because Stokely-Van Kamp was a terrific sponsor.

That winter of 1975–76, we secured Hy-Gain CB radios as our sponsor for the '76 season. In the early to mid-1970s, America seemed to be caught up in a CB radio craze. Hy-Gain was a huge manufacturer of CB radios and provided antennas and other radio gear to the military.

Our association with Hy-Gain led to the birth of my nickname, "Lone Star J. R." A few weeks before the Indy 500 we were at a meeting with the Hy-Gain folks, and they told me I need a catchy CB "handle"—or radio name—that they could use in their ad campaign.

I don't remember who actually came up with the name. But "Lone Star J. R." was perfect, because my helmet carried the Lone Star flag—my connection to my home state of Texas. Betty's CB handle was "the Yellow Rose of Texas."

The car was repainted McLaren orange, but with the Hy-Gain signage prominently displayed. Their name first appeared on the car for the second race of the season, which was at Trenton in early May.

I started in the middle of the first row at Trenton. The M16 performed beautifully the entire race and we won. Then we were off to Indianapolis to start practicing for the Indy 500.

At Indy, we set the standard as soon as we started to run practice laps.

In an attempt to slow the cars down, USAC had called for the mandatory use of a "pop-off" valve on all engines. A pop-off valve is a device installed within the turbo-charging system that limits the pressure, which in turn limits the horsepower. For the moment, speeds were reduced by approximately ten miles per hour.

For a week prior to qualifying at Indy, the track is open from nine A.M. to six P.M. for practice. During the first part of the week, we set a fast practice time at nearly 188 miles an hour, a real morale booster for the team. The next day we moved it past 188. A few days later we did better than 189.

The first day of qualifying, Saturday, May 15, 1976, didn't get going until late that afternoon because of rain. When I finally was able to run the car on the track, we were fast. During qualifying, I beat Gordon Johncock and the rest of the guys by about a half a second. No one came close to me the rest of the day. For the second time in my career, the pole position was mine.

Hy-Gain was really pleased with our early success, and their hopes were sky high. But I started thinking that if I didn't win at Indy that year, they would fire me. I never needed extra incentive before to try to win the Indy 500, but there was a little added pressure because the M16 was doing so well and the Hy-Gain people were so enthusiastic.

The 1976 Indy 500 was full of historical moments. One was the appearance of a New York-based sports car driver named Janet Guthrie, who was attempting to become the first woman to race the Indy 500. Janet, who is my age, passed her rookie driving test two weeks before the race, but her car's engine was acting up and it didn't seem like she'd qualify.

A. J. then offered her a back-up car, and though she had a pretty solid practice run, A. J. elected not to run the car after all, either because of financial reasons or because of the difficulty of assembling a good pit crew on such short notice. Janet did return to race at Indy the following year.

Also of note that year was the opening of the Speedway's Hall of Fame Museum in April. The museum displays a collection of all the cars, racing gear, and mementos from past Indy 500s and is a very impressive place.

When race day rolled around, the McLaren team was ready to make a little history of our own. More than three-hundred thousand fans came out to watch the race under overcast skies.

The green flag was waved and I whipped into the lead and held it for three or four laps before A. J. pulled by me.

Mario Andretti shot up the line from way back in the seventh row to join the leaders. A few laps later, Roger McCluskey spun in somebody's oil and smacked into the wall at turn 3. They eventually waved the yellow flag and most of the drivers came to the pits at that time. Mario's crew had some trouble in the pits and by the time he drove back onto the track he was forced to play catch-up.

It was still early in the race, and the lead had changed many times. Gordon Johncock and Wally Dallenbach, who were both racing for the Patrick Racing Team that day, each led for a time. A. J. held the lead for a while, and I did too. Mario was never able to catch the lead, but he was hanging in there despite his earlier trouble in the pits.

Gordie, Wally, A. J., Mario, Tom Sneva, Al Unser, Pancho Carter, and I were among the guys who battled during the first eighty laps. Gordie's car had handled poorly all day, but he was still about half a straightaway ahead of me. All of a sudden he started backing up, a little bit each lap. I was right on him at lap 80 when he slowed going into turn 3. I slipped by him to regain the lead. A. J. passed Gordie right after I did.

We raced another twenty laps like that, with me in the lead, Foyt in second, and Johncock third. The whole time, Tyler and I were on the radio, talking about our next move. We were still running strong and good. The M16 was handling really well.

Then the rain started and the yellow flag came out. We went around the track for a few more laps, itching for the rain to let up. I was still in the lead and A. J. and Gordie were right behind me. We were the only three on the lead lap.

But the rain didn't let up. It just got worse. It started coming down so hard that I couldn't see past the nose of the car. Eventually the red flag came out to stop the race and everybody pulled into the pits. It wasn't even one o'clock yet, so race officials decided to wait out the rain, dry off the track, and resume the race.

So we waited. And waited. And waited. An hour passed, then an hour and a half. The rain eventually let up, but the track was wet—too wet. It was so bad that it took the track crew a long time to get it dry enough for us to race again. While they worked, the drivers and their crews went back to the garages and paced.

More than two hours went by. Finally, the P.A. announcement came: "Drivers, return to your cars."

By then, Tyler and I knew that A. J. and his crew had replaced a broken front sway bar, and that Gordie and his guys had fixed whatever was wrong with their car. Tyler and I also knew that when the green flag dropped again on the restart, they both were going to be charging after me. They'd been running strong in the early stages of the race even with cars that had been handling poorly. They had even been a little faster than me at times during the race, but we'd been steady and consistently quick.

The pit crews pulled the covers off the cars and the two dozen or so drivers still in the race were strapped in and raring to go. By now, it was about four in the afternoon. It was still overcast, but everyone there that day wanted to see the race go the distance. We'd gone only 102 laps—just past the halfway point.

Speedway owner Tony Hulman was poised to announce, "Gentlemen, restart your engines," when the bottom fell out of the skies. It was a real frog-strangler. The fans scattered and the rest of us just got drenched. Because it would take another three or four hours to dry the racetrack, and because we'd lose most of the fans if we resumed the next day, USAC officials finally just called the race.

We had run only 255 of the 500 miles, but it counted. McLaren won by virtue of being in the lead when the race was called. Foyt was livid. So was Johncock. They wanted to wait and finish the race the next day, but the officials had made up their minds. The race was over, and the McLaren team had won its second Indianapolis 500.

But I was still conflicted. I also wanted the race to go on. With three fiercely competitive racers chomping at the bit to go wheel to wheel for 245 more miles, the race was shaping up to be a real thriller. But sometimes being in the right place at the right time is the name of the game.

Usually, the winner drives his car into Victory Lane so the crew can push it up the ramp and onto the podium. It was still sprinkling, so the crew pushed the car to Victory Lane and I became the first Indy winner ever to *walk* into Victory Lane. Betty walked beside me. It was the third Indy 500 in the last four years that didn't go the full two hundred laps due to bad weather. Twenty-seven of the thirty-three cars were still running when officials called the race.

After the race I saw Bill Stokely walking around in the pit area. Our former sponsor obviously remembered my prediction that we would win Indy, because when he saw me, he stopped and grinned, turned around, flipped up his coattails to expose his backside, and invited me to kick him there. Bill was a good guy with a real sense of humor. I didn't gloat.

Now McLaren faced the season-long battle for the 1976 National Championship. A team wins the championship by having an exceptionally good year and accumulating more points than anybody else on the circuit—by being the best of the best.

I had never won a national driving championship. I had won the National Sprint Car Championship in '65, but to win the prestigious Indy car championship and be able to carry the no. 1 on my car the following season meant a great deal to me.

The competition was so fierce during the 1970s and 1980s that it was very tough for any driver to win the championship. Every year from '73 through '81 I finished in the top five in the point standings and carried my number on my cars to show it.

As the 1976 season unfolded after Indy, Team McLaren found itself on a real roller coaster of a ride. A seventh or ninth place finish here, a second or third place finish there. But the whole time we stayed in the hunt in the point standings. In the end, we were battling Gordon Johncock and the Patrick Racing Team for the National Championship. But there was a battle of sorts going on within our own team as well.

Tyler Alexander, my team manager, and Denis Daviss, my chief mechanic, had been having some problems. The situation escalated to the point that Tyler sent Denis back to England. That left us without a chief mechanic for the last two races of the season. Apparently, though, McLaren's internal strife had little effect on the team's ability to win races.

We ran the two-hundred-mile race at the Texas World Speedway on the last day of October. Early on in the race, I barely escaped a "squeeze." I was going into the first turn and working in and out of traffic. Suddenly, it was like all the drivers ahead of me were standing on their brakes and backing into me. Someone checked up their speed a bit and it started a chain reaction. I turned slightly to the left and went down low through the corner and somehow avoided everybody. I was able to time it right, and passed several cars in one move.

I made a mental note of how my car handled in that situation and used that groove later in the race to pass Gordie and take the lead. The McLaren team had won another one.

We went to Phoenix to close out the season. Although we'd finished a miserable eighteenth at Phoenix seven months earlier, this was a different race and we were coming off the win at Texas the week before. Plus, I liked racing the one-mile tracks.

Going into the race, we had to finish seventh to win the National Championship. Anything better was just icing on the cake.

I was quoted in the papers as saying, "If my car lasts, I can guarantee it will win the championship." When a reporter asked me, "But what if your car fails?" I laughed and said, "Then I'll get out and run the rest of the distance. Winning the national title is very important to us. We've all worked hard to be in this position."

On lap 111, as the race was grinding on and when it counted most, an oil line popped off the car's turbo-charger, which froze up for lack of oil, and the engine overheated to put us out of the race. We lost the National Championship to Gordon Johncock by twenty points (4240 to 4220) because of a two-dollar part.

I got out of my car, unfastened my helmet, and threw it on the ground. I said some well-chosen words, too. It wasn't like me to lose my cool like that, but I was livid. To be so close to winning my first Indy car championship and have it elude me like that was one of the most disappointing things to happen to me in my racing career.

Whether Denis's presence would have made any difference in the outcome is anybody's guess. But I know I would have felt better if Denis had been there to make sure the car was in shape. Perhaps then that oil line would not have popped off. We'll never know.

☆ CHAPTER 20 ☆

Crash the Yank!

I accepted invitations to race midget cars in Australia and New Zealand in 1977 and 1978. The reason I agreed to race was the great payoff. It was also a lot of fun and the fans were great. At New Zealand's Western Springs Speedway, a quarter-mile racetrack that was built into a bowl in the land, people watched from the sides of the hills and in the trees—a natural grandstands. The Speedway was in the port city of Auckland, and at one time there was a concrete velodrome around the outside of the dirt track. The concrete track was somewhat like a high bank, and you could drive around it to warm up the cars or just for kicks.

In Australia we raced in Sydney at the Sydney Showgrounds; in Liverpool, a suburb of Sydney; in Newcastle, north of Sydney; in Canberra, Australia's capital, southwest of Sydney; and in Perth, on the western coast. There was a noticeable U.S. influence in Australia, especially in certain cities; Perth and Sydney, for example, reminded me respectively of Los Angeles and New York City in many ways. But it was tough racing there. Some of the drivers didn't always know what they were doing, but they ran hard and they loved the sport.

My first year there I drove a local car. I quickly learned that if you're going to compete, you don't want to do that. Usually the car is a local owner's second car, and his first car is the one that gets all the attention.

That first year, I took Betty, our son John, and my mom with me. I have been back eleven times since then, and not always to race midgets. I drove an Indy car there for a couple of years before I retired, and following my retirement I drove the pace car for PPG Industries in Australia at Surfers Paradise. The Indy cars ran on a street course just south of Brisbane and the Great Barrier Reef, near a beautiful, sandy beach resort.

When I raced midgets down under, I had a few run-ins, most often with local George Tatnell, the perennial champion. Going sideways down under seemed to be a recurring situation for many an American driver when he raced midget cars against the top Australian and New Zealand drivers, because the favorite pastime for many of the drivers down under—particularly the Australians—was "Crash the Yank!" Tatnell used to crash the Yanks—or at least put us in a position to find the wall on our own—with great regularity. George was leading a race one night, and all of a sudden he turned into me and nudged me just so. I spun out, and he went on to win the race. So the next race I spun him out, and he was livid. He never bothered me much after that, because I showed him I could play his game, too.

Still, we enjoyed racing against each other. George was a tough competitor. One night in Liverpool we lined up for a race, with George starting on the pole. American Hank Butcher, a West Coast midget car driver who won a lot of races in California, started on the outside of the front row. I was pole in the second row. On the warm-up lap before the start of the race, George kept squeezing Hank. As I watched this and saw sparks flying off their wheels, I thought, *What is he up to?*

Then the pace car ducked into the infield and we took off. We came off turn 4 and down the front straightaway, and George just turned right and drilled Hank into the guardrail. I was right behind Hank and I saw his right-front wheel go sailing away.

I was infuriated. I'd seen George commit a lot of blatant acts, but that was the worst yet. George pulled away from Hank as Hank's car bounced over the top of the guardrail. It's a wonder Hank wasn't seriously injured. George turned to go into the first turn, and I just "sawed" my steering wheel, turning sharply. I angrily thought to myself, *That's not the way I race.*

I decided I was going to cut across the infield, nail George broadside, and take him right to the wall as hard as I could. But just as I had devised my plan, the yellows came on, followed by the reds to stop the race. In that split second, I decided against drilling George to the wall. So I went around the track for a few minutes and then went into the pits. I realized then that that's the way they race down under.

In October of 1977, I ran another race in Australia at Bathurst, a mountainous inland city west of Sydney and home to Mt. Panorama.

The roadway in the park there is shut down once a year for a huge, one thousand-kilometer race sponsored by a european brake parts manufacturer. This annual long-distance race is one of the bigger sporting events in

Australia. In fact, it's televised all day long, for nine hours straight. At the time, it was the most-watched program of the season.

The one thousand kilometer race at Bathurst was a different kind of race. The cars were right-hand drive passenger models modified for racing, much like our NASCAR stock cars. We Yanks found it a little awkward to sit on the right side of the car and shift the standard transmission with our left hands, but it can be learned.

Near the end of qualifying, I was racing fast down a long, undulating hill. I was driving my car for the last timed lap, a good lap that I felt would get me on the clocks. The timing lights were at the end of this particular portion of the track, and I wanted to run down into the corner as far as I could and gain the advantage of tripping the clocks so I could post a better qualifying time.

But I drove the car down the hill a little too far. I was forced to lock it up and the car slid sideways off the road, bumping up against the Armco. The impact didn't really damage the car too much, other than a little dent in the fender, but the engine was dead because the brakes were locked.

At first it was very quiet down there. Then, from within the crowd that was pressed up against the barrier fence not more than twelve feet from the guardrail, I heard an Australian voice say, "Go home, Yank."

I started laughing as I fired up the car, and I waved to the fans. They all cheered and waved back. I got the car started and drove it straight across the track and into the pits. I never will forget that voice.

I went back to race midgets the next year, in late 1978, and this time I brought a car from the United States, one of Doug Caruthers's hot cars. That year we went to Perth to race at Claremont Springs. I set a track record there in qualifying with Doug's car, which, like all his midgets, handled well and ran really strong. We set a track record in Newcastle, too, and I was told a few years ago that I still hold the record.

Claremont Springs was a well-prepared, wide dirt track. Everybody who raced there tended to qualify down on the bottom; nobody used the whole racetrack. As a former IMCA dirt track racer, I'd go out and look at the whole track and pick a spot to run on. I watched those guys qualify around the bottom and thought, *There's a lot of racetrack out there where you could really keep the throttle down and whistle if you knew what you were doing.*

When I went out to qualify I just moved up into the cushion to run there. It had dried just enough that I could really get a hold of it. It wasn't deep where

I ran; I was spinning the loose dirt up and creating a little curb to run against as I went around the track. After a warm-up lap, I moved up and ran two laps flat-chat, never backing off, and set a new record. The record still stands.

In the feature, they dropped the green and everybody was all over the race-track. It was an inverted-start race—with the fast guys in the back—and those kinds of races are always exciting.

Up ahead of me, one of the drivers ran into some trouble and the yellow came out. So we slowed down and drove around the racetrack. Hank Butcher was in front of me, and he went down in the corner, swung wide, and stood on it, pressing the throttle all the way to the floor. That really alerted me to Hank's plan for the race. *Well, Hank,* I thought, *you better put a trailer hitch on, 'cause I'm gonna hook up with you and we'll both go up there to the front.*

We got ready to restart as we came off the fourth turn. We got the green flag and went into the corner. I fully expected to see Hank stay up there, pitch it into the cushion, and really stand on it. But he didn't. He followed the guy in front of him down at the bottom. So I went up into the cushion alone. I pitched it and went around the outside, passing everybody in the first and second turn, and left them all behind. I eventually won the race.

I would say I ran eight or ten races each time I went down under, and in 1978 we won the Australian-American Championship. I was not the first Yank to win it. Bob Tattersall, who raced there years before in the 1950s, was one of the first, and he also won the championship with American cars that he brought with him. He remains a hero over there. Mel Kenyon was another driver who made a name for himself there.

Another good reason to bring your own car to Australia and New Zealand was that, when the racing series was over, you could sell the car to a driver over there. You could get twice, maybe three times as much as what you could get in the United States. Then you could return to the States, buy a new car, and race over here.

But the governments got wise and started charging duties on the cars. You couldn't sell your car once that happened; the duty would come out to twice the cost of the car, and it ate up any profits. But there were ways to get around the rules. You could take your car over there, race it, and if someone wanted to buy it from you when the season was over you could sell it to them and get their money, or at least a down payment, and ship it back in pieces from the United States.

Some drivers still go to Australia or New Zealand to race, but the midgets are not as popular now as they were when I was there in the late 1970s. Sprint cars have since taken over.

My family and I really enjoyed our time in Australia and New Zealand. While we were in New Zealand, we had the chance to visit with Denny Hulme, who lived with his wife and children in the lakeside city of Rotorua. All over the city were volcanic cones or fissures that were filled with extremely hot water. The Maori, the native tribes of New Zealand, used this water to cook food. They would use a string or wicker basket to drop seafood and other foods into the water.

While we were in New Zealand, we visited the transportation museum in Auckland, where we saw some of Bruce McLaren's early cars. We also attended a road-racing event once when we had a weekend off from running the midgets. The racetrack was called Pukekohe (pooka-ko-ee). Although I didn't know it at the time, one of my future chief mechanics with McLaren, Phil Sharp, was driving that day.

Australia is also a magnificent country. It has some great tracks, like Liverpool, the Sydney Showgrounds, and Canberra. One night we were racing at the new track in Canberra, and something happened to the generator that powered the lights on the backstretch. It just up and quit and they couldn't get it restarted. It was nighttime, and track officials were fearful of an accident occurring, so we all just stood around for a while. Then somebody at the track came up with the idea of parking some cars inside the track and angling the headlights down to light up the back straightaway. It worked; we finished the race, the fans were happy, and I believe I finished third or fourth.

In Perth we raced at the Claremont Speedway, a big, three-eighths-of-a-mile track. I set a record there in qualifying, but then I got squeezed and crashed in the heat race, so I didn't get to run in the feature that night.

They entertained us splendidly in Perth. An Italian gentleman who lived in Perth let us cruise the Indian Ocean in his fifty-foot yacht. We swam, snorkeled, and had a very relaxing time. Where the water wasn't very deep, we could see the sharks down on the bottom and all kinds of marine life.

Of course, our leisure time eventually had to end, and we traveled back to the east coast to finish up the racing series before returning to America. Testing with the McLaren team in preparation for the next racing season was only a couple of weeks away.

My visits to Australia and New Zealand are something I will always treasure. The people down under are wonderful. They really make you feel welcome—even if a few of them do enjoy playing "Crash the Yank!"

☆ CHAPTER 21 ☆

Check, Please

It was time to say goodbye to an old friend.

The M16 McLaren that we had run for four years, from 1973 through 1976, was past its prime. Other teams were developing new designs that would prove tough to beat. So McLaren came up with a derivative of the M23 Formula 1 car and modified it to handle the rigors of Indianapolis-style racing. The new car was sleeker, and its nose was reduced in size so that it would punch a smaller hole in the air. McLaren, like everyone else, was placing greater emphasis on aerodynamics.

The McLaren Indy car was called the M24, and the workhorse Offy engine was replaced with a Cosworth V-8 engine. We tested the new car a lot during the winter of 1976–77. Because it was new and our competition that year was fierce, we knew it would be a struggle to do well in 1977.

Our first race, at Ontario in the beginning of March, was an early sign of that struggle. Valve problems in the engine surfaced after only eight laps and we took twenty-fifth place. Our poor finish was especially bad because we had wanted to perform well for our new sponsor, First National City Travelers Checks.

The team regrouped for the Phoenix 150 three weeks later, and our diligence paid off. We won the pole position and the race.

But our win didn't come without some trouble. It all started during the race when I tried to pass Gordie Johncock. Gordie and I were good friends, but in competing for the pole, the lead, or the victory, we always seemed to lock horns.

At Phoenix, I was on Gordie's tail and was having trouble passing him. We came off turn 2, which angles slightly off to the right and then doglegs to the left, when I noticed a white halo of smoke coming up around his rear tires. He really had the hammer down, and he was "buzzing"—spinning his tires.

I was so close to him on the inside that by the time he backed off the throttle to hook it up again, it was too late. We barely touched, but he spun out. That's an old midget car trick: you see a guy spinning his tires through the corner and you just move up and touch him gently. He'll spinout and think it's his own fault. But in this case, I didn't bump Gordie intentionally. Because we were so close, Gordie backed off and moved into me, causing his car to spin. He didn't hit anything and was able to continue the race, but the longer the race went on after he got restarted, the madder he got at me.

At the time, A. J. was leading the race and I was a lap down. I made my pit stop and returned to the track in front of A. J. I heard Tyler tell me on our two-way radio, "You've got to stay in front of A. J. so we can get our lap back if the yellow comes out."

Our car was running well, so I was able to stay in front of A. J. even though he was trying hard to get by me. It became his personal mission to pass me, and before long, he blistered his tires. The next caution period gave me the chance to come all the way around to make up the lap. When A. J. made his pit stop, I soared into the lead and won the race.

After the race, A. J. got out of his car and started barking to Gordie, "You know what they told that !#$&! Rutherford to do? To stay in front of me! Hell, they probably told him to spin you out!"

A. J. got Gordie pumped up—not that Gordie needed it—and in the process, pumped himself up. A. J. was hot. He then went down to our pit, picked Tyler up by the front of his shirt, and started threatening him. Tyler explained the situation and reminded A. J. that what we did was perfectly legal. I think A. J. was simply frustrated that he blistered his tires. Eventually he calmed down.

But Gordie was still pumped up and upset. He stormed over to the building where the post-race press conference was scheduled to be held and confronted me as I was about to go in and answer questions.

I said, "Gordie, it wasn't intentional. You were runnin' all loose right there, and we were so close that when you backed off we just touched and that was it."

But Gordie wasn't buying it. He thought I'd done it on purpose. He followed me into the press conference, yelling at me the whole time. Dozens of reporters and a number of USAC officials were there waiting for me, and they watched it all unfold.

"Gordie," I said, "this is not the time or place for this. Go on outside. I'll talk with you in a few minutes and we'll get it all straightened out."

But Gordie kept going on and on, saying I was a danger to the other drivers.

Finally I just said, "Gordie, if you don't like the heat, get out of the kitchen."

Boy, that lit him up. He reared back and swung at me, and I leaned back to avoid the blow. I lost my balance and fell backward onto a table that was set up behind me. Gordie's ring just grazed the end of my nose and drew blood. But his swing continued and his fist struck Ray Marquette, the USAC press officer, right upside his head, knocking his glasses off his face.

Some reporters grabbed Gordie and hustled him out of the press conference. I quickly apologized for the altercation and proceeded to answer the reporters' questions. Later, both Gordie and I were reprimanded by USAC for the incident. But once it was over, that was it. We never had any problems after that. In fact, Gordie and I still laugh about it to this day. And Tyler still "fondly" remembers the time A. J. Foyt picked him up by his shirt and got in his face.

Even friends can experience friction when they're regularly thrown into a "hopper," but the key, I soon learned, is to get over it.

We finished fourth at Texas the following week and eighth at Trenton the last week in April. But nothing would prepare us for what would happen at Indy on May 29.

There was a lot of hubbub before the race. After giving it her best shot the year before, Janet Guthrie was back to attempt to become the first woman to qualify for the Indianapolis 500. Although she experienced a little trouble during one of her practice runs, she did make the starting field on the last day of qualifying.

Another reason for all the public scrutiny of the 1977 Indy was that the track had been completely resurfaced after the 1976 race. A new surface would result in better grip, which would mean better handling and faster speeds. Everyone was wondering if the cars would break two hundred miles an hour on the newly resurfaced track.

In fact, Mario, Al Unser, A. J., and I all got up to speeds in the high 190s in early practice runs before we eventually busted past two hundred miles per hour. However, those were unofficial times. Tom Sneva was the first to be officially clocked at better than two hundred miles an hour. He ended up in the pole position for race day.

We ran pretty well on the second day of qualifying, but only well enough to start back in the seventeenth spot, right in the middle of the sixth row. Once again, we had our work cut out for us.

They dropped the green and Al Unser sped by his brother Bobby and Tom Sneva to grab the early lead. But I didn't stick around long enough to mix it up with any of them. Problems with the M24's gearbox knocked us out after only a dozen laps.

Chicken one year, feathers the next. We had gone from first to worst at Indianapolis. I sat and watched the rest of the race from the pits and stewed in my own dejection.

Our fortunes—and my mood—changed for the better two weeks later when we came in first at the 150-lap Rex Mays Classic in Milwaukee. During the race, Gordie piled into the wall after a run-in with Clark Templeman, and it took rescuers some time before they could even pull him out of his crashed car. They rushed him to the hospital, where he was listed in critical condition for a few hours before being upgraded to satisfactory.

That was one close race. I took the lead about two-thirds of the way through the race, but Tom Sneva, Al Unser, Pancho Carter, and a couple others were not going to just hand it to me. I had to fight off several challenges late in the race, edging Tom Sneva by five seconds to win.

The remainder of the season was a series of poor finishes interspersed with a few victories—namely at Texas and Milwaukee. We closed out the season in less than fine fashion in Phoenix when I wrecked the car in turn 2 after racing just a few laps—the second time I wrecked that season. Somehow we still managed to finish fourth in the point standings that year.

I've led a clean life and have always tried to stay on law enforcement's good side. So it must have been a surprise to my fans when they learned that I had been involved in a burglary in 1977.

The alleged crime was a pure case of misidentification, and a humorous one at that. At the time, I was serving as a spokesman for the CARQUEST Corporation. CARQUEST began in the mid-1970s with a hundred auto parts stores; it now operates nearly four thousand stores serving both the professional automotive service repair industry and do-it-yourselfers throughout North America. Since I was their spokesman, CARQUEST created life-sized, stand-up cutouts of me wearing the cap and uniform bearing their company logo. These cutouts were distributed to stores throughout the country.

One night, a truck driver in Mississippi got on his CB radio at about 4:30 in the morning and called the local police to report that a downtown store was being burglarized. The police responded quickly and converged upon the store. They peered inside the dimly lit store and saw a man standing there.

The man was yours truly. Actually, it was my cutout, as the officers quickly discovered. In the end, neither I nor my cardboard likeness was arrested for burglarizing a store.

In early 1978 I was part of a three-man team that raced the "24 Hours of Daytona" in Dick Barbour's Porsche 935.

Long-distance racing requires a different mind-set from that which Indy car racing requires. In Indy car racing, you are running flat-out the entire time, except for when you're taking the occasional pit break. In the twenty-four-hour race at Daytona, you want to save the car so you can go the full length of the race without having to take frequent pit stops. It's a different kind of racing. You're still going fast, but it's relaxing compared with racing Indy cars or anything else you run hard.

At the "24 Hours of Daytona" race, some cars whistle along at two hundred miles an hour. They're in a field with cars that are running 120 miles an hour at their top speed, so the drivers really have to be cautious. Some of the drivers have rarely, if ever, participated in that type of racing before, so they end up all over the racetrack, sometimes forgetting that they're not the only ones out there.

My car was a twin turbo and extremely fast. It had been modified considerably for racing—it had a roll cage, a single racing seat, and special suspension to handle the wider tires. The car ran well over two hundred miles an hour, and Daytona was the ideal track for those speeds. In 1978, track officials had yet to install the chicane in the end of the backstretch, so you could really open the car up. We could run flat-out off the infield course and between turns 1 and 2 and up onto the banking. By the time we got to the third turn, we would be running two hundred-plus.

Dick Barbour, a car dealer from San Diego, California, was the owner of my car. The third member of our team was Manfred Schurti, a factory pilot for Porsche who worked at their testing facility in Germany. Manfred knew the car like the back of his hand. He was from Liechtenstein and was a very fast, skilled driver. Manfred, as lead driver, and I, as the second driver, split most of the driving duties, running for ten hours each. Dick was third and ran the remaining four hours.

Our team was in the thick of it the whole time, until just after dark. Manfred, Dick, and I had each taken a turn at the wheel, and it was Manfred's turn again. He was running pretty well, but then, coming off turns 1 and 4, he cut the right-rear tire and it exploded. The car spun as it approached the front straightaway, and in doing so, tore everything on the right-rear side completely off the car.

Once he stopped spinning and gained control of the car, he drove it into the pits. Our crew put it up on the jack stands and started to work on it. They replaced the suspension and several of the parts that had been torn off in the accident. They then bolted a new, pre-made, right-rear corner onto the car. They did everything they could to align the car and make sure it was okay to race. The right-rear fender, however, was still missing.

Once the car was ready, Manfred jumped in and took off. He ran it for about two hours, and after his next pit stop I took over. I ran the car for the duration of two fuel loads; when I came back to the pits it was early the next morning. Dick didn't want to run it at that point, so Manfred took off again. Before much time had passed, the left-rear tire exploded and the left-rear corner was completely torn off the car, damaging the oil coolers in the process. Fortunately, Manfred was able to keep it under control and get it into the pits. Once again the car went up onto the jack stands. The guys must have worked on it for fifteen minutes. Because the car wasn't that hot, we felt we could just hook some hoses together in a series so that the car wouldn't require the oil coolers.

Now, with both side fenders missing and the two big, wide tires exposed, our Porsche looked like a sprint car from the back. Manfred went back into the fray with the car. He drove it for a while and then I jumped in when he brought it in for refueling. I ended up finishing the race.

The winning team included drivers Rolf Stommelen, Tom Hezemans, and Peter Gregg, and was owned by Brumos. We came in second. Diego Febles and Alex Poole's team came in third. All three cars were Porsches. After the race, the Porsche representatives had someone take a photograph of the 1-2-3 finish. That was the Porsche poster that year—one, two, and three at "The 24 Hours of Daytona."

In October of that same year, I traveled to England on a USAC-sanctioned trip to race an Indy car for Team McLaren. The first race was at Brands

Hatch in Kent, just east of London. We finished third. The next weekend we raced in the rain at Silverstone, a former Royal Air Force base south of London, and I finished fifth. I would have loved to have won for my McLaren mates, since the company was based in England, but our finishes were at least respectable.

The next racing season, 1978, was shaping up to be a truly forgettable one when we encountered one mechanical failure after another in the first three months of the season. We had problems with the valves, the clutch—you name it. I was even involved in a wreck at one of the racetracks. But as usual, there was never any blaming among the McLaren staff. We had a job to do, and when things didn't go according to plan we simply toughed it out.

Indy car racing, and the Indianapolis Motor Speedway in particular, lost a great man in October of 1977 when longtime Speedway owner Tony Hulman died of heart failure. Tony is credited with saving the Indianapolis Motor Speedway and the Indy 500 from extinction when he assumed charge of both in 1945.

After Tony died, his widow, Mary, became chairman of the board. In 1978, it was Mary who declared the start of the 1978 Indy with the command, "Gentlemen, start your engines."

Our double-digit finishes for that first three-month period of the season continued at Indianapolis, where we ended up thirteenth. Despite having damaged his wing during a pit stop late in the race, Al Unser outdueled Tom Sneva to win the race by just a few seconds. Janet Guthrie, who had finished twenty-ninth the year before, came in ninth in 1978.

Things took a turn for the better in the two months after Indianapolis, when the McLaren team got a win at Michigan and four second-place finishes. I'll never forget the Michigan race—it was perhaps the most competitive and entertaining race I've ever run.

We were given a caution late in the race with about thirty laps to go. When we got the green flag to restart, Danny Ongais—or "Danny on the gas," as we called him—and I were running 1-2. We were all over each other, racing side by side and wheel to wheel for nearly fifteen laps. At one point I thought to myself, *If the fans don't like this, they might as well load up and go home, 'cause this is as good as it gets.*

Danny tried to stick his wheel behind my left front, but I shook free of him. We battled each other until his car finally broke down from running flat-chat that hard for twenty laps. I went to Victory Lane to receive the trophy. After all the photo taking and interviewing, I saw Danny walking across the paddock toward us.

I made my way down to the gate at the end of Victory Lane and threw the gate open. He grinned really big, and I grinned really big, and we walked toward each other and hugged. We both knew that we had raced our wheels off in a one-on-one duel that gave the crowd something to get excited about. We had raced so hard for such an extended length of time, and we had walked away from it intact. And that's what it's all about.

McLaren resumed double-digit finishes in September, but made a comeback with a fifth-, a third-, and a first-place finish in October. Even with all the rough spots we encountered that season, we managed to nail down fourth place in the point standings for the second year in a row.

At the end of the 1978 season we lost our sponsorship with First National City Traveler's Checks, but were able to connect with Anheuser-Busch for 1979.

The new season started off unusually well. We took third at Phoenix in early March and followed that up with wins at both races of the Atlanta Twin 125s on April 22. Those were two tough wins; it's not easy to run twin races, much less win both, because of the problems that arise when you fire a car up a second time after it has cooled down. After the first 125-mile race, the engine cools down, and that's when the gremlins go to work. Then you have to fire it up again and race flat-chat for another 125 miles.

But with such a great crew working hard to make our car the best of the field, we encountered no major problems. In the thirty to forty-five minutes between the two races, they had just enough time to look the car over, change the tires, and refuel. You start the second race the way you finished the first one; we started first in the second race and finished first as well.

Next up was Indy, and we had to sue to get in.

The fiery pile-up in Phoenix in 1968 (left to right: me, Mario Andretti, and Roger McCluskey).

Being helped from the track after sustaining a third-degree burn to my right hand in Phoenix in 1968.

Closest run for the pole position in the history of the Indianapolis Motor Speedway, 1970.

Talking with "Big Lou" Ligino (middle) and A. J. Foyt (right) at a DuQuoin, Illinoïs, dirt race in 1973.

Proud parents John Rutherford Jr. and wife, Doris.

The Rutherford family at Indy: Betty (middle) and her parents, Norman and Carol Hoyer, pose with John and Angela in 1974.

The winner's circle at the Ontario Motor Speedway, California in 1973 (left to right: Tony Hulman, Betty, and me).

Talking with Emerson Fittipaldi during a 1974 Indy test.

Getting the checkered flag: the win at the 1974 Indianapolis 500.

Pointing to my rightful place on the Indy 500 Borg-Warner Trophy.

Betty with the spoils of victory at the 1974 Indy.

Being interviewed by ABC's Chris Economacki at Pocono,
Pennsylvania, in 1974.

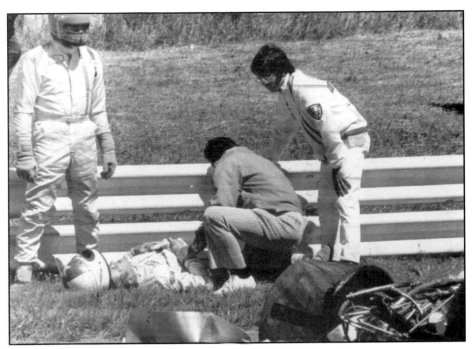

Suffering a broken left leg during a mishap at the 1974 F-5000 race in Watkins Glen, New York. David Hobbs (left) stops to give aid.

Preparing to race with a broken leg at a 1974 Michigan race. I would earn 4th place.

With Betty in Victory Lane at the 1975 World Series of Auto Racing championship car race held in Trenton, New Jersey.

Betty at work on the scoring stand during the 1975 Indy 500.

Talking with McLaren team manager Tyler Alexander in 1975.

The best engine man in racing and a longtime friend, Herb Porter, pictured here in 1975. Herb passed away in June of 1999 at the age of eighty-four.

Driving Carl Hogan's F-5000 car in Riverside, California, in 1975.

Racing Doug Caruther's midget car in Australia, 1977.

My second win at Indy, 1976.

☆ CHAPTER 22 ☆

Putting the CART before the Horsepower

Legal wrangling, not injuries or a broken sway bar, almost kept me out of the 1979 Indianapolis 500.

Trouble had been brewing for some time between race car owners and the United States Auto Club, the sanctioning body of the Indianapolis 500. The owners didn't like the way USAC was running things, particularly with regard to policymaking and rules changes, and how all of that affected the cars' engines and construction. After all, USAC was spending the car owners' money with each rule change.

The final straw was USAC's desire to put a cap on "the speed thing." The USAC wanted to slow down the newer, faster cars and in turn keep the race competitive. To accomplish this, USAC started to require that a "pop-off" valve—a spring-loaded valve that limits the amount of "boost" a turbo-charged engine can achieve—be placed on the cars' plenum chambers.

The problem was that the use of the pop-off valve was difficult to police when it was first introduced. The valves weren't consistent and they would create different results in different cars. One team's valve might stick a little, and therefore give them more boost and a better run. Another team's valve might pop open before the race, resulting in less boost and a weaker run.

On occasion, officials would allow a driver a second chance to make his qualifying run because it was ruled that his pop-off valve was faulty. It was a fiasco and just one of USAC's policies that was costing car owners money.

So the owners banded together and tried to do something about the situation. Their representatives met with USAC officials to see if they could work it out. "At the very least," the owners said, "we want more input in making the rules because we're the guys putting up the money for these teams."

USAC officials denied their requests. When the troubles continued, the owners went back to USAC and tried again to work something out. But still the answer was no. USAC allowed the election of one driver representative from each of the divisions under their control—sprints, midgets, championship cars, and so forth. I was the driver rep for sprint cars at that time, so I was privy to all USAC board actions as well as the owners' complaints.

With all the battles being fought and a few other controversies, 1978 was the beginning of the end of the United States Auto Club's role as the sanctioning body of Indy car racing.

In late April of that year, seven top USAC officials perished in an airplane crash southeast of Indianapolis. They had been flying back to Indianapolis to open the Speedway after having attended a race in Trenton, New Jersey. Two of the people on that plane were Frank DelRoy, the longtime chairman of the USAC technical committee, and Ray Marquette, USAC vice president in charge of public affairs.

It was a devastating loss, and the repercussions of the tragedy most likely contributed to the instability of the relationship between car owners and the USAC.

In early 1979, six car owners formed their own group and called it Championship Auto Racing Teams. This move pretty much split car owners into two camps. Half of the group was still loyal to USAC, and half wanted to move on with CART. It was getting messy.

In April of 1979, when the McLaren team and I were in Atlanta for the twin 125s, a federal agent came out to the track the day before the race. He served notices to our team and five others involved in the newly formed CART that said our entries for the Indianapolis 500—which was just a month away—had been denied.

The owners of the teams quickly hired a lawyer, John Frasco, to represent the six teams in CART that had been named in the court action. The six teams were the Dan Gurney team, the Pat Patrick team, the McLaren team, the Penske team, the Fletcher team, and the Jim Hall team. They sued the Indianapolis Motor Speedway to reinstate their teams on the entry list of the race that year. When Frasco drew up the court papers, however, they read *Johnny Rutherford et al. v. æ*; in other words, my name, not the names of the teams themselves, received all the ensuing media attention for the next few weeks. And boy, it got bad.

Many people interpreted this to mean that I was heading up the lawsuit against the Indianapolis Motor Speedway, which made people think that I, as a two-time winner of the race, was a hypocrite.

The whole situation destroyed a lot of friendships for Betty and me. There were people who didn't speak to us for ten or fifteen years. We received nasty phone calls and letters. In the eyes of many people, I was the bad guy—at least for a while.

Betty believes that John Frasco and his colleagues chose to name me on the court papers because I would make a good spokesperson. Whether I liked it or not, I was thrust into the spotlight whenever there was a press conference or an interview. It was a credibility issue, and since I had won Indy twice and was a seasoned racing veteran, I was deemed the most credible person to contact about the suit.

I found myself making statements based on what little I knew at the time, while the movers and shakers—Roger Penske, Pat Patrick, Jim Hall and others—remained in the background. I didn't have to accept the role, but it was my livelihood, and I was fighting to be able to support my family by doing what I'd been doing for twenty years.

In some ways, my time spent in court was easy. I was there, along with Dan Gurney, Al Unser, and a few other drivers who occasionally sat in on the proceedings. But Dan and Al and I were the only drivers to testify.

It appeared as if the defense was trying to break CART, or at least bend it. Our options in their eyes were to either adhere to the court order and not run, or give up our demands and come back to the field. The USAC's lawyers clearly didn't want to ask us questions pertaining to our livelihood—how being barred from Indy would hurt us and our families. They danced around it as long as they could, but eventually the inevitable happened, and Dan and Al and I got up on the stand and told our side of the story. We said that we made our living by racing cars, and that USAC and the Speedway were shooting us down.

The judge said, "You cannot keep these men from making a living." He ruled in the owners' favor. The six teams that sued the Indianapolis Motor Speedway could compete at Indy—no one would be denied "the right to work."

You could almost hear a collective sigh of relief from both sides. The Speedway folks were certainly relieved, because they were not enjoying all the bad publicity right before the race, and they knew how important we were to the sport and to Indy.

Though we won the lawsuit, it wasn't a big victory for CART. It was just the beginning of a long-standing rift between various factions that continues to this day. CART set about to develop a racing schedule. The USAC still had their schedule, but not enough drivers or racing teams to put on a season-long show. At Milwaukee and Pocono that year, for instance, there were maybe twelve or fourteen cars in the field. Finally the USAC called on its dirt car division and had them put pavement tires on their cars so they could run in USAC events. It was a travesty, a really bad scene.

On the other side, CART was developing more road courses for its series because there weren't enough permanent tracks to run on. CART officials would enlist cities to set up courses on the streets. By doing this, they could fill up a schedule and attract car owners from the road racing ranks. That's really what put CART on the map: the temporary street courses and the existing road courses that CART officials used to supplement their schedule. It was a fresh start for them.

My sense of relief came at the drop of the green at the 1979 Indianapolis 500. I was glad to be out there on the racetrack instead of testifying in a courtroom. I started at the eighth position and ran second or third for a time early in the race. But once again, the greatest race in the world eluded us as we ended up well back at eighteenth.

The rest of the 1979 season was a repeat of recent seasons, with several strong showings interspersed with a few pretty weak ones. Overall, we placed in the top ten in nine of fourteen races to rank us fifth in the point standings for the year.

McLaren was still doing well and winning races, but we'd lost our grip on Indianapolis. After winning the 500 in '74 and '76, we never got any closer than thirteenth. Plus, the company itself was experiencing changes in terms of direction, finances, and program emphasis. McLaren's Formula 1 division was the company's key effort in England, so there was an initial internal struggle between proponents of the Formula 1 program and proponents of the Indy car program. Teddy Mayer's Formula 1 sponsors supposedly pressured him to concentrate on that program by claiming that they would withdraw their financial backing and go elsewhere.

Meanwhile, McLaren was also fighting a lawsuit here in the States involving another driver and another racing team. In 1973, after rain had delayed the start of the Indy 500 for several hours, driver Salt Walther crashed into the outside wall on the front straightaway just before the green flag was dropped, and his car flipped over and burst into flames. He was severely burned and suffered internal injuries, and about a dozen other race cars and a number of spectators were caught up in the fiery crash. Some of the spectators who were injured in the accident sued everyone involved. McLaren was named because Walther was driving a McLaren car.

Their attorneys' fees were a financial drain, so to cut costs and protect their F-1 program, McLaren pulled the plug on Indianapolis and, as a result, set me adrift.

For the first time in years, I was left without a ride.

☆ CHAPTER 23 ☆

Ladybug on My Shoulder

☆ ☆ ☆

Team McLaren and I may have been parting company, but there remained a strong bond between us. We'd been through a lot together for the better part of the decade, and so Tyler Alexander, my McLaren crew chief, helped me take the next step in my racing career.

Tyler knew Jim Hall, the head of Chaparral Racing Ltd., from their Can-Am days. Jim had won the 1978 Indy 500 with Al Unser behind the wheel. Then, for the 1979 Indy 500, Hall and Unser teamed up again, this time in a new car that featured so-called "ground effects" that were based on Formula 1 designs. The Chaparral "2K" car, as it was called, was designed to reduce the air pressure beneath the car. With less pressure beneath the car, the normal amount of air pressure above it would push the car down, enabling the driver to get through turns faster and really fly around the track.

The car showed great potential but still needed a lot of testing. For some reason, the Hall team had to develop the car during the season. That's tough, because once the season starts you have to race the car as it is. It's best to test in the off-season, during the winter months, when you have time to discover any problems with the car and address them. The Hall team was essentially testing the car each time they raced it.

Al drove the car for the 1979 season and didn't have much success with it until the last race of the season, when he won the race at Phoenix with the Chaparral. After that season, Al and Jim disagreed over some philosophical aspects of the program, and Al quit the team. His departure coincided closely with McLaren's departure from Indy racing, so Tyler called Jim Hall and suggested he hire me to drive for his team.

Jim called me, and I went to Midland, Texas, where his operation was based. After we discussed an agreement and I toured his facility, I eagerly signed up to drive his team's state-of-the-art ground effects car. Jim also needed a chief mechanic. Fortunately, Steve Robey, an Australian mechanic with whom I had worked on Team McLaren, was also looking for a job. Steve's McLaren crewmates had nicknamed him "Abo." Steve was a great teammate and a dedicated mechanic who understood what was going on with my race cars. Just as important was that Steve knew what I liked in a race car's setup, and how I liked the car to ride and feel. We already had a strong working relationship.

In the winter of '79–'80, the Chaparral Team went to Phoenix for my first test drive with the Chaparral. Jim had set the car up exactly the way Al had wanted it when he won the last race of the 1979 season, and I could not drive that car. It wasn't comfortable for me, and really demonstrated how different drivers require different things in the setup of their race cars.

Steve suggested to Jim that they try a stiffer setup. Jim agreed, and Steve and the guys put heavier springs on the car, adjusted it, and changed the roll bars to make it ride a little more firmly. Before the day was over, we were running well under the track record.

Everybody left the test happy. The car was ready for the first race of the season, at Ontario in mid-April. We were quick in qualifying, sat on the pole, and won the race. Crucial to our success was having a great sponsor. Pennzoil had for many years enjoyed a tremendous relationship with the racing profession. The company's bright yellow race cars were always a distinctive highlight of any race.

Starting in 1980, when I began driving Jim Hall's Pennzoil Chaparral, and for many years since then, Pennzoil has helped set the standard for how sponsors should promote their teams. Pennzoil was my biggest sponsor in racing, and perhaps the sponsor that had the greatest impact on my career.

Pennzoil hired Deke Houlgate, a publicist and public relations specialist from California and one of the best in the profession. Deke was a positive, upbeat man with boundless energy. I used to kid him that he must be paid by the interview, because he could line up more interviews in a day than I would care to do. But he was good for Pennzoil and good for Johnny Rutherford.

At one point, Pennzoil wanted me to paint my entire helmet yellow and display the Pennzoil name across it. Of course, at that time I was wearing my

Texas flag helmet, and it had become my trademark. But Pennzoil persisted, and finally I offered a compromise: I would allow them to do whatever they wanted to the bottom half of the helmet, but I would not paint the whole helmet yellow.

So we painted the bottom half yellow, painted the Pennzoil signage around the bottom of the helmet, and I got to keep my trademark Texas flag on top. Everyone was happy. After all, we were an all-Texas team—Pennzoil, Hall, and Rutherford.

With a great team and a great sponsor in place, it was time to make the annual pilgrimage to the Indianapolis Motor Speedway. I was ready to pull into Victory Lane once again.

Our yellow Chaparral was too. In practice it was quick around the track, posting speeds of 192 mph or better. In fact, we had the quick time every day that month at the Speedway except for one, when rookie Tim Richmond beat us by about a half-mile per hour.

On Pole Day we bested Mario's time to earn pole position for the race, the third pole of my career. Mario's qualifying run placed him in the spot next to mine in the first row. Bobby Unser earned the outside spot next to Mario.

On race day, I was standing by my car out on the track talking with Jim and Steve when I felt something land in my hair. I reached up and flicked my hair, and when I looked down, I saw a big, orange ladybug on my shoulder. It crawled around on my shoulder for a moment before it flew off.

I just grinned and told Jim and Steve, "Hey, this is it. Just tell the rest of the guys to load up and go home. We just won the race."

After the green was dropped to start the race, Bobby shot up beside me as we moved into the first turn. I held my position and passed him across the short chute to take the early lead. Even when I slipped to second or third for a short time after my pit stops, my car was responding so well that I was always able to retake the lead.

On lap 148, that Chaparral of ours just flew past Tom Sneva to reclaim the lead once again, and moments later I ran the fastest lap of the day at better than 190 miles an hour.

With about thirty laps left, I pitted for fuel and Rick Mears went into the lead, with Sneva right behind him in second. A few laps after I returned to the track, A. J.'s car suffered a broken valve and just stopped dead in turn 3. The yellow came out. On the restart, I got by Mears and Sneva to take the lead again. Our Chaparral roared around that track to take the checkered and my third Indy 500 victory.

Tom Sneva came all the way from the thirty-third position to take second place, and Gary Bettenhausen, who was racing an old car with a rebuilt fuel system and a bunch of parts he'd gotten from other teams, came all the way from thirty-second to place third. But in the end our Chaparral proved to be too much for the rest of the field. I led the race for 119 of the 200 laps.

A big part of the reason for my success that day was that the Jim Hall team was excellent. As a car owner and a champion sports car racer, Jim not only understood the mechanics of a race car, he also understood the racing psychology and the language that drivers use to describe what they're experiencing on the track. Jim was fun to work with, and I enjoyed driving for him because we could communicate on that level.

After our victory at Indy, we took either first—in Mid-Ohio and Michigan—or second—in Milwaukee and twice in Pocono—in five of the next six races. In early August we ran in the road race at Watkins Glen, where a gearbox problem resulted in a fifth-place finish.

When we returned to Milwaukee a week later we won the two hundred-lap race, which gave us a second and a first there for the year. We also returned to Ontario, where we had started the 1980 season with a win in April, to race the California 500. Only this time, Bobby Unser took the checkered; we stumbled and finished second.

After an unexplainable fourth-place finish at Michigan three weeks later, we went to Mexico City to race on a full-blown road course. Shortly after we arrived at the racetrack, a big earthquake hit the region. We stood there, watching the ground undulate, the trees sway, and the telephone lines and electric wires swing back and forth. Betty and I got back to our high-rise hotel and found the walls of our room cracked, with two- to three-inch gaps at the corners. Plaster was all over the bed and the floor and in the bathtub. It was an eerie scene. It made us wonder if we were safe there. I had experienced smaller earthquakes in California, but this one was between a 6 and a 7 on the Richter scale.

The race itself, or at least its conclusion, was anticlimactic. I was running third, and Bobby Unser was running right in front of me in second. Al, Bobby's younger brother, was leading the race. I was really pushing the car hard to get past Bobby with a few laps to go. But I lost control, spun, and crashed. We walked away with a disappointing tenth-place finish. I really felt bad about that.

We still had one more championship race to go, but with five wins, three seconds, and a fourth and a fifth, I had earned more than forty-seven hundred points. That was all I needed. Finally, I had won the National Championship. And in doing so, we set a new record for miles covered for a racing season: more than 2,927. It was a testimony to the team, the Chaparral, and Jim Hall. The team produced a car that just did not fail. That season they gave me the opportunity to fulfill many goals and realize those dreams I had worked so hard to achieve over the years.

The 1980 season was the best season I would ever have in championship racing. But ironically, I never got to accept the National Championship trophy. Although I had legitimately won the championship by virtue of my point total, there was still one more race to run—at Phoenix.

We had a good qualifying run and started the race in the no. 2 position in the front row. I was leading after about three-fourths of the race when I returned to the track from my last pit stop. I had just passed Tom Sneva and was driving off into the sunset to take the checkered. At the same time, Dennis Firestone, a rookie driver that year, was running around at the bottom of the track. I don't know how it happened, but he let his car come up the track to take his natural line—exactly where I was running. His car's right front made contact with my car's left rear as I was going by him on the outside, and the impact spun us both.

My car's left rear whacked the outside wall, breaking the car's chassis. The car then rebounded off the wall, turned sideways so that its nose was pointing toward it, and rolled up on its rear wheel. When it flipped over, I landed on my head. The car then slid a hundred feet toward the inside pit wall and stopped.

The car was upside down and facing the inside of the racetrack. It had stopped right in front of the pits, and everybody ran out and tried to turn the car over. The roll bar had done its job, having collapsed to half its height when the car landed and skidded, but I was still pinned underneath. No one knew if I was alive or dead; they just knew they had to get that car off me. A group of guys picked up one side of the car while a couple others slid underneath and grabbed me.

It was my helmet that ultimately saved my life. It suffered the damage and kept my skull from cracking when my head hit the pavement. But, boy, did it take a beating. The brad or rivet that attached the chinstrap to the helmet had been worn down and the strap had come loose. If it had not been for my "sissy strap"—a strap attached to the left side of my helmet and tethered by a loop under my left shoulder—the slide my car took would have easily knocked the helmet off my head.

The back of my helmet sustained a three-inch-long split from the impact, and the left-rear quarter had a sizable dent. The Snell Foundation, which sets the standards for professional racing helmets, later ran a test on the same type of helmet I was wearing in that accident. To achieve a dent of that nature, they had to place a fifteen-pound weight inside the helmet and drop it to the ground from ninety-three feet. They also estimated that the speed I was traveling when my head hit the ground and the car landed on me was 135 miles an hour.

The folks at the Snell Foundation were thrilled—though I suspect I was probably more thrilled—to have approved a helmet that didn't produce "a fatal" in the face of that much destruction. You could have poked your finger through the fiberglass to the interior of the helmet on one side, where it had been ground through. It had burn marks all over it, and the face-bar in front of the helmet was cracked on both sides—one yank would have pulled it right out. But I survived with the full knowledge that, as the Snell folks said, "A helmet of any less integrity would have certainly produced a fatal."

I was kept at the hospital overnight for observation. In addition to the head injury I had sustained, I had also been burned in the crash. My helmet had slid up on my head when the chinstrap came loose, so that the eye port I normally looked through was pushed up to my forehead. When the accident caused my car's vent line to unload some methanol, sparks from the friction of the car sliding against the pavement ignited a small flash fire and I received second-degree burns on my exposed forehead. Had the helmet not slid up my head, the fire might have burned my eyes. I still shudder at that thought.

I had a terrible headache and needed to rest, so Betty attended the awards ceremonies on my behalf, even though she wanted to stay with me. But I was the national champion, so Betty had to go to collect my champion's ring and the whopping twenty-five hundred-dollar check. With the help of Jim Hall, Betty also gave my acceptance speech.

The next day I was released to go home, and spent a few weeks recuperating from the crash. Although I had nearly bought the farm, that crash proved to be serendipitous. Having witnessed how the helmet reacted during such an intense impact inspired Bill Simpson, who created the helmet, to recognize some improvements that could be made to make the helmet even safer. I've always been grateful to Bill for his diligence in the interest of driver safety.

Despite the crazy end to my season, I actually won two championships in 1980: the USAC championship, because we won Indy, and the CART championship, because of how well we fared in the other races that season. Unfortunately, because of the continuing rift between the two factions, there were no season-end point monies to be won that year—just glory.

I was also voted America's "Driver of the Year" by both the American Auto Racing Writers and Broadcasters Association (AARWBA) and the equally prestigious Olsonite panel. The Olsonite award was sponsored by car sponsor Ozzie Olson. About 100 to 150 members of the print and electronic media presented the award to me at Club 21 in New York City. The award encompasses drivers from every professional organization—USAC, CART, and NASCAR.

In addition to the Olsonite Award, Ozzie sponsored a "triple crown" award that went to the driver who accumulated the greatest number of points in championship racing's three five hundred-mile races: Indianapolis, Pocono, and Ontario. I won that award—a ring that sported a nice-size diamond—twice.

The 1980 season was an incredible season for me, all the guys on the Jim Hall team, and our sponsor, Pennzoil. We all worked so hard to do well, and our dedication paid off. But perhaps my greatest reward was carrying the coveted number "1" on my car the next year. That was sweet.

☆ CHAPTER 24 ☆

Broken Belt Drives and Broken Bones

In 1981, I celebrated my forty-third birthday by winning the Kraco 150 at Phoenix in Jim Hall's ground effects car—the same Chaparral with which we had won Indy and four other championship races in 1980.

The only difference was that this 1981 Pennzoil-sponsored car was now emblazoned with a "1" to designate the no. 1 ranking we received after winning the national championship.

The pride we felt as a team would be reflected in every race of that new season. In May we returned to Indianapolis as the defending champs, aware that the other teams would be gunning for us but confident in our car and in ourselves. Qualifying went well, and we started the race in the middle of row 2. All my contemporaries were there—A. J., Al, Bobby, Gordie, and Mario—as were some very good younger drivers such as Rick Mears and Tom Sneva. Bobby started in the pole position.

When they dropped the green flag, Bobby took off and I was right on his tail. A. J. was close behind me in third. After jockeying back and forth for several laps, I managed to grab the lead from Bobby. Things were looking pretty good after a couple dozen laps, and then the car just quit on me. I coasted to a stop on the backstretch and the car was towed back to the pits, where the crew discovered that a $4.50 belt drive had busted. My day was over and we ended up in next-to-last place at the 1981 Indy 500.

We regrouped for the next race, scheduled in Milwaukee a week later. We fared a little better there, taking sixth place. At the Atlanta Twin 125 races two weeks later, we earned the pole position for the first race with a near-record speed of more than two hundred miles an hour. We took second in the first race and third in the second.

Then it was on to Michigan. It was at this race that Betty founded the Championship Auto Racing Auxiliary (CARA) with twelve other drivers' wives. CARA was to serve as a support group and charitable organization within the auto racing community. Since the late 1960s, Betty had been aware of the need for a support group among drivers' wives, whom she expected were experiencing the same types of frustrations with track policies—such as the one that didn't allow wives into the pit area after a race—as she was. She felt as though the racing community wasn't as close-knit as it should have been—people rarely talked together after races, instead choosing to return to their respective motor homes. She feared that we were isolating ourselves from one another, even though we were all on the same battleground together.

She received little response to her suggestion to form a support group until the early 1980s, when twelve women decided they would be interested in forming an organization. The members elected Betty as their founding president, a position she would hold for four years. In 1996, CARA's members elected Betty as their director emeritus. She has enjoyed her involvement with CARA over the years, which has not only provided fun and camaraderie, but also is fulfilling in its role as a charitable organization.

For me, the race at Michigan wasn't as momentous. We experienced the first in a long and unhappy string of mechanical failures when we cut a tire and spun out, resulting in a twenty-second-place finish. In later races we ran into different problems, but it was always something—a burned piston, a wreck, a pit stop fire.

The fire occurred in Phoenix, at the last race of the season. I brought the car in for a pit stop to refuel. Some of the fuel spilled, and when I side-stepped the clutch to pull back onto the track, the fuel sloshed onto the red-hot headers and ignited.

I was going around the warm-up lane, heading for the second turn to pull out onto the backstretch and rejoin the fray, when it got hot in the cockpit— real hot. I got on the radio and yelled, "Jim! This thing's on fire! I'm gonna have to get out of it somewhere around here!"

I pulled the car up to the fire station in the first turn. They were ready with their extinguishers and doused the fire until it was out. The irony of the whole situation is that I actually had the presence of mind to reach up and push the fire bottle button—the on-board fire extinguisher—and it didn't work.

I quickly unhooked my belts and got out of the car. I noticed that my left shoulder was smoldering and that the flame-retardant material on my uniform was bubbling. I yelled to a fireman that I was on fire. He ran over and rubbed the uniform with his gloved hands to get the embers off.

Once I had determined that I was okay, I felt something hit me lightly in the back. I turned around to face a fan standing there holding his program and a pencil. Evidently he had stepped over the cable that divided the racetrack from the infield so he could drunkenly ask for my autograph. I was hot and dirty, and a second ago I had been on fire. The fireman who'd just put out the embers on my uniform picked up the fan and dropped him back on his feet about a yard from where he'd been standing. That was the end of that.

I've had fans try to get my autograph when I was dining out, in the bathroom, or standing in an elevator, but never when I was on fire. However, I was a race car driver and I guess that fan found it so exciting that he couldn't help himself—especially after knocking back a few.

Over the years I have encountered many terrific fans. In the early 1970s, Raeanna Ellis, with Betty's help, founded the Johnny Rutherford Fan Club. Jean Scotte, of Zanesville, Ohio, is the current club president. Jean has multiple sclerosis, but she doesn't let that hold her back; she has done a marvelous job in handling her duties and responsibilities, which include answering fan mail and compiling the newsletters. Jean is a J. R. fan extraordinaire. I am honored that anyone would think enough of me to belong to the Johnny Rutherford Fan Club.

In 1982, A. J. Foyt and I were the first two race car drivers to be inducted into the Texas Sports Hall of Fame. It was a great honor to be recognized by my state as a sports celebrity and to have many of my friends and family members present at the induction ceremonies to celebrate with me.

The 1982 season started out reasonably well with a fourth-place finish at Phoenix and an eighth-place finish at Indy, but deteriorated into a season of more double-digit finishes than I care to dwell on.

On top of all that, in mid-August I was leading the Pocono 500 when a tire blew on lap 137 and I crashed the car. I suffered a broken right hand and wound up finishing twelfth. But my itch to race was too strong, and I was back behind the wheel two weeks later to race in the Riverside 300, where I finished third.

We closed out the '82 season with pair of poor showings that included the season finale at Phoenix on November 6. Shortly thereafter, Jim Hall decided to retire the team. I was devastated. It had been a great three years with Jim, Pennzoil, and rest of the Chaparral guys, highlighted by the Indy win and the national championship in 1980. But now I had to find another ride.

That proved to be more difficult than I imagined. In fact, 1983 was really the beginning of the end for me in racing, because I was entering a marketplace I no longer understood. When my racing career began, in the late 1950s, it was always cut-and-dry—the driver, if he had talent, was hired to drive a race car. The new procedure was that the driver had to bring in sponsorship dollars before he or she was given a car to drive.

It became clear to me that racing teams were looking for younger drivers who had connections with sponsors and dollars. I still managed to parlay my ability and desire into further success for the next several years, but I was forced to make a transition into this new marketplace, which was light years away from my early "handshake" days of racing.

☆　☆　☆　☆　☆

My 1983 season was a disaster. I was driving for Pat Patrick in a Wildcat chassis sponsored by Connie Ray's Sea Ray Boats, and on top of being winless, I failed to qualify for Indy when I slammed into the wall in turn 3 during practice. For my efforts I wound up with a broken right ankle and a broken left foot.

I managed to qualify for only six races the whole year, and I didn't finish a single one. It was my worst season ever, but it had its rewards. I did obtain the use of a Sea Ray boat in the summer thanks to our sponsor Connie Ray. Those sea boats were luxurious and very comfortable, and a nice way to relax in the off-season.

Betty and I knew that the 1984 season had to be better. And it was, though not by much. At the 1984 Indy 500, I got a last-minute ride in A. J. Foyt's third car. But I didn't have a crew, so Jim Ellis and Betty tried to put one together for me. Jim and A. J. found enough guys to service my car when I came in, but they didn't have anybody in the pits who could "talk to the wall"—to Jim, who held my signboard—and tell him what was happening. Betty was already in charge of the timing and scoring, but since we didn't have anyone else to help out, she wore two headsets that day—one to talk with Jim to tell him what lap we were on and the speed I was running for that lap, and the other to talk to me and the crew. Betty had to tell me when to pit, and she later told me that she had been truly scared that she would miscalculate my fuel level. At the time she was thinking, *This is the worst place in the world for a wife to be.* Betty has never wished me out of a race and she didn't wish me out of that one. But she was relieved when it was over.

I finished twenty-second at Indy in the car co-owned by A. J. and his partner, Jim Gilmore. I also raced their car in the Michigan 500 and the Pocono 500, finishing seventh and twenty-eighth, respectively.

Oddly enough, I had my best finish in 1984 when I subbed for Rick Mears at the Sanair race in Quebec, Canada. During a practice run, Rick smashed his car, and as the car slid his feet were dragged under the guardrail. It was a scary, horrible accident, and Rick didn't return to racing until the following year.

Rick's car owner, Roger Penske, hired me to replace Rick in the race, and we took fifth. I was kept on for the final two races of the season, a move that reunited me with my old sponsor, Pennzoil.

The first race was at Michigan. Generally, I had posted fast times and good finishes at Michigan over the years, and I was looking forward to racing there again. Derrick Walker was my crew chief on the Penske team. One of the guys on his crew, Ken Anderson, was incredibly knowledgeable about shock absorbers and chassis settings. Ken built us a set of shocks for the qualifying run that took absolutely every bump out of the Michigan racetrack, a notoriously bumpy track.

At that race, we set a new world record for Indy cars on a closed course, a new world record for qualifying, and a new track record at Michigan International Speedway. We ran just over 215 miles an hour. Although the record didn't last long, it remains something I'm very proud of.

In 1974 and from 1976 through 1979, I participated in the International Race of Champions (IROC), an annual series for drivers of note from oval tracks and road courses alike. Some of the best drivers in the business are invited to race against one another in cars with identical specifications. In 1984, I ran my last IROC series.

Drivers from Formula 1, NASCAR, and Indy racing are all represented at IROC. The first year I ran the IROC, we raced Camaros, which were virtually stock cars with just a roll cage and a custom-made engine. The stock car racers who participated might have had an advantage over the other drivers, because the Camaros were basically the same kind of car they raced in NASCAR, but it wasn't much of an advantage. IROC was a fun, competitive series, and I enjoyed running in it.

In 1985 I signed a deal with the Alex Morales Racing Team. Alex was a long-time, stalwart car owner from the West Coast who had run sprint cars at Ascot as far back as the '20s and '30s. Johnny Capels, who is now the president of the United States Auto Club, was the team manager and chief mechanic on the Morales team, and one of the most thorough mechanics I have ever worked with. He could put a car together so it didn't fall apart.

I really enjoyed my three-year association with that team and our sponsor, Vermont-American Tool Company, a hardware company that made hand tools and anything that cut wood or metal, such as drill bits and saw blades. We had a little bit of success together and a thrill or two along the way.

Our season began with my efforts to qualify for the 1985 Indy 500. On Sunday, May 19, I got bumped late in the day, on the last day of qualifying. But with about ten minutes left before the gun sounded to signify that the thirty-three-car field was set, I got back out there and stood on it at more than 208 miles an hour to reclaim a starting position.

In the race itself, we started in the next-to-last row but finished sixth. It was my best showing at Indy since I had won the race in 1980.

The season, however, had its share of troubles, including a number of wrecks late in the season. But we finished in the top ten six times that year and did well in the points standings. Our best finishes in 1985, in addition to the sixth at Indy, were our ninth-place finish in mid-June at Portland; a fourth- and ninth-place finish at a pair of races at Michigan, one in late July and one in late September; and a win at Sanair, where I had subbed for Rick Mears the year before.

Sanair was a treacherous little racetrack. It was less than a mile long, triangular shaped, and very fast. I was running in third quite late in the race when the two lead cars got tangled up. The caution flag came out while the crew went to work cleaning up the track. They were still trying to get equipment out of the way when we came around, so we were given the white flag and the yellow flag, which meant that there was one lap remaining and that it would be run under caution.

Coming off the fourth turn, with me leading the race under the caution, we saw that they were bringing out the checkered flag. But someone had also turned the green light on under the flag stand. The flagman was getting ready to wave the checkered flag while an official was trying to turn the last hundred yards of the last lap into a green-flag situation.

This was unheard of and, in fact, illegal. The drivers had already been told they had one more lap to go, and that the lap would be run under caution. As we came around and headed for the finish line, I heard Pancho Carter rev his engine and change gears to try to pass me. I got my car in gear and jumped on the throttle, but he beat me by maybe a foot or two at the finish line. However, given the situation with the flags, I had legitimately won the race. But when I pulled into Victory Lane, Pancho was already there. The officials had given him the win.

Of course, we protested. The hearing took place a couple of weeks later. The jury consisted of Bobby Hillin, a former car owner; Rodger Ward, a retired driver; and Tom Binford, the track steward at the Indianapolis Motor Speedway. We presented our case, and when we were through Rodger just rolled his eyes and said to all of those present, "Look, you threw the yellow and the white. That means there was only one lap left, and it was denoted as a caution lap."

They awarded our team the victory. It was my first Indy car win in three years, but none of us were jumping up and down at the news. For one thing, my crew never got to celebrate in Victory Lane after the race. For another thing, Pancho Carter wouldn't give us the trophy. It was a bad scene. We did finally get three trophies—one for Alex, one for me, and a little one to display at the shop. It was sad that things turned out that way, but it was just another example of CART officiating at that time.

The team did even better, overall, in the 1986 season. We kicked things off with four consecutive top-ten finishes, including an eighth-place finish at Indy, and raced well—though not spectacularly—for the next two months.

Then we prepared to run one of the hardest races on the Indy car schedule—the Michigan 500. The track is a wide, modern, paved oval with high banks, which along with the sustained speed it requires makes the race difficult to run. You have to run virtually flat-out around that track, at more than two hundred miles an hour, for five hundred miles—roughly two and a half to three hours of racing.

I had qualified mid-field, and before the start of the race I thought about my plan of attack. I knew I couldn't run it flat-out for twenty laps. I would have to back off and breathe it in the corners a little bit, running a steady speed and staying within sight of the leaders.

When they dropped the green flag I was right in the hunt. Everything went according to my plan. Capels had given me a good steady race car that would run the distance if I didn't put a strain on it.

I was running smoothly, staying in the same lap with the leaders, and I thought, *Boy, I ought to pick up the pace—sneak up a little bit and see if I can get with the leaders.* But just as the thought entered my mind, Roberto Guerrero spun in turn 3 and swatted the wall, scattering junk all over the racetrack. We were given a yellow. Then I started thinking, *Boy, maybe I better stay put and just keep doin' what I'm doin'.*

After the crew cleaned everything up, we got the green and I started running along very nicely. Again I started thinking about picking up my pace and moving up to the leaders. Just about that time, Mario lost it. He swatted the wall and started going backwards down the racetrack. I was on the brakes and looking at him eye to eye, trying to figure out which way he was going to go so I could go somewhere else.

In the end, I was able to swerve under him before we clipped each other. I saw him in my mirror as I went by, and then I saw him turn and dart down the track. I just barely got by.

As a result of Mario's mishap, they brought out the yellow again. We ran around under the yellow and I started thinking that maybe I should just hold my pace. But when we got the green, the hard-charger in me got that urge again, and I thought, *I better pick up the pace.*

When yet another driver did a gilhooley—which is dirt track lingo for "spinout"—it became glaringly obvious to me that I was right where I was meant to be. I just let the race drone on, lap after lap, and held my pace. My pit stops were exciting by comparison. And sure enough, the very next time I heard that inner voice say, *Better get movin' there, J. R.,* I saw Geoff Brabham and Al Unser Jr. get into it. They both spun coming off turn 2, and once again the yellow came out.

There weren't many laps left, and by this time I found myself in the lead, with Josele Garza, a talented young driver, right behind me. The crew cleared the track and the green flag was dropped. With less than twenty laps to go I was thinking, *Kid, if you're gonna keep up with this old man, you better stand on the gas, because here we go.*

I stood on it and didn't back off. I'd been running 210 miles an hour, a conservative pace, earlier in the race. Now I was doing 217. This was it. It was time to put it all on the table, and Josele couldn't handle me. I steadily pulled away from him and ran 217 the rest of the way.

Before I knew it, I had won the race. Man, what a great thrill. I'd won my first big race in almost a year. And at forty-eight years old, I became the oldest driver to ever win a five hundred-mile race—not bad for an old dirt track boy from Texas. My victory reminded me of the adage, "Old age and treachery has won out over youth and inexperience."

But did I hear any congratulatory exclamations from my contemporaries like Mario? Not on your life. Instead they said, "Ah, if I hadn't dropped out, you wouldn't have won," or "I had you in my sights till my car blew a piston"—real heartwarming stuff like that. But I probably would have said the same thing if I had been watching any of them celebrating in Victory Lane after that trial. A win is a win no matter how you get it.

The rest of the 1986 season went reasonably well for us. Although we didn't take any more victories, we finished thirteen of the seventeen races we entered and wound up in the top ten in eleven of those races.

In 1987 we suffered a reversal of fortunes. The first half of the season went well—we posted four top-ten finishes in our first seven races—but then things turned sour midseason when we experienced one mechanical failure and double-digit finish after another.

On the upside of things, I was voted into the Indianapolis Motor Speedway Auto Racing Hall of Fame that year. I feel very fortunate to have been inducted into the Hall of Fame while I could enjoy it. Too many times, it seems, people are inducted into their respective sport's halls of fame or given awards after they're gone. That happened to one of my very best friends not long ago.

Herb Porter, who was my crew chief for a couple of years as well as my mentor, was one of the most brilliant engine-builders ever to get grease under his nails. Herb was eighty-four when he was finally recognized and voted into the Hall of Fame. The night before the induction ceremonies, he was involved in a car crash on the interstate and was hospitalized with many broken bones. He was already battling emphysema and diabetes, and it all just worked against him. Herb didn't get to attend his induction ceremony or thank everybody like he wanted to. He passed away about a month later.

I cherish the honor of being inducted into the Hall of Fame, which was that much sweeter because I was able to appreciate it and thank everyone for the recognition. It was a time of reflection for me, and it felt good to publicly express my gratitude to so many people.

Little did I know at the time that 1987 would be my last full season of racing.

CHAPTER 25

It Was Time

In 1988, although I didn't know it at the time, I ran my last race at the Indianapolis Motor Speedway.

That year I was driving for famed drag racer Kenny Bernstein. Kenny also owned Indy cars, and his No. 1 driver during that period was Jim Crawford. However, Jim had broken both of his ankles in a crash during a qualifying run for the 1987 Indy, and it appeared he wouldn't be able to run again in 1988. So the Bernstein team hired me, and I started the preseason testing with a V-6 Buick in a Lola chassis. The engine was strong, but it was typical of a push rod engine—it had a lot of internal moving parts, so its sharp edges tended to wear with running, causing the engine to lose its effective power.

The team and I prepared and fine-tuned the car for weeks, and then one day Crawford showed up at the track. He was still on crutches, and he wanted to race for Bernstein in the upcoming Indy. Now, I had proven years ago that a driver can still race with a broken leg, but Jim just didn't look ready for that.

Nonetheless, Jim's surprise appearance suddenly changed the attitude on the Bernstein team. He was their guy. I wasn't. Their priority now was to set up the car I had been testing to match Jim's needs, which was completely different from the way they had set the car up for me. From then on, the situation between the Bernstein team and I, which had been fairly businesslike anyway, became a struggle. I was upset by this new turn of events and they knew I was upset. But I soon realized that I would only generate hard feelings by complaining or questioning their decisions, so I simply backed off and accepted the hand I was dealt.

Like most drivers who find themselves in this situation, I did not want to have a teammate because I felt it would divide the team effort. Most teams don't have the funds or the number of crew members to handle two cars and two drivers. The no. 2 driver always gets the leftovers. And although I had worked with some great teammates in the past—Don Branson and Jim Crawford among them—I preferred being a team's sole driver.

Unless a driver is prepared from the beginning to be a team's second driver, problems can arise. For instance, late in my career I was the second driver for a team that was unable to develop two new race cars in time for the Indianapolis 500. So the owner bought one Lola for the team's No. 1 driver, Danny Sullivan, and gave me some sponsorship money to take to another team. I took it to A. J. Foyt's team and drove for him that year at Indy.

Driving for A. J., my longtime friend and rival, while also being his team-mate, was tough. The only positive thing about that situation was that A. J. and I could drive the same race car. It was the only time I've been able to jump right into another driver's car and like its setup. His cars suited me.

For the most part, I wasn't used to being a team's second driver; I had been the No. 1 driver for McLaren for seven years, Jim Hall for three, and Alex Morales for three. Eventually the Bernstein team was able to get things sorted out, and Jim and I both wound up driving for them in Buick V-6s. I still was-n't happy with my car's handling, particularly with the suspension, but I took what I was given and made the best of it.

Unfortunately, that wasn't good enough—for the team or for me. I barely made the starting field on "Bump Day" and ended up in the next-to-last row for the race. I was never a serious contender that day, which ended for me when the suspension broke and caused me to crash into the wall in the first turn a little more than halfway through the race. The impact tore the wheels off the right side of the car, but I was okay. Crawford, on the other hand, was in the thick of it for most of the day and finished sixth in a race won by Rick Mears.

I ran one other championship race that season, in early August at the Michigan 500. A. J. was ill and I subbed for him. I was doing okay for a while, but then the car caught on fire in the pits after about 130 laps. That put a stop to my race day and my 1988 Indy car season.

After 1988 I focused on finding the right set of ingredients that would pro-duce a competitive team. Having enjoyed success for a dozen years or more, I knew what it would take to put together a winning combination. But the nature of the profession was changing with regard to the level of sponsorship that teams needed to offset the costs of doing business. The money that was crucial to being truly competitive and "raceworthy" was substantial, and this put me at a distinct disadvantage. Once I had become a winner, anything less was very distasteful. As I heard Paul Newman once say, "Once you've had steak, why would you settle for hamburger?"

In 1989 after a brief respite from racing, owner John Menard returned to Indy—on April 1. Menard decided he wanted to run a car in Indy that year, and hired me to drive for his team. He and his colleagues quickly ordered a car and hired Phil Casey as the crew chief. They got the car the week before the track opened. Phil and his guys had to work virtually around the clock that entire week to get the car ready for practice and qualifying. On top of everything else, the engines the team had to work with were second hand, and not really producers.

I qualified for Indy in the Menard/Glidden car at better than 213 miles an hour, but I got bumped on the last day. Only a few minutes were left to make the field, so A. J. quickly and kindly offered me a back-up car with which I could try again to qualify. I took him up on his offer, got the car going pretty strong around the track, and ran a lap at 217-plus mph—a good enough speed to get me back into the starting grid for race day.

But during the first practice lap prior to qualifying, the car's engine blew and knocked me out of the running. It was the first Indy I had failed to qualify for in twenty-five attempts. I was upset about my loss, but just as much for Phil and the rest of the team. They worked so hard to get things sorted out on that car, only to feel the frustration of not qualifying.

For the first time in many years, I had an awful lot of free time. Now, whether I liked it or not, a heavy schedule of Indy car racing was replaced with a number of other pursuits and offers. I competed in the Celebrity Cutting Horse Futurity in Fort Worth and finished a respectable seventh. I signed on to do various color commentary gigs for CBS, NBC, and ESPN on the CART, NASCAR, and Trans Am circuits, and hosted *Motorsports Gallery*. I stayed busy for the rest of the 1989 season, but I still wanted to race.

Sometimes I had to look overseas for opportunities. That year, I traveled to Macao, a Portuguese territory along the southeastern coast of China, to participate in the "Race of Champions" at the Macao Grand Prix. An Indy car sponsor, Teddy Yip, hosts the annual race, which is run in the city's streets. It's treacherous but fun. We drove Mazda Miatas, the little roadsters, and as many as eighteen to twenty cars started in the event. The only problem for some of the drivers was having to shift left-handed. Of course, I had raced cars with that configuration in Bathurst, Australia, in 1977, so adapting wasn't a big problem for me.

The entire trip was fabulous. In Macao, we visited a Chinese factory where they manufacture junks—houseboats made of solid teakwood and powered by diesel engines. Some of the junks were made to last more than a hundred years and some people are born, live, and die on these boats. They never come ashore. It's incredible to think about.

After the 1989 Indianapolis 500, I hooked up with Jeff Stoops, a businessman from Indianapolis who at the time owned a large freightliner truck business and some car dealerships. I ran a couple of races with Jeff that year, and he was my sponsor for the five hundred-mile race at Michigan, where I placed tenth.

Jeff was a former sprint car owner, but he wanted to run an Indy car. Chris Paulsen, a friend of mine from Indianapolis and a real craftsman, was the team's crew chief. The Stoops team had an '89 race car they offered to let me drive for the 1990 Indy, which would have been fine if not for a troublesome USAC rule change that greatly affected the aerodynamics of older cars.

USAC officials felt they needed to decrease the cars' downforce because speeds were escalating to what they viewed as unacceptable levels. So they invoked a rule that required the existing '89 cars to insert a wedge of a specified size into the tunnels on the bottom of the car to diffuse some of the downforce that was generated.

Because of our car's design, the diffuser ruined our aerodynamics. The downforce was less effective when we added the wedges. In fact, it made our car, and any cars like it, very unsafe.

In the meantime, Lola, our car's manufacturer, built a new chassis designed around USAC's parameters, and it was fast. The new '90 Lolas, without the diffusers, were much faster than the '89s with the diffusers. In practice runs at the Speedway before qualifying, the newer Lola chassis were faring much better than the older ones. I know, because I crashed twice in three days, and the second time hurt.

Chris and the guys had taken the car apart and had decided to try a different setup. They put it back together and we took it out on the track. I wasn't even going fast yet when the car suddenly spun in the third turn just like it was on ice. The downforce had vanished. The car slammed into the wall so hard that it started to disintegrate and became airborne. When the car stopped, I was taken to the hospital. I suffered a concussion and a hairline fracture of my left leg, which matched the hairline fracture of my right leg that I got during an earlier test.

Even more upsetting than the accident was the fact that Jeff had ordered a 1990 car, but at the last minute got cold feet and sold it to another team. We had an older car that the crew tried very hard to make right, but it was a useless effort. They should have saved their money.

For two straight years I had lost an opportunity to race at Indy. On top of that, the Stoops team ordered a new Lola and changed drivers for the rest of the season. I wasn't even afforded the courtesy of a phone call—I learned from a radio news story that I no longer had a ride.

By that time I was getting up there in years; I was fifty-two and my age was working against me. It was a bitter pill to swallow, because I wasn't ready to leave competitive racing. I'd been in the game for thirty-two years and I had no intention of retiring. But there simply wasn't an opportunity out there for me to continue the way I wanted to, the way I knew it had to be in order to be successful.

I spent the 1990 season driving the PPG pace car at CART races and doing more television work for CBS and NBC. I was named honorary chairman for the Motorsports Racing Hall of Fame of America induction dinner. Betty and I did some work for charitable organizations and traveled.

That year we visited the island of Kyushu, Japan, one of the country's southernmost islands, where a new racetrack had been built. The track was called Autopolis—a cross between *automobile* and *Indianapolis*. The man who had built the Autopolis, which was a road course situated in a mountain valley, had bought twenty Sabres from USAC to race on the track. The Sabre was a rear-engine, independent-suspension car very much like an Indy car. In fact, the Sabre was one of the designs the USAC submitted when the formula was being changed at the Indianapolis Motor Speedway.

Many different types of cars were showcased at the race, from beginner go-carts and competition carts to Formula Vs and open-wheel race cars. The Sabre was unquestionably the fastest and most top-of-the-line car there. A number of drivers from the United States—including George Snider, Billy Vukovich III, Tony Bettenhausen, Stan Fox, and myself—were brought to Japan to demonstrate the Sabres. Our first trip to Japan was great and we had a lot of fun, especially when we went to see a Japanese country-western cover band.

Back home, I decided that I needed to just kick back and wait for something to develop. But nothing came. Nobody called. The 1991 season was a washout.

I then decided to go to work on getting some sponsors together for the '92 season. Nearing the eleventh hour, I was turned on to an outfit in Dallas that seemed like a genuine possibility. It was a fairly new business, and the executives said they were very interested in sponsoring me because it would give them national exposure. It seemed like a perfect match. They were willing to pay us nearly six million dollars over a three-year period, and I don't think you could have come up with a better plan than they offered.

Derrick Walker, who had been a key member of Roger Penske's team and later headed up Porsche's Indy team, offered to field a second car for me—Scott Goodyear was driving his other car—and things seemed to be looking up. But when the time came for Derrick to buy the car, we had no money. All we had was the sponsor's initial promise of a certain amount of money for operating costs, and when Derrick phoned them they assured us the money was on its way. He bought the car—a secondhand car from Carl Haas, the Lola distributor, which turned out to be a piece of junk—and the crew went to work on it.

The sponsor's chief officials came to the Speedway and we held a press conference to announce our 1991 racing program. Then they left and went back to their home base in Dallas. We still had no money, but they assured us that the check was in the mail.

We waited and waited for the money, but nothing ever appeared. The car was painted with the sponsor's name and we had our uniforms. Everything was ready, yet not one penny came in. We started checking into the business from every angle and had an attorney look into the matter as well, and soon discovered that they were frauds. They had been pocketing the money from their venture—redeemable coupons that schools could put toward computer equipment and other necessities, which sold for twenty-five thousand dollars a clip. Eventually they went to jail.

We had uncovered their scheme, but it was of little solace to us. It was embarrassing—our would-be sponsors had done everything right, except give us the money.

The situation was hard for me personally and professionally. I went to another company where friends were kind enough to give us the money to at least try to qualify the car for the 1992 Indy. But when I took the car out on the track to see what it could do, we realized just how junky it was. Derrick had tried to make a silk purse out of a sow's ear, and it couldn't be done. He had worked so hard to get that thing working properly, and even tried to round up pieces to make all four corners of the car match. It was too little, too late. We failed to qualify.

Suddenly, things were quite clear. It was time. But it was hard for me to admit that, after more than thirty years as a professional race car driver, I was leaving the sport I had dedicated my life to. Even when I was injured, even when the victories were few and far between, I felt I was riding the crest of a wave. I was racing. That was enough. I was *racing*. But then the wave crashes on the shore and it's over.

There were moments—days, even—when I thought, *No, I still feel good. I can do this. I want to race and I can race.* But then the reality of my situation would set in and I would see the big picture: These guys didn't want a fifty-four-year-old driver. They wanted young guys. The owner's fear is that a veteran driver, especially one who has had success at the highest level of the sport, could get hurt or killed in his car. In fact, some owners even revealed this to me.

I was pondering how to gracefully bow out. I was wrestling with how I'd even force the words out of my mouth: "I'm through."

I didn't *want* to say it. I was never a quitter and I didn't want to start now, even if the truth was staring me in my face.

Betty, of course, had sensed for some time that my career was winding down and would soon end. She sensed it when the rides weren't there, when the cars were worthless, when the sponsor turned out to be a fraud. But she remained true to her word and never once pushed me in any direction. We both knew it had to come from me. It had to be my decision.

I had two choices. I could fold my tent and silently steal away. Or I could break clean—make an announcement and see what happened. But I was worried about what I would do after racing. As far back as 1988, when things started getting rough, I was not only looking for my next ride, I was looking for a life after racing. Nothing was visible then and it wasn't any clearer when I decided to announce my retirement. I couldn't bring myself to make a clean break. Betty and I went back to the Speedway in '93 to watch the race and just be present in case a car opened up and a team needed a driver. I was stubborn. I had put myself in limbo.

I did race in Indianapolis in 1993; it just wasn't the Indy 500. I participated in the Fast Masters, auto racing's first attempt at a race similar in concept to golf's Seniors Tour. We raced Jaguar XJ-220s, each of which was reputed to be worth about $220,000. Bobby Unser and I ran 1-2 in our preliminary race to qualify for the finals. My car experienced some problems, and I finished sixth or seventh. Bobby won the final event and took home the grand prize—one hundred thousand dollars.

What happened at Indy that year probably, in a subtle or subconscious way, influenced my decision to face my own reality. A. J. was hitting speeds of 220-plus in a morning practice and seemed destined to start yet another Indy.

But A. J.'s protégé, Robby Gordon, later hit the wall during a practice run, and the accident seemed to really bother A. J. He got into his car, took a farewell lap around the track as he waved to the fans in the stands, and called it a career. My longtime friend and rival had taken the next step. And I was getting closer to that step myself.

As one Rutherford's racing career was waning, another's was just beginning.

In the early 1990s, I saw our son, John, run his first race. The event, at Mid-Ohio Raceway in Lexington, Ohio, was a "licensing" race—one of several regional events that John was required to run in order to obtain a license in the Sports Car Club of America, the SCCA.

It was my first real opportunity to watch my son drive a race car, and in doing so I gained a whole new respect for his mother. Until that moment, I had no idea what it was like to watch a loved one drive out of the pits and disappear around the corner, and then wait for him to come back. I realized that Betty had been doing this for thirty years.

Betty got quite a kick out of watching me watch John. My jaw muscles tensed and popped out as I watched him run through the turns we *could* see. It was quite an experience and a real eye-opener for me.

I am proud of our son. I can't say it's fun to be worried for his safety, but that's part of the game. I've had to accept the fact that John is pursuing a career in racing, and I hope he has great success at it.

At the start of the 1994 season, Mario announced that the upcoming Indy 500 would be his last race. Then, at the Indy 500 that year, Al Unser Sr., another of my contemporaries, announced his retirement.

It was like a release for me. It was now obvious what I had to do. I was the last one of the group. There was no point in lingering, no point in fooling myself any longer. Heck, I was older than Al.

When it dawned on me what I had to do, I didn't say anything to anybody. I don't think I even told Betty. A couple of days after Al called a press conference to announce his retirement, I went to A. J.'s garage. I walked in and said, "A. J., you busy?"

Win #3 at the Indy 500, 1980.

Steve "Abo" Roby, me, and Jim Hall at the 1980 Indy 500.

This one nearly got me: upside down at the 1980 Phoenix.

I finally win the national champion title in 1980. Pictured here at Indy 500 in 1981.

A world record at Michigan International Speedway: with the crew and official time of 215.189 on September 22, 1984.

Another record: at age forty-eight, I became the oldest driver ever to win a five hundred-mile race when I won the 1986 Michigan 500, a record that still stands today.

With Betty and crew after the Michigan 500 victory in 1986.

On the platform with Pancho Carter (3rd place) and Josele Garza (2nd place).

My last Indy 500, 1988.

A hard crash in Stoops's car at Indianapolis Motor Speedway, 1989.

Driving Derek Walker's car, I made my last attempt to qualify for the Indy 500 in 1992.

Conference: discussing with Phil Casey and John Menard Jr. my first failure to qualify for Indy in twenty-four years.

Tony George giving me my last green flag at my Indy retirement in 1994. The car is the same one A. J. Foyt retired in the year before.

Taking the last checkered flag at Indy: Jim Ellis, who held my signboards for twenty-one years, with one final message.

With General Norman Schwarzkopf at the Indianapolis Motor Speedway in 1991.

Thanking A. J. while Betty looks on with mixed emotions about my retirement lap at Indy in 1994.

The family on vacation in Steamboat Springs.

With son, John, at F-2000 Race at the Indianapolis Raceway Park.

With Mari Hulman George in The Suite at the Indianapolis Motor Speedway, 1991.

With Jim Haynes, my "right-hand" man, in front of the Olds Alero IRL pace car at the Texas Motor Speedway, 1998.

Angela and Craig with Grant, six-months old; Evan, twenty-two months old; and Conner, four-years old, 2000.

My mother and stepfather, Mary and Norm Vediner, celebrating their 50th wedding anniversary.

Life off the track still has its thrills: riding in the National Cutting Horse Association's Futurity celebrity-cutting event in Fort Worth, Texas.

In the "booth" with Bob Jenkins for ESPN television coverage of Laguna Seca.

Macho man: on my Harley at the Texas Motor Speedway.

My P-51 flying days: Arriving at Michigan International Raceway to test the McLaren race car (left) and my P-51 Mustang WWII fighter plane on the ramp and ready to aviate.

"No," he said. "What do you want?"

"I'm going to announce my retirement. Have you got a car I can take a last lap around the Speedway in?"

He didn't say one word. He just looked me right in the eye, and then spun around and yelled at one of his guys as he pointed to a car, "Get that car ready and roll it out! Rutherford's gonna retire and he wants to take a ride around the track."

It was the same car in which A. J. had taken his last lap around the Speedway the year before. That car made history—a four-time winner and a three-time winner each took his last lap around the Indianapolis Motor Speedway in it. While A. J.'s guys rushed to get the car ready, I went back to the motor home and told Betty what I was going to do. She just said, "Well, okay." We went out in front of the track just before that day's qualifying runs began. The word had spread like wildfire, and Speedway President Tony George, the late Tony Hulman's grandson, came over to me and said, "We'll make sure this is all done right. We'll have Tom Carnegie announce it over the P.A. system."

Everybody pitched in to make it a proper send-off. Now it was up to me not to blow it, because I had not driven a race car around the Speedway in two years. It was the next-to-last day of qualifying and there were thousands of people in the stands. I got into A. J.'s car and we fired it up. Tom Carnegie, the longtime announcer at the Speedway, got on the P.A. system and said, "Ladies and gentlemen, please direct your attention to the south end of the pits. Three-time Indy 500 winner Johnny Rutherford is pulling out to make his last laps around the Speedway. He is retiring."

Tony George himself started my final laps. He dropped the green flag and I drove by him, making a big production of it.

When I pulled out onto the track in that race car I felt a thrill. So many memories came flooding back to me as I took those last laps, memories of qualifying, racing, times in the pits, talking with my crew chiefs on the two-way. The feelings and the smells and the vibrations were almost more than I could handle.

The flagman gave me the checkered flag and I made another lap before I pulled into the pits for the last time and shut it off. The second I stepped out of the car it started to sink in. *It's over.*

Betty and I both were teary-eyed, and when Tom Carnegie walked over with his microphone to interview me, it was hard for me to talk. I don't even remember all that I said. I know I thanked the fans for their loyalty to racing.

There would be no more worrying about rides or looking for an opportunity or trying to find sponsorship dollars. The question now was "What am I going to *do*?"

Betty and I had our investments. I could do television and continue the pace car program for PPG Industries at the CART races. Plus, I could accept more speaking engagements. I would be able to make a decent living doing those things.

But really, what was I going to *do*? I'd never been one to sit around. I liked to move around. I was used to traveling. I was used to getting my hands dirty. I was used to being a race car driver.

☆ CHAPTER 26 ☆

Leaving Gasoline Alley

☆ ☆ ☆

When I was racing, getting knocked out of a race for any reason was always vexing for me: But at least I could look forward to the next race. This was different.

I now had to adapt to days and nights without the one thing to which I had devoted much of my youth and all of my adult life.

Of course, I still had connections to the sport, thanks to speaking engagements and the fact that I was still driving the pace car at CART-sanctioned Indy car events. But I missed being in the cockpit and actually competing in the races.

Ironically, I only drove the pace car for the Indianapolis 500 once. The pace car manufacturer—which varies from year to year—always has the right to choose the driver. In 1997, Oldsmobile officials asked me to be their company's celebrity driver, and I was honored to accept. After that, I drove the pace car at every one of the Indy car races that season.

No longer a race car driver, I was still looking for a purpose, something to get involved in. That purpose revealed itself to me in 1995.

That year, Speedway President Tony George created the Indy Racing League. His intent was to nurture American drivers by giving them more opportunities to race while reducing costs involved in racing at that level. The IRL was inevitable. Tony and his advisers saw the need to protect the future of the Indianapolis Motor Speedway and Indy car racing in that vein.

The IRL was in direct competition with CART, Championship Auto Racing Teams. When CART was formed in the late 1970s, it was exactly what it needed to be. Everybody was pulling in the same direction and looking at the big picture. But as often occurs in a situation like that, soon one party or one interest group was calling the shots.

CART supporters will say I'm full of bull or that my decision to work with the IRL is a result of sour grapes, but CART is just not the type of organization I want to be affiliated with. Everyone involved is out for his own piece of the pie. I can't fault them for turning the organization into a moneymaking business, but it has evolved into a situation in which only a few people are actually making money. It's the Golden Rule: "Them that has the gold, rules."

In the end, only a few live off the rest, without whom there would be no show. The reason for this one-sidedness is that the more financially able owners become the exclusive distributors or manufacturers for this chassis or that engine or those parts. By building and leasing this equipment, they're making money off the rest of the competitors.

Maybe I'm all wet. Maybe I just haven't accepted the fact that racing is show business. But when I left CART, there was no place for the past champions, no use for their expertise. In fact, there was no organized promotion of CART's current drivers to increase awareness or fan support—a system that very obviously works in the NASCAR ranks. CART seemed to have little regard for the past and the Indy 500, which was more responsible than any other entity for giving Foyt, Unser, Mears, Andretti, and Rutherford their celebrity status.

The type of racing I made a career out of was based on competition between teams, owners, and sponsors. That's the way it should be. Now it seems that car owners want to control the show, which, when CART was founded, was because they had the most invested in the venture. Today, the sponsors invest the most, yet control remains with the owners. It seems that so much of racing today is about control, or just plain greed. Only a handful of teams and drivers always end up in the top five or six, because only a handful of car owners can really afford to play. That, to me, is scary, especially when thirty-three cars are needed to stage the Indy 500.

I don't want to label any racing organization as good, bad, or indifferent, but the competitive nature of the IRL as it is now, and the races the IRL produces, seem to be a lot better than the other programs. That's what Tony George intended when he created the Indy Racing League.

Tony was protecting his turf from those owners in CART that wanted to have more control of his track than he was willing to relinquish. Basically,

CART started in very much the same way. The United States Auto Club would not let the owners have more say in rules making. Well, they should have had more say, as should all other racing participants—to a point. But to allow a situation to develop in which the owners run the program is like letting the inmates run the asylum.

The Indy Racing League has proven a point. It opened the doors for sprint car drivers, Silver Crown car drivers, and midget car drivers who would not have had an opportunity, under the CART regime, to race at the great Indianapolis 500. It was frustrating for any young American driver to realize that racing's premier event was out of his reach unless he could come up with the money to put himself into the driver's seat of an Indy car. We lost Jeff Gordon from open-wheel racing to stock car racing for that reason.

In putting together his staff, Tony George asked Jack Long, who'd had success in developing other racing programs, to contribute his expertise in helping establish the IRL. I had known Jack for a long time, so when he called me and asked if I would work with him in the new IRL, I immediately agreed, eager to be a part of any program that dealt with the Indianapolis Motor Speedway and racing.

All of a sudden, things fell in place.

I was given the title of Director of Special Events, which encompasses driving the pace car at the races and working with the rookie orientation program. It was a fresh beginning for me. I enjoyed the chance to impart some of my knowledge of racing to the younger drivers coming through the rookie program, and was again involved with and contributing to the auto racing profession. This was a new racing organization, and though we experienced growing pains and had to overcome our share of obstacles that first year, it was exciting for all of us. It was like a brand-new baby: it had to be cared for, given guidance, and nurtured. I was thrilled to be a part of it all.

To watch the IRL grow from a struggling entity in 1996 to a polished, credible organization four years later has been a true joy. Although there is always room for improvement, the entire staff has made a concerted effort to pull together and make the IRL even stronger. You could search for a long time for the right people to do a job, and you couldn't come up with a better staff than we have the Indy Racing Northern Lights Series right now.

Tony George has come a long way from the young boy who didn't say a whole lot. He reminds me a lot of his grandfather, Tony Hulman. He was a man of few words, but when he talked you listened, and you knew what he said was right. Tony George and the entire Hulman-George family have been great friends of mine for many years. I admire and respect them all for what they have done with the Indianapolis Motor Speedway.

Tony's decision to hire Leo Mehl was another step in the right direction. Leo was the director of racing for Goodyear, and I met him back in 1964, the first year they came out to test at Indianapolis. I was fortunate to be driving one of the cars that was testing the new Goodyear tires. Leo was one of the engineers, and I have admired his tenacity and abilities ever since.

Brian Barnhart, a young man with a great mind and a great deal of talent, served as Al Unser Jr.'s crew chief when "Little Al" won the Indy 500. Tony George recognized Brian's abilities and put him to work, first as superintendent of the Indianapolis Motor Speedway and then as the Director of Racing Operations. He's done a superb job and I've enjoyed working with him.

Phil Casey is our Technical Director. I drove for Phil on a few occasions, and earned my first single-digit number in racing when he was my mechanic. He, too, has a tremendous mind, and knows a lot about racing and what the league needs.

Tiffany Hemmer, Manager of Administration, and her colleagues at the Indy Racing Offices all pull in the same direction and work for the same end result. With team players like these, Indy Racing absolutely cannot fail.

I enjoy working for such a dedicated organization. And, from a strictly personal standpoint, my involvement with the IRL created what I had been looking for: that elusive life after racing.

☆ CHAPTER 27 ☆

Life after Racing

☆　　☆　　☆

Once I decided to retire from racing, I was able to devote more time to the hobbies I had been developing all my life. I have always prided myself on being well rounded, and I suppose I've followed in the footsteps of my dad, who was adventurous and enjoyed the challenge of exploring many different life paths.

My greatest passion outside of driving a race car is flying an airplane. Because of my dad's love of aviation, I grew up around airplanes and came to love them as well, so learning to fly was something I had always wanted to do. In late 1963, my rookie year at the Indianapolis Motor Speedway, A. J. Foyt, Parnelli Jones, and I all started flying on virtually the same day. We formed the "500 Flying Club," but given our busy racing schedules, I'm the only one of the group who ever received a pilot's license.

The first planes we learned to fly were of the old design. One was a sixty-five-horsepower Aeronica Champ. We had a lot of fun with that little plane. It seemed that A. J., for some reason or another, couldn't take off very straight. Whenever A. J. went out on the runway to prepare to take off, Parnelli and I would run out there and just bust a gut laughing as A. J. tried his hardest to keep the plane in the centerline. My problem was just the opposite; I wasn't very good at landing. I hadn't yet gotten the hang of getting that rear wheel down. So whenever they heard me in the pattern, A. J. and Parnelli would run out to the edge of the runway and get their jollies laughing at me trying to land the plane without hurting myself.

After those first few months, I drifted away from flying because racing was again taking up most of my time. In 1966 or '67, car owner Jim Hayhoe, who was also a Piper Aircraft dealer in Washington at the time, brought two or three airplanes to Indianapolis. We resumed the 500 Flying Club with several new members from the racing community, and it was then that I decided to seriously pursue obtaining my pilot's license. To do this, I enlisted the help of Johnny Poulsen, A. J. Foyt's chief mechanic and a respected flight instructor. I credit Johnny with getting me ready to take my check ride and preparing me for becoming a licensed pilot.

I had passed the written pilot's exam and Johnny and I were going to go out in the plane one afternoon so that he could check me out for the flight phase of my test. Johnny was performing double duty, flying with another student that morning. I was scurrying around, getting ready to leave for the airport, when I received a phone call informing me that John's plane had crashed in Crawfordsville, Indiana, and that both he and his student had been killed.

John's death was a tough loss for me and the racing community. It made me wonder about the dangers of flying and question whether or not I should carry on with it. In the end, I went ahead and did my check ride with another instructor and two days later took my test and passed. During the test, I felt as though Johnny were riding in the backseat, watching over me and tapping me on the shoulder whenever I made a mistake. I obtained my license in 1967, and have enjoyed being a pilot ever since.

In 1970 I had the privilege of being made an honorary member of the Blue Angels, the Navy Flight Demonstration Team. As a result of my affiliation with the team, I was invited to go aboard two aircraft carriers, the USS Independence in the mid- to late 1970s and the USS Ranger some years after that. I flew on a delivery craft that brought parts and personnel from shore to the Independence, and spent a night aboard the ship getting a taste of what Navy life was like. Many years later, I spent three days and two nights aboard the Ranger, while the crew prepared for Desert Storm. I was guided all over the ship, even to the LSO platform, where I watched the fighters come in and perform arrested landings. My experiences aboard those carriers are something I will always remember.

After I won Indy in 1974 and had some extra money to play with, I bought a P-51 Mustang, something I had always wanted. One of the top fighters of World War II, the P-51 was very fast and agile. Flying a P-51 was just like driving an Indy car; I had to stay focused and on top of what I was doing at all times. I have owned two P-51s in my lifetime, and aside from racing, flying those planes was the most relaxing time of a very busy period in my life.

In 1980, my military aviation interests took me in another direction—television. I appeared on a show for the ABC network called *American Sportsman* and spent two days at Reese Air Force Base in Lubbock, Texas, an advanced training base where they fly T-38s—twin-engine, supersonic jets used in training exercises. I flew for two hours in the backseat of a T-38 and underwent extensive emergency training. From there, we went to Nellis Air Force Base in Las Vegas, where I had the opportunity to fly in an F-15. We performed a lot of air-to-air combat maneuvers with an F-4 Phantom, and for a while I got to live the life of a fighter pilot.

That same year I had a chance to do television coverage of the air races in Reno, Nevada. The event spotlighted World War II fighter planes that had been modified for racing. The sportscaster gave his opening remarks from the control tower and then "threw it" to me in my P-51. While I was airborne, I talked about the differences between flying a plane and driving a race car—my two greatest passions.

If I weren't a race car driver, I would definitely want to be a fighter pilot. The pilot, like a race car driver, goes to the edge. I always enjoyed the thrills of playing fighter pilot, such as when my friend, Steve Summers, who served as a fighter pilot in Vietnam, took me on a flight in an F-105, the mainstay of our forces in Vietnam in the 1960s. We went up with three other airplanes and flew to Fort Sill, Oklahoma, where we dropped practice bombs and shot the guns at targets—which is also known as strafing. We then flew to Shreveport, Louisiana, where we met up with refueling tankers and refueled in the air. It was an exciting experience for a race car driver, who was used to refueling on the ground.

In 1982, I sold my P-51 Mustangs. Our son, John, got his pilot's license, and I decided to get an airplane he could fly too. I found a Decathlon, a small, high-wing plane similar to a Piper Cub. It was not quite like flying a P-51, but it was fun. That was the last of my airplanes; however, I didn't lose touch with the world of aviation.

In the mid-1990s, I was involved in a promotional program for Commander Aircraft in Oklahoma City, Oklahoma. Betty and I flew a Commander 114-B—a four-place, single-engine, performance aircraft—to several places around the country, where I would meet with some of the company's dealers or potential customers. In turn, the dealers would come to the Indy car races, where they would have an opportunity to visit with potential buyers and the people who currently flew their planes.

The airplane was very comfortable to fly, and I had the opportunity to take it across the United States two or three times to various races and locations. My stint with Commander lasted two or three years, and in that time I came to know some great people and have a lot of fun.

Another lifelong interest I have cultivated over the years, and perhaps yet another influence of my father, is drawing and painting. In 1971 and '72, I was given the opportunity to showcase my work in The National Art Museum of Sport show, "Art and the Athlete." I contributed six pieces to the exhibit, including pencil sketches and a couple of oil portraits. The entire collection formed an exhibition that opened at Madison Square Garden and then toured the United States a month or two later. To have my artwork viewed by people across the country and be a part of this exhibit was a real honor and very gratifying.

I have had numerous opportunities to do commission work as well. In the mid- to late 1960s, I did four pieces for the Goodyear Tire and Rubber Company, and completed a shaded pencil drawing for Larry Truesdale, who was then the head of racing for Goodyear. I've done portraits of Joe Leonard, a top driver of the time, and Lloyd Ruby, my old friend and a fellow racer from Wichita Falls, Texas. I also painted an oil portrait of my close friend, Don Branson, after he was killed in a sprint car accident in California in 1966. It hung, on loan, in the United States Auto Club offices for years until Betty and I added a trophy room to our home, where I now display the painting. I'm very proud of that piece.

As may be expected, I have developed other hobbies that are slightly more action-oriented than my artistic efforts. In the 1970s, Betty and I took up off-road motorcycle riding for recreation, and years later I bought a Harley-Davidson Dyna low-rider model. We even rode in the street bike Colorado 500, an annual bike ride hosted by Wally Dallenbach, the retired director of competition for CART. We covered something like nine hundred miles in four days of riding. Betty rode every mile on the backseat of my Harley. I'm not sure she would want to do that again unless we found a more comfortable seat for her to ride on.

I guess you could say I'm a fan of many speed-related activities, such as flying, riding motorcycles, and skiing. In 1977, I had an opportunity to go with my best friend, Charlie Hillard, and his family to Steamboat Springs, Colorado. I immediately fell in love with the place, and took Betty back with me later. Eventually, Betty and I returned and purchased a condo there with our friends, Jim and Raeanna Ellis. We have since sold that condo but now have a larger place in Steamboat Springs that is close to the ski slope and has "ski in, ski out" access.

Betty and I only started skiing after we had embraced Steamboat Springs. Betty is now an avid skier, and our children, John and Angela, are very accomplished at the sport as well. John showed an aptitude for skiing at a very young age, and even had an opportunity to pursue skiing as a profession. Angela and her husband, Craig, with a little help from Betty and me, will be watching their children, Conner, Evan, and Grant, take to the slopes when they get a little older.

In line with my competitive nature are two of my special passions—riding cutting horses and hunting quail. Riding cutting horses has become a passion of mine in recent years. The National Cutting Horse Association holds its big futurity in December at the Will Rogers Coliseum in Fort Worth, and my participation has allowed me many opportunities to meet football players, entertainers, and other celebrities. All of us ride in the event as amateurs—although some more than others.

The cutting horse event in rodeos and horse shows today mimics the competitions that have been held among ranch hands for years. It involves riding into a group of maybe twenty cattle, choosing three or four of them, and then allowing your saddle horse to single one out.

It can be a humbling experience for the rider. Sometimes the horse goes one way, and the rider is left hanging in midair. The rider must master his or her technique and be able to anticipate the horse's movements. And, of course, he or she has to watch the cow and determine which way it's trying to feint.

As with the cutting horse competitions I've been involved in, I have met some very nice people in the various quail hunts and sporting clay competitions I've attended. Several celebrity hunters, including actor Dale Robertson and country music artist Roy Clark, compete with me at the Grand National Quail Hunt in Enid, Oklahoma.

General Chuck Yeager, another avid quail hunter, is also an acquaintance of mine. We run into each other at two or three different annual hunts. The fact that I owned P-51s kind of lights him up, and I've enjoyed our chances to talk about fighter planes and his exploits in Europe with the P-51. General Norman

Schwarzkopf hosts a sporting clay event that I attended as well. Both Generals are race fans.

Of course, some of my interests are directly related to racing. I have long been interested in the history and pageantry of auto racing, and in June of 1999 I was privileged to take part in a very special event called the Goodwood Festival of Speed, located at the Goodwood estate about ninety minutes southwest of London. The three-day festival draws approximately one hundred thousand people per day to view vintage race cars of all types.

Many of the world's drivers of note from years past, including Sterling Moss, Sir Jack Brabham, John Sertees, Derek Bell, and Jacky Icks, were in attendance. The Indianapolis Motor Speedway contingency was composed of Rodger Ward, Parnelli Jones, Tony George, and me. I drove the car in which I finished second at the 1975 Indy 500, a McLaren M16 chassis that was sponsored that year by Gatorade. The car had been restored to running condition, and it was impressive. I had the opportunity to drive it twice a day for three days. It was great fun to get back into the cockpit again.

I also was able to catch up with some of my old mates from my McLaren days, including my chief mechanic, Denis Daviss, and one of my crew chiefs, Phil Sharp. I renewed old acquaintances and formed some new ones. Lord March, the owner of Goodwood, was a wonderful host, and the Goodwood Festival of Speed was a truly grand spectacle. Betty and I had a magnificent time, and I hope to go back someday.

Obviously, my career in racing has afforded me many exciting opportunities outside of the sport, whether it be competing in charity events with the National Cutting Horse Association or flying in the backseat of a super-sonic military jet. Betty and I have even had the privilege of visiting the White House on four occasions. We were invited by presidents Nixon, Ford, Carter, and Reagan to be their guests at various functions.

I enjoy leisure-time pursuits, too, including reading, watching movies, and going out to dinner for my favorite food—Tex-Mex. Living in Texas, I guess that's natural. I also enjoy traveling, and have had many opportunities in my life to travel the world. My favorite place to visit is Australia. I especially enjoy visiting Sydney and Melbourne, and wherever I go in Australia, the people are wonderful. That country has some of the best race fans anywhere.

While I do love visiting other parts of the world, Fort Worth, Texas, is home, and has been for most of my life. I enjoy being here and being a part of the community's traditions and values. I can't think of any other place I'd rather live.

The definition of retirement, according to the dictionary, is "to withdraw from action or danger; to withdraw especially for privacy; to move back, to withdraw from one's position or occupation; conclude one's working or professional career." But not for me. I only retired from the cockpit of a race car, not from living.

☆ **APPENDIX 1** ☆

Racers, Rivals, Friends

Late one night, after a day of interviewing, looking at family photos, and perusing old newspaper clippings, David asked me to relate stories of some of the drivers I had known over the years. I realized later that I also wanted to include some friends from other walks of life who mean a great deal to me. Here, then, are stories about some of the racers, rivals, and friends I've known over the past forty years.

Mike Anderson

Mike has been my friend for a number of years. He worked on my stock car pit crew in 1981, when I drove for the Levi Garrett team. Mike has even worked on my son John's car and helped him get a ride for the 24-hour Race at Daytona in the mid-1990s.

Mike lives in Lighthouse Point, Florida, with his wife, Tory, and they have two sons. We talk once or twice a month to learn what's going on with each other and to share jokes. He and Tory have even visited Betty and me in Steamboat Springs and skied with us out there. I really enjoy being with Mike and his family. This has been a genuine case of super fan becoming super friend.

☆　☆　☆　☆　☆

Mario Andretti

Mario got his first ride in an Indy car in late 1964. The race was in Trenton, and he backed into a fence and finished well out of the pack. I was there for the race, and I heard Clint Brawner say, "Boy, I wouldn't hire that kid on a bet."

Two weeks later, Mario had signed a contract to run for Brawner, and the rest, as they say, is history.

Born in Italy in 1940, Mario migrated with his family to Nazareth, Pennsylvania, in the mid 1950s. Mario's first love was road racing. He and his twin brother, Aldo, who was also a driver of some note until an accident in the late '60s curtailed his racing career, got their start by rebuilding an old car and racing it locally.

Mario was multitalented; he could race just about any kind of car on any kind of track and do well. Sprints, midgets, stock cars, Indy cars, Formula 1—you name it, Mario raced it. He was a rookie at Indianapolis in 1965 and four years later he won the race. He won the USAC National Championship in '65 and '69, and had great success in Europe. He is a world champion race car driver.

Buzz Barton

Buzz Barton ran midgets for years; he was one of my favorite drivers when I was a kid growing up in Tulsa. A talented and wise race car driver, he was a premier driver in the '40s and '50s.

Buzz had a soft heart, a wild sense of humor, and a great ability to tell stories. He also had the foulest mouth of any human being I've ever met. He didn't care who was standing around. He'd say something foul even if the queen of England was standing next to him.

I learned a lot racing against Buzz. He was the kind of driver who would spin you out and make you think it was your own fault. He was smooth. Although I didn't travel with Buzz, we became friends on the circuit, and later raced together when I was in IMCA.

Tony Bettenhausen Sr.

At first it was the name: Bettenhausen. It just caught my ear. But it was after I saw him drive—when I first ventured to the Midwest in 1960 to race sprints—that I really started to admire him and the way he drove.

He had such an air of confidence about him. He sat bolt upright in a race car and made it look easy, and I always liked that about him. I tried to pattern my style after Tony, and considering that he was a two-time national champion, I chose a good role model.

In 1961, when Tony was driving for Lindsey Hopkins, Paul Russo asked Tony to help him sort out some problems he was having with his roadster. The car didn't feel right to Paul and he wasn't able to run with any speed. Tony obliged, and a day or two before qualifying started he took Paul's car out onto the track. As he was coming down the front straightaway, a bolt fell out of the front suspension and the axle rolled over and broke the steering. The car climbed up on the wall and flipped several times. It landed down by the South end of Tower Terrace, outside of the track, where railroad rails, cut and buried in the concrete, formed part of the fencing. The car sheared off five of those uprights and then burst into flames. Tony was killed instantly.

That day I was in Morris, Illinois, working for a guy who owned an anhydrous ammonia plant, a tractor dealership, and the race car I was driving in IMCA races in the area. I was taking a break from my duties—which included unloading tank cars into the company's holding tanks—and was listening to the radio in the shop. A newscast came on, and the newsman was nearly crying as he said, "We have just learned that race car driver Tony Bettenhausen has been killed at the Indianapolis Motor Speedway during practice."

I cried. Tony was my hero. It was a sad day for all of us.

Clarence Cagle

I met Clarence Cagle in 1963, my rookie year at the Indianapolis Motor Speedway. The former superintendent of grounds for the Speedway, Clarence is one of the finest gentlemen I've ever known—and a man with great integrity. He was instrumental in making the Indianapolis Motor Speedway what it is today. The Speedway was his racetrack. He knew everything there was to know about the track, and he took great steps to make sure that nothing went wrong under his watch.

People didn't mess around with Clarence. He is very knowledgeable about a number of things, including racing. He is the kind of guy you better not tell a lie to, because he will remember, and even if he doesn't hold it against you he will consider you untrustworthy. And you don't want Clarence against you; you want him on your side.

I treasure my friendship with Clarence, a friendship that lasted throughout my career and continues to this day.

Jim Chapman

Jim Chapman, the quintessential Southern gentleman, was named head of the PPG Racing Program when it was created. He hired me to drive the pace car at every CART event before I started working with the Indy Racing League, and I always appreciated the way he ran the program.

Jim was a journalist by profession. More than fifty years ago, Ford Motor Company selected Jim to accompany Babe Ruth on Babe's farewell tour. Jim told some wonderful stories about the baseball Hall of Famer and treasured the good luck coin that Babe gave him.

Over the years, Betty and I developed a great friendship with Jim; in fact, he loved to dance with Betty, who is a very good dancer. Even when he was in his late seventies, Jim could still move across a dance floor, and Betty was his favorite dance partner.

Bill Cheesbourg

Bill was one of the guys at the Indianapolis Motor Speedway who always seemed to pick up a late ride. He was able to jump into just about any car and qualify it for the race.

Bill was a pretty good shoe. Real steady. Good guy.

He also had this hostility toward cars with bright lights.

He stored a ball peen hammer behind the seat in his hopped-up Ford truck. I've heard it told more than once that if somebody pulled up behind him at a stop light or stop sign with their headlights on bright, Bill would put his truck in neutral and set the brake.

Then he'd grab his ball peen hammer from behind the seat, get out of his truck, and walk back to the other car, where he'd calmly know out both of the headlights. Then he'd get back in his truck, wait for the green light, and drive away.

So you just didn't want to have the lights on bright when you pulled up behind "Cheese," because he'd dim them for you.

Sid Collins

Sid Collins was the voice of the Indianapolis Motor Speedway. When the radio network began, Sid anchored the broadcast team that called the race every year.

Sid set a lot of standards that still prevail today. He was the gentleman who coined the phrase, "The greatest spectacle in racing—the Indianapolis 500!" He was a good friend, and we often talked about racing. I loved listening to him reminisce about the old days at the Brickyard, the tradition of the great race, and the idiosyncrasies and superstitions of some of the drivers.

Pete Conrad

In November of 1980, I raced in a "Pro-Celebrity Challenge" race at Watkins Glen, New York. The pros—including Dan Gurney, Parnelli Jones, and myself—competed against celebrities from other professions, such as Kent McCord of *Adam-12* fame, singer-songwriter-actor Paul Williams, and actor Robert Hays, who starred in *Airplane!*.

The race was set up so that the celebrities took off under the green flag and the professional drivers, based on lap speeds during practice, were staggered behind them. But the event was on the level—it would be a race like any other.

The green flag was dropped and the celebrities took off. Going into turn 9, I caught up with Pete Conrad, one of the Apollo astronauts who walked on the moon, and a good friend of mine. Parnelli and Dan were in front of me, and we were racing to the front. As we came off turn 9, I moved over to the inside and started to go by Pete.

As we approached turn 10, the last turn before the pit straightaway—the long straightaway down to turn 1—I decided I shouldn't be where I was because Pete probably didn't see me—or, at least, he didn't acknowledge me. So I got out of the throttle and stood on the brakes hard. I started backing out just as he turned to the right to go through turn 10, and my left front bumper caught his right rear bumper. The motion turned him and he went up on the FIA curbing, which is like a curb, only it comes up from pavement level at an angle and is painted with red and white stripes.

Pete's car tipped up in the air on two wheels, turned over, rolled once, and started flipping end for end. He flipped six times like that and landed upside down. I thought, *My God, I've just killed an American treasure.* It scared me to death.

I pulled down, stopped my car, and got out. I went back to Pete's car, afraid of what I might find. The emergency crew got to the scene right away and the guys were pulling him out from underneath his car. Pete was okay—shaken, but okay. God, what a relief that was.

When we saw each other after the incident, we would kid about it. He'd tell the story and then I'd tell the story and we'd compare the two versions. Pete would exclaim, "You were pushing me out of the way!" He actually introduced me to people by saying, "Yeah, Rutherford here gave me my highest launch."

Pete and I later had an opportunity to work together on the television channel SpeedVision, doing some air shows. Pete was the authority on aviation and I was the aviation buff.

Tragically, Pete died in a motorcycle accident in California in 1999. I will always remember the good times we had together, our friendship, and our conversations.

Dale Earnhardt

In the late 1970s, I ran NASCAR races for Johnny Ray, a car owner from Talladega, Alabama. Johnny had put a lot of money into his car, a late-model Chevrolet. Since most of my time was devoted to running Indy cars, I wasn't able to race Johnny's stock car too often. I could run in the big races, such as the Daytona 500 in February, because the Indy racing season had not yet started. When I couldn't run for Johnny Ray, he'd put someone else in the car.

Such was the case at a race at the Atlanta International Raceway in November of 1976. Johnny told me he wanted to put a rookie in the car to give the guy a chance to show him what he could do. On the day of the race, Johnny called me to say that the rookie driver he had hired had crashed the car. Evidently, the car was having some problems and the rookie hit the outside wall on the backstretch and then hit the inside wall at turn 3. The car flipped over and ended up at the bottom of a ravine inside turn 3. Johnny said the guy had crashed up the car pretty good. I told Johnny I was sorry for him, and asked him if the young driver was okay.

"Oh, yeah," Johnny told me, "he's fine. He just feels bad about crashing the car."

"By the way, John," I asked, "who was the new guy you hired?"

"A kid from over in the Carolinas by the name of Dale Earnhardt," he said.

That's right—the same Dale Earnhardt who would end up winning NASCAR's Winston Cup championship several times. He's a superb race car driver—and the same driver who started out by crashing the stock car I ran in the off-season.

Emerson Fittipaldi

In the autumn of 1974, months after I won the Indianapolis 500 for the first time with McLaren, Emerson Fittipaldi came to the Indianapolis Motor Speedway and took his first ride in an Indy car—my Indy car. But he decided—perhaps it was a mutual decision between Emerson and his McLaren team because of potential scheduling conflicts—that it would be best if he concentrated on Formula 1 racing in Europe. He eventually won the world title driving for McLaren.

In a few instances over our years of racing together, I became the keeper of Emerson's briefcase. The first time occurred after an IROC race in Talladega, Alabama. After the race we were all rushing to catch our planes, and I noticed that Emerson's briefcase was left sitting on the ground. I picked it up, and when Betty and I caught up with him at the airport, I asked him if he had forgotten anything. He looked around and said, "Oh, my gosh, I've lost my briefcase!" I handed it to him, and he was visibly relieved that he hadn't lost it. He thanked me and we went our separate ways.

Later, at a race in Michigan, Betty and I flew into town and went to a rental car office to pick up a car. The clerk at the desk asked me if I was with the races and if I knew Emerson. He said Emerson had left his briefcase in the office when he got his car and asked if I could take it to him. So once again I collected my fellow driver's briefcase and took it to the track. When I saw him, I said, "Emerson, where's your briefcase?" He looked puzzled, and when I told him he had left it in the rental car office and that I had it in my car, he said, "I really owe you, Johnny."

Betty and I have not collected anything yet, but it became a source of amusement for Emerson and us over the years.

Emerson—"Emmo"—is quite a guy and a tremendous race car driver. A warm, wonderfully funny man, he's a joy to be around.

Pete Folse

Pete Folse was an IMCA champion. Like other championship drivers, he was a strong competitor. His success wasn't based on luck—he was tough and drove hard. He raced the Hector Honore "Bardahl Deuce," one of the premier cars in IMCA. The black car had a Hillegas chassis and a 270 Offy engine and handled really well.

Pete, a gravelly voiced welder from Tampa, Florida, was a real piece of work. He traveled from racetrack to racetrack in his turquoise and white '55 or '56 Chevrolet Nomad station wagon. I made some trips with Pete and I liked riding with him—he was a good teacher and really knew his stuff.

On occasion we would share a room to cut down on expenses. Pete would get up in the morning, pour himself a water glass full of vodka, and drink it down. Then he'd light up a cigarette, draw deeply, and say, with the smoke pouring out of his mouth and nostrils, "Ahhh . . . now we can get goin'!" I don't know how guys did that kind of thing, but they did. And I couldn't argue with Pete's success.

I enjoyed being around Pete. He was a fun guy, and we shared some laughs even if we didn't share the same ideas about breakfast.

A. J. Foyt

I still think that A. J. was the best driver to ever strap on a racing helmet. He won in every car he drove. An engine builder, chassis man, mechanic, and car owner, A. J. has done it all and he's done it well.

I always enjoyed watching A. J. and Parnelli race against each other. They were great nemeses and were battling each other on the sprint car circuit when I started racing in the early 1960s. On any given day, it was a toss-up as to who was going to win.

When I raced against A. J. it was tough duty. Texas is our home state, and we both had our contingents of fans. At one race in Texas, I saw A. J. Foyt "up close and personal" on a caution flag. He was leading the race and I was in second when the yellow came out and the pace car pulled in front of us.

We were on a two-mile track, and our team wasn't sure whether we could make it to the end of the race on the fuel we had left in the tank. I thought our

4-cylinder Offy could make it, and the consensus on the team was that A. J., with his V-8, would be short on fuel for the remaining distance.

He and I were running 1-2 behind the pace car. Soon we received word that we only had a couple more laps to go before we could resume battle. But just as the pace car was getting ready to turn into the pits so we could get the restart, A. J. pulled up inside the pace car. He actually blocked the pace car so the driver couldn't pull into the pits. Instead, the driver had to continue around the track for another caution lap, and as he did, A. J. ducked into the pits.

I was so dumbstruck that I missed my chance to follow A. J. into the pits. So he went in alone, got a full tank of fuel, whipped back onto the track, and with a fresh load of fuel in a car that was running plenty fast, he was able to race flat-footed the rest of the way without worrying about fuel consumption. I don't even remember who won that race. All I remember is A. J.'s sly move.

A. J. often had a tiger in his tank when he raced the rest of us, but one day he met his match in a lion.

We were in DuQuoin, Illinois, and a lion act was part of the show. The animal weighed at least four hundred pounds, but it was fairly tame and it would respond to its handler's commands. On this particular day the lion was a bit testy—not unlike A. J. now and then. Everything was going okay at first. A. J. was petting the lion and clowning around. Then the lion swatted at A. J., and A. J. backed up and turned around like he was going to run. Suddenly, the lion pounced on him. It wrapped one of its paws around A. J., pulled him back, and slammed him to the ground.

The lion wasn't gnawing on A. J., but A. J. was certain that that was going to be the lion's next move. When the handler finally pulled the lion off A. J., my old racing buddy was more somber than I've ever seen him. He got up and dusted himself off, and it seemed like he didn't know whether to laugh, cry, or throw up.

Mari Hulman George and Family

Mari George has been involved in racing virtually all her life. Her father, the late Tony Hulman, bought the Indianapolis Motor Speedway in 1945, and over the years Mari has been involved in all facets of the business. Mari owned midgets, sprints, and championship cars for many years, and her husband, noted racer Elmer George, enjoyed a fulfilling career, racing a variety of cars and managing the Indianapolis Motor Speedway. Mari is very knowledgeable about the racing profession. I have always liked and respected her—she's a racer at heart.

Mari and her family are racing royalty, but they don't put on any airs. They're hardworking, pleasant people. Mari's son, Tony George, is the president of the Indianapolis Motor Speedway and founder of the Indy Racing League. He has done a fabulous job of running the Speedway and developing and nurturing the IRL.

The family tradition carries on, thanks to Mari, Tony, and the rest of their family. Tony's son races midgets in the United States Auto Club, and Tony's sisters, Nancy, Josie, and Kathi, all sit on the Indianapolis Motor Speedway Board of Directors. Mari serves as chairman of the board. They are responsible for an ongoing chapter of American history—the Indianapolis Motor Speedway—and do a tremendous job of ensuring that the Indy 500 and Indy car racing as a whole remain a vibrant part of our culture.

Dan Gurney

Dan isn't always mentioned in the same breath with other racing greats, particularly when the subject is Indy. But his influence on racing here and abroad is still felt today. Make no mistake about it: Dan was an exceptional driver and an exceptional talent—most notably in road racing.

Dan built his own cars in the mid-'60s, and his Formula 1 car was a direct precursor to the state-of-the-art Eagles. It was because of him that the direction of rear-engine Indy car racing changed in this country. His All-American Eagle was like the Watson roadster of years before—everybody had to have one.

Dan is a superb engineer—one of the best—and he has a sharp wit, too. We've had a lot of fun over the years whenever we've gotten together at the racetrack or at some function. I've always respected him for his intelligence, his wit, and his decency. Auto racing has had few ambassadors as good as Dan Gurney.

Tony Hulman

Tony Hulman, the longtime president of the Indianapolis Motor Speedway, was a tremendous and fair businessman who really understood how to make things work. He was energetic and astute, and preferred a hands-on approach to everything. He could fly to three cities and attend six meetings in one day. I think at one time he sat on more than forty boards of directors around the Midwest.

Tony was the best thing to happen to the Indianapolis Motor Speedway after World War II. He not only made it work—he made it flourish.

In 1977 Tony underwent surgery for a heart ailment, and he never recovered. I went to his funeral—a grand funeral for a grand man, but such a sad day. He meant so much to so many people. Tony had an incredible smile and never forgot a name. He was one of the gentlest men I've ever known.

Jim Hurtubise

Jim was a tremendously talented race car driver, first and foremost. He was the first driver to really go 150 miles an hour at the Speedway, though it was unofficial. Jim was a racer, pure and simple, and he was well liked and respected by people throughout the racing community.

Jim was also a bit of a character. He had this strange habit of never taking enough clothes with him when he went to a race. He'd show up at the track for a race and he wouldn't have his shoes, his flame-retardant long-john racing underwear, or even his helmet.

Jim and I were about the same size, so it became a habit with him to stop by and borrow my stuff. He'd even borrow some flame-retardant underwear to wear for the race. At the end of each season, around Christmas, Betty and I would receive a package in the mail from Janie Hurtubise, Jim's wife, containing all of the underwear, freshly laundered, I had lent Jim over the season. We soon learned I was not the only driver whose gear Jim had borrowed, because Janie once said to Betty, "Do you know how many packages I have to send out each year?"

There are stories still circulating about Jim that go way, way back to before he was racing at Indy. Jim—his nickname was "Herk"—was in the Coast Guard or the Navy, I can't recall which, and stationed at one of the naval bases along the East Coast.

He used to jump ship on race nights and swim ashore to race at the local track. He had his gear stored someplace and he'd go get it and head to the track. Then when his night of racing was over, he'd store the gear and swim back to his ship.

In 1964, Jim's hands were burned horribly at a championship race in Milwaukee. The doctors had to put pins into his hands so that they would remain stationary and heal faster, and Jim had them bend his fingers so he could get them around a steering wheel when he returned to racing. Although he was never really as effective after his accident as he was before it, Jim was a real talent and a good guy who loved to race.

Bob Jenkins

Bob Jenkins and I have worked together for many years on radio, TV, and as co-emcees of several events. He is always the anchor, and I am the expert analyst. Bob is a real pro who is relaxed and keeps me in line most of the time. Seldom does he become flustered, but I have many times. The first Indy 500 that I was in the "booth" with Bob, I was like a first timer to the race. I had never seen all of the pageantry of the Indy 500, or even the balloons that are released just before its start. I completely forgot where I was and began to "ooh" and "ahh" at the magnificent sights. Bob took it all in stride and merely said "Oh yes, you never have seen any of this before, have you?" How's that for expert commentary?

Parnelli Jones

Parnelli Jones remains one of the world's greatest drivers. A calculating and smooth driver, he could race anything—sprint cars, Indy cars, stock cars, off-road cars. Parnelli was a sprint car champion and an Indy 500 winner, but his forte was off-road racing. That's when he would let it all hang out; he would just stand on the gas and do whatever he wanted out there in the desert. When he raced anything he made it look effortless; he never got in trouble, and he virtually never crashed.

Once, during a stock car race at Riverside, he was black-flagged for a relatively insignificant infraction. He was leading the race when he was called into the pits, and by the time he got back onto the track he was dead last. So he drove like a wild man—but smooth. He made his way in and out of traffic and back up through the field, passing one driver after another until he retook the lead. As he sped past the officials' stand, he stuck his hand out his window and gave them the "international" middle-finger salute. It was like he was saying, "There! Whaddya think about that!"

Though he'll never admit it, Parnelli helped me out at the Speedway when

I was a rookie. I went out to practice one day when Parnelli was warming up. We were both on the track, and he came by me as we were heading down the straightaway. But rather than rip around the track, leaving me in his wake, he just pulled over and held at my speed.

When he sensed that I was ready to open up my car a little bit, he didn't just stand on it and drive away. He waited on me. He let me run for two laps behind him around the Speedway. He was still inching away, but he kept me right there behind him.

Parnelli was showing me the groove. He was showing me exactly where to go and what he was doing at certain places along the track. Once I had built up to speed, he stood on it, as if to say, "Okay kid, that's enough. You're on your own."

I was able to stay with him for a while and watch his line so I could imitate his run. We ran another lap before he started pulling away; by then I was getting a little shaky on the unfamiliar track.

On that day in May of 1963, I gained some insight into what I needed to do to build up my speed and my confidence, thanks to a talented and famous race car driver who let a rookie watch him at the Indianapolis Motor Speedway. I'll always be grateful to him for that.

Jud Larson

Jud was as much of a hard-charger in a race car as there ever was. He had been racing since the 1940s, and was an old-timer when I met him.

Jud was a big, burly guy, and kind of snaggle-toothed. He also had a heart as big as all outdoors. When he got a few in him, he really became the life of the party. One night, after a banquet we had attended in Houston, Texas, a group of us went over to Ebb Rose's house. Jud had had a couple of toddies, and he sat down at the piano and started singing Shall We Gather at the River. Ebb and I joined in, and we had quite a sing-along around the piano.

This little get-together was special to me because Jud was one of the drivers I had watched race midgets back in Tulsa when I was nine or ten years old. He was one of the top names in midget racing then, and later got an opportunity to race big cars.

One day at the racetrack Jud experienced what some people assumed was a heart attack. As far as I know, it was never determined whether or not Jud had a heart problem, but whatever it was kept him out of the race that day. After that incident the medics would not pass Jud on his physical, so he dropped out of racing for a while, moved to Kansas City, and tended bar. He settled down for a time, but soon he got the itch to race again and decided to make his comeback.

One night in 1966, when I was recovering from the two broken arms I received in the Eldora Speedway crash, I was wakened by the phone ringing at about three or four in the morning. It was Bill Marvel, a friend of mine who worked for the United States Auto Club, calling from Reading, Pennsylvania.

The news was devastating: Red Riegel and Jud had crashed at the sprint car race in Reading and both had been killed. Jud was a good friend and an inspiration. It was hard for me to believe he was gone.

Ken Lowe

Ken Lowe and I have been friends since meeting in 1964 when Ken worked for the Goodyear Tire & Rubber Co. racing division, and I was a regular on the Goodyear Tire testing program. In the late 80's we once again worked together when I drove the PPG pace car for the CART races, and Ken supervised the pace car program for PPG.

Ken and I share a variety of interests—racing, airplanes, motorcycles, pace car programs, Goodyear tire testing, vintage motor vehicle collecting, snow country, and rum raisin ice cream. We even joined the "Macho Man" club together. While in Vancouver, British Columbia, for a race, Ken arranged for us to pick up some motorcycles so that we could ride and enjoy the beautiful Northwest. It began to rain, but we rode anyway—for one hundred miles—in the rain and cold. That trip definitely qualified us for the club. No one said it was the smartest thing we ever did!

Roger McCluskey

I was running my IMCA sprint car on a USAC temporary permit at New Bremen, Ohio, when I first encountered Roger McCluskey, who was about two or three years ahead of me on the Indy scene. And boy, was I impressed.

If you gave an inch, he'd take it—and then sit back and wait for you to slip another inch. Then he'd take that one, too, and before you realized it, he'd made up enough inches on you to be on your rear and ready to go wheel to wheel with you. The guy was absolutely tenacious, but he was also patient—a great combination in a race car driver. He won the National Sprint Car Championship several times and was a USAC stock car champion as well.

I was watching from the pits with A. J. Foyt the day Roger broke his arm in Reading, Pennsylvania, prior to the 1964 Indy. We saw Roger go into the turn, and it didn't look right. Roger wasn't in the right place for the speed he was carrying. The next thing we knew, the car was flipping in the first turn. We took off running, and by the time we reached the car it had stopped on the track. It was right side up, but Roger was slumped over the wheel, against the shoulder harnesses, and both of his arms were hanging down by his side.

Some track guys got there first and were tending to him, but A. J. and I both thought they were going about it all wrong. I jumped onto the bumper of Roger's car and placed my hands on Roger's helmet so they wouldn't move his head, and A. J. started throwing guys out of the way. Then he came over and started working on freeing Roger from the car.

When the track medical staff arrived, they found Roger unconscious and his breathing was somewhat labored. A. J. unhooked Roger's seat belts and harnesses while I put my arms under his from behind, and with the help of the medical staff we were able to gently lift him out of the car and put him on the stretcher. One of Roger's arms was broken—it would be several months before he could get behind the wheel of a race car again.

Some of the adventures Roger and I shared were away from the track. Betty and I were coming back from Salem, Indiana, in 1966 with Roger and his wife, Evelyn, after watching Roger race sprint cars. This was some time after my Eldora mishap, so by then my left arm was out of the cast and my right arm was in a splint but it wasn't healing well, as I mentioned earlier.

Some guy pulled up beside Roger on the highway. He was acting a bit strange, when he suddenly sashayed in front of Roger. This guy had his wife and two or three kids with him in the car. He was really acting goofy. I think he must have been suffering from what we call "road rage"— but heaven knows why.

Roger still had on his driving suit and the leather boxing shoes we wore back then, the ones with the thin soles so we could feel the throttle when we raced. The four of us were heading into Indianapolis when this guy started hassling us. After he pulled in front of Roger and made sashays, he slammed on his brakes so that Roger had to slam on his brakes or swerve to avoid hitting the guy. We all thought, What in the world is this idiot doing? What does he want?

Well, we drove through a suburb; the guy in front of us and stopped at a stop light. In fact, just as the light changed he made a sudden stop that forced Roger to really stand on the brakes to avoid rear-ending him. The guy jumped out of his car, ran back to Roger's side of the car, and tried to fight Roger through the window.

That did it. Roger had had e-nough. He opened his door, knocking the guy back a few feet, and stepped out of the car. I'd been sitting in the back, on the right, and by now I'm getting out of the car and circling around to where Roger and this guy are ready to go Fist City. And though Roger's wearing his boxing shoes, which might have been apropos, they were oil-soaked and a little slippery.

This guy comes at Roger, draws back, and just as Roger's getting ready to swing, he loses his footing and slips. The guy now has a blow to the chops measured for Roger's face. He's standing there with his feet apart when I get to the two of them. I can't do anything with my arms but I\m wearing cowboy boots and I've got g-o-o-o-d footing. So I dropped-kicked that clown right where it hurts and he doubles over. That took all of the fight, all of the weirdness, out of him. When he dropped to his knees, Roger and I got back in the car, back ep, and the four of us took off from the intersection. Only trouble was, one of us accidentally stepped on this guy's glasses in the fracas. Hope he had a spare pair to use on the rest of his journey.

It wasn't funny then. But now, looking back on it more than 30 years later, it takes on the aura of a slapstick comedy. Just a little side trip along the way to kind of spice up a big day of racing.

Roger was one heck of a guy. We shared a lot of laughs and spent some great times together way back when.

Rick Mears

Rick is a true racer. He simply wanted to race, and not just for the money. Like me, he wants to stay involved in racing (it is an addiction, you know), but I'll bet he still likes to be able to go out in his boat and do a little fishing, too.

There were several occasions when 4-time Indy 500 winner Rick Mears and I raced each other—and I don't mean at the Indianapolis Motor Speedway. Rick and I would race to see who could get from the Watkins Glen track to the ice cream parlor first.

One car was a stick shift and the other was an automatic. Obviously, the stick shift was a little faster, so Rick and I would switch cars every time we raced. Loser bought. Naturally, our driving skills came into play. I think it was about an even deal over time. More importantly, the ice cream was good!

Danny Ongais

Danny and I went wheel to wheel at Michigan in 1978, just one year after his rookie season. That race was possibly the most exciting race I've ever competed in, and who knows what might have happened if Danny's car hadn't have given up on him with ten laps to go. He proved to me that day that he was a fair and trustworthy competitor. I'd race with Danny any day.

Danny raced long-distance sports cars, as well as Indy cars, with a lot of success. And although he's not a rookie anymore, he could probably jump back into a long-distance sports car today and be a challenger like he was then—he's that good. Even this late in his career, Danny could still be a factor on the Indy scene if he tested and practiced enough.

Paul Page

When Sid Collins—who is also a great friend—retired as the voice of the Indianapolis Motor Speedway, Paul Page took over. I've known Paul for many years—he is a great fan of racing and a marvelous historian—and the two of us have had the opportunity to travel and work together over the years. Paul and I have not seen much of each other in recent years because of the CART-IRL controversy. He is still in television, and is one of the best racing anchors in the business. We share a love for flying and racing, and between the two of us we have some great stories.

Jon Potter

Jon Potter, a former member of the Indianapolis Sheriff's Department, is the executive director of the Championship Drivers Association. Jon is also a talented musician he plays the piano and has sung at the Grand Ole Opry.

He's one of those individuals you can't help but like.

One night on our way back to Indy from the Mid-Ohio Raceway in Lexington, Ohio, we stopped to eat at a Cracker Barrel restaurant. When Potter saw the huge line of people waiting for tables, he walked over to the manager and asked him, You know who I've got here?

"Isn't that Johnny Rutherford?" the manager asked.

"Yes it is," Potter replied, "and I could probably get him to sign some autographs for you. But he needs to eat first, since we've had a long day at the racetrack."

We were seated right away and the manager gave us both a free meal; after dinner I signed autographs for about half an hour. That's the kind of guy Potter is: he can get anything done or get anybody to donate.

Jon is tremendous individual, and I've always enjoyed my friendship with him and his wife, Karen—alias *Beverly Jean*.

John Poulsen

M-80s were standard equipment for many race car drivers and others in the racing profession. I know John seemed to like them. One time he wanted to give some folks a good scare as he drove by in his car, so he lit the fuse and started to toss the cherry bomb out the window.

Trouble was he'd forgotten to open the window first. He smashed his hand against the glass and knocked the cherry bomb onto the floor. He tried to grab the thing with his right hand while he rolled down the window with his left, but the thing went off and blew off the end of his thumb.

My favorite John Poulsen story has to do with another preoccupation of his—Volkswagens. He had it in for "bugs." I don't know why that was. I'm not sure anybody has ever been able to explain it. Maybe he disliked them so much because they were too slow or too ugly for his taste.

John had a hopped-up pickup truck that he used to push his race cars. That meant that, like most push trucks, it had a big oak bumper on the front that would get up against the bumper of a race car and push it until it started.

Well, he loved to catch Volkswagens on the highway. If the situation presented itself and the traffic was light, he'd ease up behind the Volkswagen, gently move his big oak bumper into the VW's bumper, and accelerate up to about a hundred miles per hour. Then he'd let 'em go.

One time when John did this, the guy went way off the highway, bounded out into the desert for about three hundred yards, and stopped in a swirl of dust and sand.

Glad I didn't have "a beetle."

Jim Rathmann

Jim Rathmann is truly one of the sport's greatest pranksters. I actually witnessed one of the best pranks he ever pulled, at the Speedway in the mid-'60s.

Late one night, I was standing outside the garage gate talking with someone when a Cadillac pulled into the driveway behind the Tower Terrace and between the garages. The Speedway used to employ some older guards to watch over things at night, and one of them was sitting in his folding chair when the car approached. A woman with blonde hair stuck her head out the driver's-side window and said, "Yoo-hoo! How are you!?" Then she gunned it right down the center alley between the two rows of garages, turned the corner, and disappeared.

The old guard was beside himself. He jumped up off his folding chair and gave chase. He was waddling and yelling after the blonde, "Ma'am! Lady! You can't be in here! Ma'am, please!"

I thought he was going to have a heart attack. He got on his walkie-talkie and alerted the other guards, and soon a contingent of old guards was walking around in search of the mysterious blonde. But they couldn't find her anywhere.

I started walking over to my garage, and when I cut through a row of buildings I came upon the empty Cadillac in front of one of the other garages. I walked around the car and quickly assessed the situation: Jim Rathmann, who was bald, must have found a blonde wig and borrowed the Cadillac. He had parked the car in front of his garage, where his guys were working on his race car, and had thrown the wig under the front seat of the Caddy. Seconds later, the old guard that had been chasing after the blonde arrived at Rathmann's garage, practically hyperventilating.

"Where's that woman?!" he asked me.

"What woman?" I asked.

"This is her car! Did you see her?!"

"No. There's no woman here. Honest."

Nobody ever found the mystery woman, at least not the guards. Rathmann still loves to tell that story.

Troy Ruttman

Many people who knew Troy in his younger days say that he was the greatest race car driver they've ever seen. And he did have a lot of talent. He was exceptionally strong in sprint cars, and in 1952, when he was only twenty-two, he won the Indianapolis 500 driving J. C. Agajanian's dirt car. Although roadsters were coming into vogue, Troy drove that dirt car, with its narrow chassis, to victory.

I met Troy when I first arrived at Indianapolis in 1963 and raced against him several times over the years. A few years later, we went to Terre Haute to do some publicity for an upcoming sprint car race, and I soon discovered that Troy was still popular with the fans, even though he had not been fully active in racing for a couple of years. It was amazing to see how many fans came out to see him that day.

Years later, I did an autograph-signing event with Troy at a Bradenton, Florida, racetrack. We reminisced a little about the old days, and it seemed like he hadn't changed a bit. He was the same soft-spoken Troy I'd met years before.

Troy passed away a few years ago from cancer. That day we lost one of the true gentlemen of Indy car racing.

Don Shepherd

One time, the two of us were pulling our race car behind a pickup truck. I was driving and Shepherd was sitting on the passenger side. We pulled into some city for gas or something to eat, and as we're heading down one street, we notice a construction site on the corner of where we had to stop for a red light.

We were real close to the curb, and next to us a cement truck had just dumped a load of concrete, which some workers were spreading out and working to form a new sidewalk section. One guy had the barrel of his truck revolving at high speed so it would clean out all of the interior, and he had a water hose trained on the chute.

Well, with the freshly poured concrete and the water he was spraying, a nice little puddle was forming. Shepherd was smoking a cigarette and as he reached down under the seat, I realized what he was going to do. He always carried the cherry bombs in the truck, under the seat.

"Watch this."

Don took his cigarette, lit the fuse of the cherry bomb, and pitched it out the window. It landed right in the puddle of wet concrete, in front of the guy with the water hose. The guy saw the cherry bomb. He saw Don throw it and he saw it land. He just grinned, laughed real loud as though we were the chumps, and he turned the hose on it.

Cherry bombs are waterproof. You can drop them into water and they'll burn right down and explode anyway. The guy is standing there, spraying that cherry bomb with the hose, and just as the light changed the M-80 went off.

The explosion covered him from head to toe with wet concrete and water. There was a big blob of concrete dripping off the end of his nose, and he couldn't open his eyes because he had wet concrete all over his face. He was the funniest looking thing I ever saw. Thank goodness the light changed, because I'm sure that in another few seconds he was going to come over and pop us one. We peeled out in the truck and just about laughed ourselves sick.

Please note: I never threw any cherry bombs in any of these stories.

Tom Sneva

Tom Sneva won the Indianapolis 500 in 1983 and has long been considered a tremendous competitor in professional racing. He came from the Pacific Northwest, where he worked as a school teacher and principal, and he turned out to be a tremendous driver.

Tom now owns a golf course in Scottsdale, Arizona, and has made quite a success of it. Naturally, he has a golf cart. It runs on a motorcycle engine and Tom describes it as "the fastest golf cart in the world." He has gotten that thing up to 104 miles an hour.

When Tom and I last spoke, he told me that he and some other gentlemen were looking to build an ice rink in Phoenix. He started thinking that he could put a hot engine into a Zamboni machine and have the fastest Zamboni in existence.

That's Tom Sneva.

☆ ☆ ☆ ☆ ☆

Bobby Unser

His unofficial title could have been "King of the Cherry Bombs," but Bobby Unser was truly one of the most gifted race car drivers I ever ran against. His record speaks for itself—like me, he won three Indy 500s in his career.

He was an intense driver, and one of the toughest competitors I've ever encountered. Away from the track, he was an outgoing, funny guy, as well as a real prankster.

If you were with Bobby Unser, say, at a restaurant, and he briskly walked past you and said in a low voice, "Let's get out of here," you got up and followed him out the door because something was up. Bobby had figured out how to set a time fuse on an M-80, or "cherry bomb." An M-80 is like a mini stick of dynamite. It'll blow a commode off the face of the earth. I know—I've seen it done.

Many a urinal, commode, water pipe, and towel dispenser has been dispatched by the Unsers. Yes, even Bobby's younger brother Al was an occasional culprit. I sometimes wonder if their middle name wasn't "Mayhem." But Bobby was the one in the family who really took delight in pulling pranks.

Perhaps my favorite Bobby Unser story involves a hotel fire extinguisher. We were all in Langhorne, Pennsylvania, running a race there. We stayed in a nice hotel, and the trick was to find out who was in which room so that you could play a prank on them. Bobby was looking for my old crew chief, Herb Porter, and when he couldn't find him he decided to take action. He called the desk clerk and found out which room Herb was staying in.

Bobby, having probably knocked back a couple of toddies by then, found the room, grabbed the nearest fire extinguisher, shoved the hose under the door, and sprayed the inside of the room, laughing and carrying on the whole time.

Only it wasn't Herb's room. It was the room of a clothing salesman who was staying at the hotel. The guy had racks of men's clothing just inside the door, and Bobby doused them all with soda solution from the fire extinguisher.

The police came, but of course Bobby was long gone by that time. They never pegged him specifically as the culprit, but the hotel manager had his suspicions. So did a number of other people. Guess which hotel the drivers could never go back to.

Al Unser Sr.

I've always said that if I were a car owner, and I was putting together a team to win the big races, I would hire Al Unser to drive my car. Al knew where he was going and what he wanted to do. He was probably one of the more calculating and successful drivers in the history of Indy car racing.

The entire Unser clan has a record that speaks for itself. Al; his son, Al Jr.; Al's brother, Bobby; and Bobby's son, Robby, and nephew, Johnny, are all very competitive people and very talented drivers. They are a formidable team in racing.

Al performed well in stock cars, dirt cars, and, of course, Indy cars—he won four Indianapolis 500s. He was low-key off the track and on; he was a discreet prankster and a subtle competitor. He'd almost lull the other drivers into believing he wasn't really a threat, and then—look out! He was racing by them. It was always a pleasure to race against him.

Rodger Ward

Rodger Ward was a mentor to me; he gave me advice when I was driving for Herb Porter, his former chief mechanic, and later when I started driving for his former team, A. J. Watson's Leader Cards team. Having worked with these people in the past, Rodger was able to tell me what to expect from my car owners and chief mechanics. When I went to work for chief mechanic A. J. Watson and car owner Bob Wilke, I got the car that Rodger had driven—a rear-engine car in which I would later win my first championship race.

I've always thought a lot of Rodger, both as a successful driver and as a person. He's still a good friend, and we see each other three or four times a year. We had a great time together in June of 1999, when we were among the drivers invited by Lord March to participate in the "Goodwood Festival of Speed" in England.

Johnny White

Johnny White and I raced IMCA together. Johnny was a real clown, but he was also a good race car driver and, like me, a hard-charger. A tremendous craftsman, Johnny built many race cars, including some midgets for Carl

Forberg, who raced at Indy back in the early '50s, and a sprint car in which he was later injured.

In a USAC sprint car race in Allentown, Pennsylvania, White bumped A. J. Foyt and spun him out. A. J. was furious. He went up to Johnny after the race, and in front of all the people in the grandstands he tried to jerk Johnny out of the car and whip his butt. But White had left his seat belts and shoulder harness intact and held onto them for dear life so that A. J. couldn't drag him out of the car. Frustrated, A. J. grabbed Johnny's head and squeezed until the Fiberglas in Johnny's helmet started to crack.

Johnny White helped me learn how to run the high banks, and I passed along what he taught me to the younger drivers coming into Indy car racing. Because of what Johnny taught me about running the high banks, I was always pretty successful on the "hills."

Smokey Yunick

Everybody knows Smokey. He was a legend when he was still active in racing, and the years have done nothing to diminish his reputation.

Smokey's hearing is gone. Shot. It's unfortunate, but very loud engines do take their toll. A few years ago he and I were once again at the International Motor Sports Hall of Fame for the induction ceremony luncheon. A large gathering of about 300 people was present. President George Bush, who was in town for another function, was the honored guest.

Smokey had just had surgery on his ears, but he was still unable to hear well. Because he couldn't hear himself when he talked, he talked very loudly even if you were quite close to him.

Smokey and I were seated at the same table, across from each other. The two of us conversed by using a pad and pencil, writing notes and questions to each other and then passing the pad across the table.

Soon, Smokey got a little frustrated with that routine, and just as they got ready for the invocation, Smokey, in a very loud voice, boomed out, "Boy, this is some deal, huh, John!"

Of course, everybody in the room heard him and absolutely cracked up. God bless Smokey!

Friends from the Big Screen and Little Screen

Bob Schieffer, veteran CBS White House correspondent and news anchor for many years, was a classmate of mine. I went to North Side High School in Fort Worth with Bobby Schieffer.

I have not seen a lot of him in recent years, although he did make a special trip home when the city of Fort Worth honored me with a banquet following one of my victories at the Indianapolis 500.

"Tool Time" Tim Allen, on television's popular show Home Improvement, is someone I've known for several years. Race car driver Michael Andretti and I did a cameo appearance on Tim's show a few years ago.

Tim is a race nut, a real gearhead. I've always enjoyed talking with Tim about racing and other shared interests.

Bob Wilke, a big, slightly ominous-looking man, was a widely regarded American character actor who usually portrayed villains or "shifty" types in westerns. He appeared in *20,000 Leagues Under the Sea*, *Kill the Umpire*, and *Stripes* to name just three of his films. Bob, who should not be confused with car owner Bob Wilke, was one of my good friends and fans.

He enjoyed racing so much, and came to Indianapolis every year to see the Indy 500. He also occasionally went to some of the other races out west.

Bob's hobby was gluing seashells together to make figures of people. He made an entire seashell family for Betty, and we still have it on display.

"Bad Man Bob Wilke," as he was called, passed away several years ago. He was anything but bad. A great guy, Bob was.

James Garner, one of the most popular actors of television and movie fame is also a tremendous race fan. Perhaps that is why he appeared in the movie *Grand Prix*.

Betty and I see Jim every now and then. He used to come to Indianapolis every year to catch the Indy 500, but he got busy with films and his television show, *The Rockford Files*. Recently, Jim has been back to Indy, and we hope he continues to return every year as other celebrity favorites like Florence Henderson and Jim Nabors do.

Florence Henderson and Jim Nabors are kind of synonymous with the Indy 500. Jim has sung "Back Home Again in Indiana" and Florence has sung our National Anthem before the start of the race.

They have been good friends of ours for many years. Betty and I always enjoy seeing them at the Speedway and, if their respective schedules permit, we get to have dinner with them—usually at the Speedway grounds or at Mari Hulman's house.

Friends We've Made along the Way

Not all that long ago, Betty and I were coming back from the East in our Newell motor coach.

Near Columbus, Ohio, I think, a guy driving a big rig and accompanied by a woman riding in the passenger seat pulled up alongside us in their semi. The guy got on his CB radio and asked if we were in a rock group. I guess the motor coach made Betty and me look the part.

I got on our CB and told him who we were—"Lone Star JR" and "the Yellow Rose of Texas." One thing led to another, and pretty soon Betty and I were practically learning this couple's entire history. I got around to telling the two of them that Betty and I were heading to Indianapolis.

You guessed it. He said he and his wife were going there, too. And because it was their anniversary and his wife was riding with him on this trip, he wanted to take her to dinner at a nice restaurant in Indianapolis. Did we know of any place that served good food but wasn't going to cost a lot?

The only thing we could think of where they could get a decent dinner that was inexpensive and had a big enough parking lot where he could pull his truck in was the Sizzler over on the west side of town. Well, then they invited us to have dinner with them, and I accepted.

We stopped at the restaurant, and while I gave them a tour of the inside of our motor coach, Betty gave me a look that said, "What are you doing? We don't even know these people."

The four of us went in and I bought their dinner for them as an anniversary gift. They were actually very nice, and pleasant. They thanked us, we said our good-byes, and that was it. We never heard from them again. To be honest, I don't even recall their names. Oh, well, seemed right at the time.

Zoom of the Unknown Fan

One of my favorite fan stories involves a man who gripped an amber bottle in one hand while losing his grip on reality.

It was my first year of racing modified stockers at the Devil's Bowl Speedway in Dallas. The drivers and their cars were competing in a preliminary race to qualify for the featured event. I had my car in the pits on the infield. What I witnessed from my vantage point was probably pretty much the same thing that Moses witnessed when he parted the Red Sea.

One of the cars lost a wheel, which started bounding down the track and then hit a guardrail. Normally a catch-fence in front of the grandstand would have stopped the tire, but the tire hit the guardrail in such a way that it bounced high over the catch-fence and landed on the footpath in front of the grandstand.

From there, the tire started bouncing and rolling up through the grandstand. The fans quickly parted to give the tire a clear path to wherever it wanted to go. Or at least, most fans got out of the way.

As the tire bounded all the way up the stands, a couple standing in the top row remained virtually motionless. In fact, they had their arms linked. The man was holding an amber-colored bottle in his free hand.

The spinning tire, with an agenda known only to itself, bounced right for the couple with their arms still interlocked.

The man yelled, "I've got it!" as his free hand reached up to grab the tire. And then the couple disappeared.

When we all saw the tire take them up over the grandstand we thought they'd had it. Fortunately, people had parked their cars directly below, and right up against the back of, the grandstand, and the couple landed on either the hood or the roof of a car. It gave them some bruises, but otherwise they were all right.

I don't know how much of the contents of that amber bottle the guy had consumed, but it was enough to impair his judgment. So please, folks, leave the tire-changing to the guys on the pit crew. They're gulping water and sports drinks.

☆ APPENDIX 2 ☆

Career Highlights

Second only to the legendary A. J. Foyt in Indy Car seasons . . . Second in all-time starts (315) to Foyt's 359 . . . fifth in all-time Indy Car victories (27) tied with Rick Mears and sixth in all-time pole positions (23) . . . His $4,209,232 ranks 11th among all-time earnings . . . One of only four drivers to have reached the plateau of 300 or more Indy car starts . . . One of only eight drivers to win three Indy 500s . . . Indianapolis victories in 1974, 1976 and 1980 with the last two wins coming from the pole position . . . In 315 Indy Car starts, has finished in the top-five 99 times and in the top-ten 157 times . . . Won CART national championship in 1980 . . . In 59 career 500-mile race starts, has five victories, six seconds and 25 top-ten placements to share third place tie among all-time drivers with Mario Andretti.

1962 Indy Car debut with ride in Hoosier 100.

1963 Pole winner and 100-mile race winner, Daytona 500. Set new world and track record in qualifying at Daytona. Passed rookie test and started first Indianapolis 500. Ran in all twelve championship races, taking seven top-ten placings and finishing 10th in Indy Car standings.

1963 Started 15th at Indy and and placed 27th.

1965 Won first USAC Championship race, Atlanta 250. USAC Sprint Car Champion—winning seven races.

1967 Qualified 19th at Indy and finished 25th.

1969 Took 11th in driver standings.

1970 10-mile Indy 500 qualifying speed only 1/100th of a second slower than polesitter Al Unser—the closest qualifying race in Indy 500 history.

1972 Qualified eighth at Indy and finished 27th. Picked up seventh place in season standings.

1973 Set one lap and four lap Indianapolis 500 qualifying records at 199.071 mph and 198.413 mph (4 lap average), and finished 9th in the race. Won Ontario 100 and Michigan 125. Finished third in final season standings.

1974 Won his first Indianapolis 500, followed with a win in the Pocono 500. Set the current Pocono track record with a race speed of 156.701. First driver to win two 500s in one year. Also won Ontario 100 and the Milwaukee 150 Championship races to finish second in the USAC Championship point standings. Triple Crown champ with 2nd in Ontario, California 500. Named "Driver of the Year" by the American Auto Racing Writers and Broadcasters Association, also named Racing All-American. Finished 7th in the IROC series.

1975 Won Phoenix 150 and was runner-up at Indianapolis 500 to Bobby Unser, finished second in points to A. J. Foyt. Competed in ABC's "Super Stars" and finished 2nd in the World Series of Auto Racing series.

1976 Won the rain-shortened Indianapolis 500, also won the Trenton 200 and Texas 200; finished 2nd to Gordon Johncock in the USAC championship point standings.

1977 Won Phoenix 500, Texas 200, and both Milwaukee 150 and 200; finished 3rd in USAC championship point standings. Won the Australian Midget Car Championship.

1978 Ran a career-high 18 events and had eight top-five placings to take fourth in points. Won Michigan 200 and Phoenix 150. Placed 4th in the USAC championship point standings. Finished 2nd Daytona 24 hour with Barbour Porsche.

1979 Competed on CART championship circuit, winning both of the Atlanta Twin 125s and finishing in the top ten in nine of 14 races to finish 4th in the point standings.

1980 Won his third Indianapolis 500, becoming sixth driver to win the race three times. Also won the Ontario 22, Mid-Ohio 250, Michigan 200 and finished in the top five 10 times during the 12-race Indy car series to win the USAC and CART championships. Set record for most consecutive racing miles completed in competition. He was voted "America's Driver of the Year" by both the AARWBA and the prestigious Olsonite panel. The City of Hope's panel of 150 sportswriters also voted him a Victor Award as auto racing's "Man of the Year." In his hometown, the Fort Worth Advertising Club presented him with a Dateline Award for being Fort Worth's most newsworthy citizen.

1981 Won the Kraco 150 at Phoenix. Won pole position with near record 200.512 mph in Atlanta Twin 125. Set a new track record of 135.890 mph qualifying on the pole for the rained-out Milwaukee 200. Led two NASCAR Winston Cup races, Daytona Firecracker 400 and Michigan Champion 400. Finished 3rd in Watkins Glen. Finished 5th in points.

1982 Finished 8th At Indianapolis 500. Suffered broken right hand at Pocono 500.

1984 Replaced Rick Mears at Sanair, Canada for 5th place finish. Set new world record for Indy cars at 215.189 mph at Michigan International Speedway on September 24 in Penske-Pennzoil Z-7. Ran 6 of 16 races, finished 22 in point standings. Ran IROC series and finished 7th.

1985 Won at Sanair, Canada—first win since 1980. Ran 14 of the 15 races. Finished in top ten 6 times and finished season tied for 10th in the points standing. The teams also finished 120th in "UA CAN" Award completing 2698.744 miles of racing. 12th in the Dana Pit Crew championships, and 7th in the Triple Crown Award. The team also was the winner in the Concours at Long Beach and Miami for the best-looking car and crew.

1986 Qualified 12th for the Indy 500 and finished 8th after a week's rain delay of the race. Won Michigan 500 and became the oldest to ever win an Indy Car event. Drove in 17 races and finished 13. Finished in top ten 11 times and completed the season 11th in the tight point standings with 78 PPG points. The team finished 5th in the "US CAN" Award for miles completed. Tenth in the Pit Crew Championships and 3rd in the Triple Crown Award.

1987 Qualified for Indy 500 in 8th and finished 11th. Was voted into the IMS Auto Racing Hall of Fame, and was also voted a charter member of the Fort Worth Sports Hall of Honor and Boys Clubs of America's Alumni Celebrity Hall of Fame.

1988 Qualified 30th and finished 22nd at the Indy 500. Finished 18th as a substitute for A. J. Foyt at Michigan 500. Was awarded "Sportsman of the Year" for the Corvette Challenge. Was elected to the Texas Auto Racing Hall of Fame.

1989 Qualified for Indy 500 with a time of 213.097, but bumped from field. Finished 10th in the Michigan 500 and 13th at the Pocono 500. 7th place finish at the invitational Macau Race of Champions. Won TV's "Star Shot" and finish 7th in the Celebrity Cutting Horse Futurity in Fort Worth, Texas.

1990 Named honorary chairman for the National Motor Racing Hall of Fame induction.

1991 Received the Lifetime Achievement Award from the Toronto Indy Festival Foundation. Full-time Pace Car driver.

1992 Received Louie Myer Award for contributions to racing. Returned behind the wheel of PPG Pace Car

1993 Placed 2nd in qualifying and finished 7th in the Fast Masters series. Named the Ambassador of Motorsports by the Cleveland 500 Foundation. PPG Pace Car Driver.

1994 Officially retired from racing, taking final lap at the Indy 500.

Awards and Honors:

1963 Outstanding Rookie
Honorary River Oaks JC

1964 Hoosier Hundred Sportsmanship Award

1965 Most Improved Driver
National Sprint Car Championship

1967 Most Outstanding Race Driver

1969 1st Jim Clark Award

1970 USO Tour to Vietnam

Honorary Blue Angel

1973 Extra Mile Award

1974 Fort Worth Newsmaker of the Year

1974, 1976
Driver of the Year AARWBA-Jerry Titus Award
Jim Malloy Award
Tony Bettenhausen Award
Martini & Rossi Award Runner-up
Nominated Victor Awards
Nominated Gillette Cavalcade of Champions
Recipient of the Vanderbilt Cup

1974, 1976, 1977, 1978, 1979, 1984
International Race of Champions

1974, 1976
Super Stars Participant

1974, 1976, 1980
Johnny Rutherford Day in River Oaks and Fort Worth, Texas

1976 Driver of Year for Sport Magazine
Eddie Sachs' Award (nominated 9 times)
Triple Crown Award - 1976 and 1980

1980 Winner Victor Award for Racing

Olsonite Driver of the Year
National Driving Championship USAC and CART
Fort Worth Advertising Dateline Award

1981 Texas Sports Hall of Fame

1983, 1989
Jigger Award

1983 Distinguished Alumnus Award, Fort Worth ISD

1987 IMS Auto Racing Hall of Fame
Fort Worth Sports Hall of Honor - charter member
Boys Clubs of America's Alumni Celebrity Hall of Fame - charter

1988 Texas Auto Racing Hall of Fame
Sportsman of the Year for Drivers in Corvette Challenge

1990 Lifetime Achievement Award - Toronto, Canada

1992 Louie Meyer Award - Indianapolis Hall of Fame

1992 Top Gun - Grand National Quail Hunt

1993 Ambassador of Motorsports - Cleveland

1995 Sprint Car Hall of Fame

1996 International Motorsports Hall of Fame
Motorsports Hall of Fame of America

1997 CARA Award for Giving

1998 Honored as "Best of Texas"- national media in Dallas

1999 U.S.A. Honoree at Goodwood (England) Festival of Speed

Invited to the White House—
Nixon-1971, Ford-1976, Carter-1978, Reagan-1980
CART Pace Car Driver for PPG - 1990-1995
Listed in Who's Who
Honorary Chairman of Texas Cancer Society
Honorary Chairman Indiana Heart Association

INTERNATIONAL MOTOR CONTEST ASSOCIATION (IMCA) CAREER RECORD

DATE	LOCATION	Q	HEATS	F	CAR # & OWNER	TYPE TRACK
08/14/60	LaCrosse, WI	6	4 - 4	11	#42 Heath	Dirt-1/2 mile
08/14/60	LaCrosse, WI (night)	5	2 - 3	7	#42 Heath	Dirt-1/2 mile
08/20/60	Cedar Rapids, IA	10	5 - 4	10	#42 Heath	Dirt-1/2 mile
08/26/60	St. Paul, MN	22	4-6-14-10	24	#42 Heath	Dirt-1/2 mile
08/30/60	St. Paul, MN	23	8-scratch	23	#42 Heath	Dirt-1/2 mile
09/04/60	St. Paul, MN	16	3	10	#42 Heath	Dirt-1/2 mile
09/05/60	Bethany MO	5	2 - 4	5	#42 Heath	Dirt-1/2 mile
09/10/60	Topeka, KS	13	2	—	#4 Peacock	Dirt-1/2 mile
09/11/60	Topeka, KS	12	—	12	#4 Peacock	Dirt-1/2 mile
09/14/60	Spencer, IA	—	4 - 3	9	#4 Peacock	Dirt-1/2 mile
09/18/60	Hutchinson, KS	3	3 - 4	4	#42 Heath	Dirt-1/2 mile
09/21/60	Hutchinson, KS	2	4 - 5	15	#42 Heath	Dirt-1/2 mile
09/26/60	Oklahoma City, OK	8	4	7	#42 Heath	Dirt-1/2 mile
09/29/60	Oklahoma City, OK	10	2 - 3	10	#42 Heath	Dirt-1/2 mile
10/01/60	Shreveport, LA	8	5 - 3	7	#42 Heath	Dirt-1/2 mile
10/22/60	Shreveport, LA	10	4 - 3	—	#42 Heath	Dirt-1/2 mile
10/23/60	Shreveport, LA	9	6 - 4	6	#42 Heath	Dirt-!/2 mile

Finished 22nd in Points with 13 Races

DATE	LOCATION	Q	HEATS	F	CAR # & OWNER	TYPE TRACK
02/11/61	Tampa, FL	14	1 - 1	8	#42 Heath	Dirt-!/2 mile
02/15/61	Tampa, FL	13	2	9	#42 Heath	Dirt-1/2 mile
02/18/61	Tampa, FL	13	2	6	#42 Heath	Dirt-1/2 mile
02/19/61	Tampa, FL	13	4	10	#42 Heath	Dirt-1/2 mile
05/27/61	Houston, TX	8	5 - 3	5	#42 Heath	Paved-1/2 mile
05/28/61	Shreveport, LA	2	3 - 3	9	#42 Heath	Dirt-1/2 mile
06/11/61	Des Moines, IA	16	1	11	#42 Heath	Dirt-1/2 mile
07/04/61	Cedar Rapids, IA	6	5 - 3	11	#42 Heath	Dirt-1/2 mile
07/16/61	Terre Haute, IN	22	4	—	#73 Wilson	Dirt-1/2 mile
07/28/61	Kansas City, KS	10	4 - 1	6	#73 Wilson	Dirt-1/2 mile
08/12/61	Oskaloosa, IA	1	5 - 1 - 2	4	#73 Wilson	Dirt-1/2 mile
08/13/61	Austin, MN	1	3	3	#73 Wilson	Dirt-1/2 mile
08/19/61	Sedalia, MO	NT	—	—	#73 Wilson	Dirt-1/2 mile
08/20/61	Sedalia, MO	19	1 -	—	#73 Wilson	Dirt-1/2 mile
08/26/61	St. Paul, MN	9	3	6	#73 Wilson	Dirt-1/2 mile
08/29/61	St Paul, MN	8	5 - 1	3	#73 Wilson	Dirt-1/2 mile
08/30/61	St. Paul, MN	9	3	12	#73 Wilson	Dirt-1/2 mile
09/01/61	St. Paul, MN	6	3	7	#73 Wilson	Dirt-1/2 mile
09/03/61	St. Paul, MN	6	—	16	#73 Wilson	Dirt-1/2 mile
09/09/61	Topeka, KS	10	—	—	#73 Wilson	Dirt-1/2 mile
09/10/61	Topeka, KS	9	—	12	#73 Wilson	Dirt-1/2 mile
09/13/61	Spencer, IA	8	—	—	#73 Wilson	Dirt-1/2 mile
10/07/61	Birmingham, AL	5	2	7	#73 Wilson	Dirt-1/2 mile

Finished 16th in Points with 15 Races

DATE	LOCATION	Q	HEATS	F	CAR # & OWNER	TYPE TRACK
02/07/62	Tampa, FL	7	2	3	#63 Beatson Chevy	Dirt-1/2 mile
02/10/62	Tampa, FL	7	2	—	#63 Beatson Chevy	Dirt-1/2 mile
02/14/62	Tampa, FL	7	2	6	#63 Beatson Chevy	Dirt-1/2 mile
02/17/62	Tampa, FL	7	2	2	#63 Beatson Chevy	Dirt-1/2 mile
05/13/62	Schereville, IN	2	1-1	1	#63 Beatson Chevy	Paved-1/2 mile
05/26/62	Mt. Clemens, MI	9	1	13	#63 Beatson Chevy	Dirt-1/2 mile
05/29/62	Anderson, IN "500"	1*	(Leep in relief)	5	#63 Beatson Chevy	Paved-1/4 mile
05/30/62	Mt. Clemens, MI	6	1	4	#63 Beatson Chevy	Dirt-1/2 mile
06/17/62	Des Moines, IA	2	4	5	#63 Beatson Chevy	Dirt-1/2 mile
06/24/62	Winchester, IN	3	4	1*	#63 Beatson Chevy	Paved-1/2 mile
07/04/62	Cedar Rapids, IA	2	3	1	#63 Beatson Chevy	Dirt-1/2 mile
07/15/62	Salem, IN	4	1	1	#63 Beatson Chevy	Paved-1/2 mile
07/22/62	Winchester, IN	3	4-1	3	#63 Beatson Chevy	Paved-1/2 mile
07/27/62	Minot, ND	6	2-3	3	#63 Beatson Chevy	Dirt-1/2 mile
07/28/62	Minot, ND	10	5	9	#39 Melton	Dirt-1/2 mile
07/31/62	LaCrosse, WI	3	6-4	SCR	#63 Beatson Chevy	Dirt-1/2 mile
07/31/62	LaCrosse, WI		Feature Only	5	#8 Cahill Bros.	Dirt-1/2 mile
08/01/62	LaCrosse, WI	4	1	12	#63 Beatson Chevy	Dirt-1/2 mile
08/05/62	Hibbing, MN	5	3	4	#63 Beatson Chevy	Dirt-1/2 mile
08/09/62	Eldon IA	6	1	2	#63 Beatson Chevy	Dirt-1/2 mile
08/11/62	Springfield, MO	4	2-2	3	#63 Beatson Chevy	Dirt-1/2 mile
08/12/62	Cedar Rapids, IA	5	3	5	#63 Beatson Chevy	Dirt-1/2 mile
08/14/62	Denison, IA	2	2-2	1	#63 Beatson Chevy	Dirt-1/2 mile
08/16/62	Wausau, WI	3	3-3	2	#63 Beatson Chevy	Dirt-1/2 mile
08/18/62	Sedalia, MO	7	2	6	#41 Hyneman	Dirt-1/2 mile
08/19/62	Des Moines, IA	1	4	6	#54 Herring	Dirt-1/2 mile
08/23/62	Des Moines, IA	1	4-2	4	#63 Beatson Chevy	Dirt-1/2 mile
08/25/62	St. Paul, MN	13	9-SCR	—	#63 Beatson Chevy	Dirt-1/2 mile
08/26/62	St. Paul, MN	eye injury—did not run			#63 Beatson Chevy	Dirt-1/2 mile
08/28/62	St. Paul, MN	16	1	7	#22 Kern	Dirt-1/2 mile
08/29/62	St. Paul, MN	—	—	17	#22 Kern	Dirt-1/2 mile
09/02/62	Lincoln, NB	7	4	9	#63 Beatson Chevy	Dirt-1/2 mile
09/03/62	Lincoln, NB	7	1	12	#63 Beatson Chevy	Dirt-1/2 mile
09/06/62	Lincoln, NB	7	2	14	#63 Beatson Chevy	Dirt-1/2 mile
09/13/62	Spencer IA	3	2-2	5	#63 Beatson Chevy	Dirt-1/2 mile

Finished 5th in Points with 34 Races

* record

SCR - scratched

1955—'62 Lifetime Points in Active Drivers—Rank is 13th

USAC CAREER RECORD

FEATURE STARTS

YEAR	CH	ST	SC	SP	M	F5	SE	TOTAL
1962	4	-	-	7	1	-	-	12
1963	12	1	-	6	4	-	-	23
1964	11	3	-	14	2	-	-	30
1965	15	-	-	20	1	-	-	36
1966	1	-	-	1	1	-	-	3
1967	16	-	-	10	2	-	-	28
1968	17	-	-	10	4	-	-	31
1969	14	-	-	3	2	-	-	19
1970	14	2	-	4	-	-	-	20
1971	10	1	4	1	1	-	-	17
1972	9	-	2	1	3	-	-	15
1973	13	4	2	-	-	-	-	19
1974	13	1	-	-	-	2	3	19
(IROC, World Series Sprint & Midget)								
1975	12	1	1	-	2	-	2	18
(World Series Stock & Champ Car)								
1976	13	1	-	-	-	-	1	15
(IROC)								
1977	14	-	-	-	4	-	1	19
(IROC)								
1978	18	-	-	-	-	-	1	19
(IROC)								
1979	1	-	-	-	-	-	-	1
1980	5	-	-	-	-	-	-	5
1981	1	-	-	-	-	-	-	1
1982	1	-	-	-	-	-	-	1
1983	-	-	-	-	-	-	-	-
1984	1	-	-	-	-	-	-	1
1985	1	-	-	-	-	-	-	1
1986	1	-	-	-	-	-	1	2
(Hoosier Dome Midget)								
1987	1	-	-	-	-	-	-	1
1988	1	-	-	-	-	-	-	1
1989	-	-	-	-	-	-	-	-
1990	-	-	-	-	-	-	-	-
1992	-	-	-	-	-	-	-	-
TOTALS:	219	14	9	77	27	2	9	357

KEY: CH= Championship Division (Indy Cars)
ST=   Stock Cars
SC=   Silver Crown Championship (Dirt) Car
SP=   Sprint Cars
M=   National Midget
F5=   Formula 5000
SE=   Special Events (RCA Dome Midgets, IROC, World Series of Auto Racing)

USAC CHAMPIONSHIP CARS

DATE	LOCATION	TRACK NAME
09/15/62	Indianapolis, IN	Indiana State Fairgrounds
09/23/62	Trenton, NJ	New Jersey State Fairgrounds
10/28/62	Sacramento, CA	California State Fairgrounds
11/18/62	Phoenix, AZ	Arizona State Fairgrounds

Race scheduled for 100 laps but halted after 51 laps due to Elmer George's accident.

04/21/63	Trenton, NJ	New Jersey State Fairgrounds
05/30/63	Indianapolis, IN	Indianapolis Motor Speedway
06/09/63	Milwaukee, WI	Wisconsin State Fairgrounds
06/23/63	Langhorne, PA	Langhorne Speedway
07/28/63	Trenton, NJ	New Jersey State Fairgrounds
08/17/63	Springfield, IL	Illinois State Fairgrounds
08/18/63	Milwaukee, WI	Wisconsin State Fairgrounds
09/02/63	DuQuoin, IL	DuQuoin State Fairgrounds
09/14/63	Indianapolis, IN	Indiana State Fairgrounds
09/22/63	Trenton, NJ	New Jersey State Fairgrounds
10/27/63	Sacramento, CA	California State Fairgrounds
11/17/63	Phoenix, AZ	Arizona State Fairgrounds

03/22/64	Phoenix, AZ	Phoenix International Raceway
05/30/64	Indianapolis, IN	Indianapolis Motor Speedway
06/07/64	Milwaukee, WI	Wisconsin State Fairgrounds
06/21/64	Langhorne, PA	Langhorne Speedway
07/19/64	Trenton, NJ	New Jersey State Fairgrounds
08/22/64	Springfield, IL	Illinois State Fairgrounds
08/23/64	Milwaukee, WI	Wisconsin State Fairgrounds
09/07/64	DuQuoin, IL	DuQuoin State Fairgrounds
09/26/64	Indianapolis, IN	Indiana State Fairgrounds

#relieved Bobby Unser for 15th place in the #8D Gordon VanLiew machine.

10/25/64	Sacramento, CA	California State Fairgrounds
11/22/64	Phoenix, AZ	Phoenix International Raceway

03/28/65	Phoenix, AZ	Phoenix International Raceway
04/25/65	Trenton, NJ	New Jersey State Fairgrounds

#Race scheduled for 100 laps, halted by rain after 87.

05/31/65	Indianapolis, IN	Indianapolis Motor Speedway
06/07/65	Milwaukee, WI	Wisconsin State Fairgrounds
07/25/65	Indianapolis, IN	Indianapolis Raceway Park
08/01/65	Atlanta, GA	Atlanta International Raceway

Q	F	OWNER & CAR #	TYPE TRACK	DISTANCE
18	15	#17 Fred Sclavi	1 Dirt	100 Laps
22	14	#19	1 Paved	200 Laps
17	7	#15 Ollie Prather	1 Dirt	100 Laps
11	11	#15 Ollie Prather	1 Dirt	51 Laps#
22	10	#27D George Walther	1 Paved	100 Laps
26	29	#37R Kostenuk-Tucker	2.5 Paved	200 Laps
19	20	#27R George Walther	1 Paved	100 Laps
5	7	#37D Ed Kostenuk	1 Dirt	100 Laps
17	16	#37D Ed Kostenuk	1 Paved	150 Laps
2	5	#46D Racing Associates	1 Dirt	100 Laps
9	7	#46D Racing Associates	1 Paved	200 Laps
6	10	#46D Racing Associates	1 Dirt	100 Laps
2	4	#46D Racing Associates	1 Dirt	100 Laps
18	6	#46D Racing Associates	1 Paved	200 Laps
2	17	#46D Racing Associates	1 Dirt	100 Laps
1	11	#46D Racing Associates	1 Dirt	100 Laps
9	21	#10D Racing Associates	1 Paved	100 Laps
15	27	#86R Racing Associates	2.5 Paved	200 Laps
14	22	#10D Racing Associates	1 Paved	100 Laps
1	12	#10D Racing Associates	1 Dirt	100 Laps
14	17	#10D Racing Associates	1 Paved	150 Laps
8	17	#10D Racing Associates	1 Dirt	100 Laps
12	5	#86R Racing Associates	1 Paved	200 Laps
6	7	#10D Racing Associates	1 Dirt	100 Laps
7	18#	#10D Racing Associates	1 Dirt	100 Laps
3	14	#10D Racing Associates	1 Dirt	100 Laps
15	23	#10RE Racing Associates	1 Paved	200 Laps
21	15	#24RE Racing Associates	1 Paved	150 Laps
10	11	#6D Walter Beletsky	1 Paved	87 Laps#
11	31	#25 Ebb Rose	2.5 Paved	200 Laps
17	15	#93 J. Frank Harrison	1 Paved	100 Laps
15	11	#2D Leader Card	80 Laps	
5	1	#2RE Leader Card	1.5 Paved	167 Laps

DATE	LOCATION	TRACK NAME
08/08/65	Langhorne, PA	Langhorne Speedway
08/14/65	Milwaukee, WI	Wisconsin State Fairgrounds
08/21/65	Springfield, IL	Illinois State Fairgrounds
08/22/65	Milwaukee, WI	Wisconsin State Fairgrounds
09/06/65	DuQuoin, IL	DuQuoin State Fairgrounds
09/18/65	Indianapolis, IN	Indiana State Fairgrounds
09/26/65	Trenton, NJ	New Jersey State Fairgrounds
10/24/65	Sacramento, CA	California State Fairgrounds
11/21/65	Phoenix, AZ	Phoenix International Raceway
03/20/66	Phoenix, AZ	Phoenix International Raceway
05/30/67	Indianapolis, IN	Indianapolis Motor Speedway
06/04/67	Milwaukee, WI	Wisconsin State Fairgrounds
06/18/67	Langhorne, PA	Langhorne Speedway
07/02/67	Mosport, Canada	Mosport Park
07/02/67	Mosport, Canada	Mosport Park

#Race scheduled for 40 laps, halted after 6 due to rain.

07/22/67	Indianapolis, IN	Indianapolis Raceway Park
07/30/67	Langhorne, PA	Langhorne Speedway
08/12/67	St. Jovite, Canada	Mt. Tremblant Circuit
08/19/67	Springfield, IL	Illinois State Fairgrounds
08/20/67	Milwaukee, WI	Wisconsin State Fairgrounds
09/04/67	DuQuoin, IL	DuQuoin State Fairgrounds
09/09/67	Indianapolis, IN	Indiana State Fairgrounds
10/01/67	Sacramento, CA	California State Fairgrounds
10/22/67	Hanford, CA	Hanford Motor Speedway
11/19/67	Phoenix, AZ	Phoenix International Raceway
11/26/67	Riverside, CA	Riverside International Raceway
03/17/68	Hanford, CA	Hanford Motor Speedway
03/31/68	Las Vegas, NV	Stardust International Raceway
04/07/68	Phoenix, AZ	Phoenix International Raceway
05/30/68	Indianapolis, IN	Indianapolis Motor Speedway
06/09/68	Milwaukee, WI	Wisconsin State Fairgrounds
07/07/68	Castle Rock, CO	Continental Divide Raceway
07/20/68	Indianapolis, IN	Indianapolis Raceway Park
07/20/68	Indianapolis, IN	Indianapolis Raceway Park

#2nd Race.

07/28/68	Langhorne, PA	Langhorne Speedway
08/03/68	St. Jovite, Canada	Mt. Tremblant Circuit

Q	F	OWNER & CAR #	TYPE TRACK	DISTANCE
11	8	#2D Leader Card	1 Paved	150 Laps
11	13	#2RE Leader Card	1 Paved	150 Laps
2	4	#2D Leader Card	1 Dirt	100 Laps
13	24	#2RE Leader Card	1 Paved	200 Laps
4	5	#2D Leader Card	1 Dirt	100 Laps
18	6	#2D Leader Card	1 Dirt	100 Laps
9	16	#2RE Leader Card	1 Paved	200 Laps
11	6	#2D Leader Card	1 Dirt	100 Laps
7	22	#2RE Leader Card	1 Paved	200 Laps
15	18	#12 Leader Card	1 Paved	150 Laps
19	25	#45 Weinberger/Wilsek	2.5 Paved	200 Laps
15	12	#47 Weinberger/Wilsek	1 Paved	150 Laps
22	10	#47 Weinberger/Wilsek	1 Paved	100 Laps
11	14	#45 Weinberger/Wilsek	Paved	40 Laps
14	14	#45 Weinberger/Wilsek	Paved	6 Laps#
14	13	#45 Weinberger/Wilsek	Paved	80 Laps
4	20	#45 Weinberger/Wilsek	1 Paved	150 Laps
21	15	#47RE Weinberger/Wilsek	2.6 Paved RC	36 Laps
12	16	#45D Weinberger/Wilsek	1 Dirt	100 Laps
15	25	#47RE Weinberger/Wilsek	1 Paved	200 Laps
13	11	#45D Weinberger/Wilsek	1 Dirt	100 Laps
17	16	#45D Weinberger/Wilsek	1 Dirt	100 Laps
11	5	#45D Weinberger/Wilsek	1 Dirt	100 Laps
14	23	#45RE Weinberger/Wilsek	1.5 Paved	134 Laps
15	22	#47RE Weinberger/Wilsek	1 Paved	200 Laps
20	8	#45RE Weinberger/Wilsek	2.6 Paved RC	116 Laps
14	20	#96RE Eisert Racing	1.5 Paved	134 Laps
10	11	#96RE Eisert Racing	3 Paved RC	50 Laps
10	17	#96RE Eisert Racing	1 Paved	150 Laps
21	18	#18RE Alan Green	2.5 Paved	200 Laps
10	4	#18RE Alan Green	1 Paved	150 Laps
14	20	#96RE Eisert Racing	2.66 Paved RC	57 Laps
15	24	#22RE Michner Petroleum	2.5 Paved RC	40 Laps
	20#	#22RE Michner Petroleum	2.5 Paved RC	40 Laps
8	25	#16RRE Don Gerhardt	1 Paved	100 Laps
10	5	#22RE Michner Petroleum	2.6 Paved RC	38 Laps

DATE	LOCATION	TRACK NAME
08/03/68	St. Jovite, Canada	Mt. Tremblant Circuit
#2nd Race.		
08/18/68	Milwaukee, WI	Wisconsin State Fairgrounds
09/22/68	Trenton, NJ	New Jersey State Fairgrounds
10/13/68	Brooklyn, MI	Michigan International Raceway
11/03/68	Hanford, CA	Hanford Motor Speedway
11/17/68	Phoenix, AZ	Phoenix International Raceway
12/01/68	Riverside, CA	Riverside International Raceway
03/30/69	Phoenix, AZ	Phoenix International Raceway
04/13/69	Hanford, CA	Hanford Motor Speedway
05/30/69	Indianapolis, IN	Indianapolis Motor Speedway
06/8/69	Milwaukee, WI	Wisconsin State Fairgrounds
06/22/69	Langhorne, PA	Langhorne Speedway
07/06/69	Castle Rock, CO	Continental Divide Raceway
07/19/69	Trenton, NJ	New Jersey State Fairgrounds
07/27/69	Indianapolis, IN	Indianapolis Raceway Park
08/17/69	Milwaukee, WI	Wisconsin State Fairgrounds
08/24/69	Dover, DE	Dover Downs
09/01/69	DuQuoin, IL	DuQuoin State Fairgrounds
09/06/69	Indianapolis, IN	Indiana State Fairgrounds
09/14/69	Brainerd, MN	Donnybrooke Raceway
09/21/69	Trenton, NJ	New Jersey State Fairgrounds
10/29/69	Kent, WA	Seattle International Raceway
11/16/69	Phoenix, AZ	Phoenix International Raceway
12/07/69	Riverside, CA	Riverside International Raceway
04/04/70	Sears Point, CA	Sears Point International Raceway
04/25/70	Trenton, NJ	New Jersey State Fairgrounds
05/30/70	Indianapolis, IN	Indianapolis Motor Speedway
06/07/70	Milwaukee, WI	Wisconsin State Fairgrounds
06/14/70	Langhorne, PA	Langhorne Speedway
07/04/70	Brooklyn, MI	Michigan International Speedway
07/26/70	Indianapolis, IN	Indianapolis Raceway Park
08/22/70	Springfield, IL	Illinois State Fairgrounds
08/23/70	Milwaukee, WI	Wisconsin State Fairgrounds
09/06/70	Ontario, CA	Ontario Motor Speedway
09/07/70	DuQuoin, IL	DuQuoin State Fairgrounds
09/12/70	Indianapolis, IN	Indiana State Fairgrounds
09/19/70	Sedalia, MO	Missouri State Fairgrounds
10/03/70	Trenton, NJ	New Jersey State Fairgrounds

#Race scheduled for 200 laps, halted by rain at 176 laps.

Q	F	OWNER & CAR #	TYPE TRACK	DISTANCE
	5#	#22RE Michner Petroleum	2.6 Paved RC	38 Laps
13	11	#22RE Michner Petroleum	1 Paved	200 Laps
17	5	#22RE Michner Petroleum	1 Paved	200 Laps
5	16	#22RE Michner Petroleum	2 Paved	125 Laps
11	25	#22RE Michner Petroleum	1.5 Paved	167 Laps
22	17	#22RE Michner Petroleum	1 Paved	200 Laps
17	6	#22RE Michner Petroleum	2.6 Paved RC	116 Laps
12	24	#36 Michner Petroleum	1 Paved	150 Laps
12	4	#36 Michner Petroleum	1.5 Paved	134 Laps
17	29	#36 Michner Petroleum	2.5 Paved	200 Laps
7	5	#36 Michner Petroleum	1 Paved	150 Laps
8	15	#36 Michner Petroleum	1 Paved	150 Laps
12	11	#36 Michner Petroleum	2.66 Paved RC	57 Laps
14	22	#36 Michner Petroleum	1 Paved	134 Laps
30	-	#36 Michner Petroleum	2.5 Paved RC	40 Laps
31	-	#36 Michner Petroleum	1 Paved	200 Laps
7	7	#91 Leader Cards	1 Paved	200 Laps
12	14	#32D Tim Delrose	1 Dirt	100 Laps
21	-	#32D Tim Delrose	1 Dirt	100 Laps
12	11	#36 Michner Petroleum	3 Paved RC	34 Laps
19	12	#36 Michner Petroleum	1.5 Paved	200 Laps
6	19	#36 Michner Petroleum	2.25 Paved RC	45 Laps
18	4	#36 Michner Petroleum	1 Paved	200 Laps
11	5	#36 Michner Petroleum	2.6 Paved RC	120 Laps
9	5	#18 Michner Petroleum	2.5 Paved RC	60 Laps
9	20	#18 Michner Petroleum	1.5 Paved	134 Laps
2	18	#18 Michner Petroleum	2.5 Laps	200 Laps
6	14	#18 Michner Petroleum	1 Paved	150 Laps
-	-	#18 Michner Petroleum	1 Paved	150 Laps
6	3	#18 Michner Petroleum	2 Paved	100 Laps
12	17	#18 Michner Petroleum	2.5 Paved RC	60 Laps
2	11	#18 Michner Petroleum	1 Dirt	100 Laps
8	21	#18 Michner Petroleum	1 Paved	200 Laps
3	31	#18 Michner Petroleum	2.5 Paved	200 Laps
7	11	#18 Michner Petroleum	1 Dirt	100 Laps
24	-	#18 Michner Petroleum	1 Dirt	100 Laps
9	12	#18 Michner Petroleum	1 Dirt	100 Laps
14	4	#18 Michner Petroleum	1.5 Paved	176 Laps#

DATE	LOCATION	TRACK NAME
10/04/70	Sacramento, CA	California State Fairgrounds
11/21/70	Phoenix, AZ	Phoenix International Raceway
02/26/71	Rafaela, Argentina	
02/26/71 *#2nd Race.*	Rafaela, Argentina	
03/27/71	Phoenix, AZ	Phoenix International Raceway
04/25/71	Trenton, NJ	New Jersey State Fairgrounds
05/29/71	Indianapolis, IN	Indianapolis Motor Speedway
06/06/71	Milwaukee, WI	Wisconsin State Fairgrounds
07/03/71	Pocono, PA	Pocono International Raceway
07/18/71	Brooklyn, MI	Michigan International Speedway
09/05/71	Ontario, CA	Ontario Motor Speedway
10/03/71	Trenton, NJ	New Jersey State Fairgrounds
10/23/71	Phoenix, AZ	Phoenix International Raceway
03/18/72	Phoenix, AZ	Phoenix International Raceway
04/23/72	Trenton, NJ	New Jersey State Fairgrounds
05/27/72	Indianapolis, IN	Indianapolis Motor Speedway
06/04/72	Milwaukee, WI	Wisconsin State Fairgrounds
07/15/72	Brooklyn, MI	Michigan International Speedway
07/29/72	Pocono, PA	Pocono International Raceway
08/13/72	Milwaukee, WI	Wisconsin State Fairgrounds
09/03/72	Ontario, CA	Ontario Motor Speedway
09/24/72	Trenton, NJ	New Jersey State Fairgrounds
11/04/72	Phoenix, AZ	Phoenix International Raceway
04/07/73	College Station, TX	Texas World Speedway
04/15/73	Trenton, NJ	New Jersey State Fairgrounds
05/30/73	Indianapolis, IN	Indianapolis Motor Speedway
06/10/73	Milwaukee, WI	Wisconsin State Fairgrounds
07/01/73	Pocono, PA	Pocono International Raceway
07/15/73	Brooklyn, MI	Michigan International Speedway
08/12/73	Milwaukee, WI	Wisconsin State Fairgrounds
08/26/73	Ontario, CA	Ontario Motor Speedway
09/02/73	Ontario, CA	Ontario Motor Speedway
09/16/73	Brooklyn, MI	Michigan International Speedway
09/16/73	Brooklyn, MI	Michigan International Speedway
09/23/73	Trenton, NJ	New Jersey State Fairgrounds
10/06/73	College Station, TX	Texas World Speedway
11/03/73	Phoenix, AZ	Phoenix International Raceway
03/03/74	Ontario, CA	Ontario Motor Speedway

Q	F	OWNER & CAR #	TYPE TRACK	DISTANCE
8	13	#18 Michner Petroleum	1 Dirt	100 Laps
6	6	#18 Michner Petroleum	1 Paved	150 Laps
13	7	#17 Vollstedt Ent.	2.874 Paved RC	53 Laps
	20#	#17 Vollstedt Ent.	2.874 Paved RC	53 Laps
2	21	#18 Patrick Petroleum	1 Paved	150 Laps
10	17	#18 Patrick Petroleum	1.5 Paved	134 Laps
24	18	#18 Patrick Petroleum	2.5 Paved	200 Laps
11	6	#18 Patrick Petroleum	1 Paved	150 Laps
12	7	#18 Patrick Petroleum	2.5 Paved	200 Laps
8	10	#18 Patrick Petroleum	2 Paved	100 Laps
5	26	#18 Patrick Petroleum	2.5 Paved	200 Laps
-	-	#18 Patrick Petroleum	1.5 Paved	200 Laps
4	22	#18 Patrick Petroleum	1 Paved	150 Laps
3	13	#18 Patrick-Michner	1 Paved	150 Laps
-	-	#18 Patrick-Michner	1.5 Paved	134 Laps
8	27	#18 Patrick-Michner	2.5 Paved	200 Laps
10	21	#16 Don Gerhardt	1 Paved	150 Laps
15	16	#16 Don Gerhardt	2 Paved	100 Laps
13	2	#16 Don Gerhardt	2.5 Paved	200 Laps
10	3	#16 Don Gerhardt	1 Paved	200 Laps
24	10	#16 Don Gerhardt	2.5 Paved	200 Laps
15	6	#16 Don Gerhardt	1.5 Paved	200 Laps
7	5	#16 Don Gerhardt	1 Paved	150 Laps
6	4	#7 Bruce McLaren Racing	2 Paved	100 Laps
5	15	#7 Bruce McLaren Racing	1.5 Paved	100 Laps
1	9	#7 Bruce McLaren Racing	2.5 Paved	200 Laps
8	5	#7 Bruce McLaren Racing	1 Paved	150 Laps
7	5	#7 Bruce McLaren Racing	2.5 Paved	200 Laps
3	2	#7 Bruce McLaren Racing	2 Paved	100 Laps
4	18	#7 Bruce McLaren Racing	1 Paved	200 Laps
4	1	#7 Bruce McLaren Racing	2.5 Paved	40 Laps
4	31	#7 Bruce McLaren Racing	2.5 Paved	200 Laps
2	3	#7 Bruce McLaren Racing	2 Paved	63 Laps
2	1	#7 Bruce McLaren Racing	2 Paved	63 Laps
3	4	#7 Bruce McLaren Racing	1.5 Paved	134 Laps
3	2	#7 Bruce McLaren Racing	2 Paved	100 Laps
-	-	#7 Bruce McLaren Racing	1 Paved	150 Laps
2	1	#3 McLaren Cars	2.5 Paved	40 Laps

DATE	LOCATION	TRACK NAME
03/10/74	Ontario, CA	Ontario Motor Speedway
03/17/74	Phoenix, AZ	Phoenix International Raceway
04/07/74	Trenton, NJ	New Jersey State Fairgrounds
05/26/74	Indianapolis, IN	Indianapolis Motor Speedway
06/09/74	Milwaukee, WI	Wisconsin State Fairgrounds
06/30/74	Pocono, PA	Pocono International Raceway
07/21/74	Brooklyn, MI	Michigan International Speedway
08/11/74	Milwaukee, WI	Wisconsin State Fairgrounds
09/15/74	Brooklyn, MI	Michigan International Speedway
09/22/74	Trenton, NJ	New Jersey State Fairgrounds
09/22/74	Trenton, NJ	New Jersey State Fairgrounds
11/02/74	Phoenix, AZ	Phoenix International Raceway

DATE	LOCATION	TRACK NAME
03/02/75	Ontario, CA	Ontario Motor Speedway
03/09/75	Ontario, CA	Ontario Motor Speedway
03/16/75	Phoenix, AZ	Phoenix International Raceway
04/06/75	Trenton, NJ	New Jersey State Fairgrounds
05/25/75	Indianapolis, IN	Indianapolis Motor Speedway

#Race scheduled for 200 laps, halted after 174 by rain.

DATE	LOCATION	TRACK NAME
06/08/75	Milwaukee, WI	Wisconsin State Fairgrounds
06/29/75	Pocono, PA	Pocono International Raceway

#Race scheduled for 200 laps, halted after 170 by rain.

DATE	LOCATION	TRACK NAME
07/20/75	Brooklyn, MI	Michigan International Speedway
08/17/75	Milwaukee, WI	Wisconsin State Fairgrounds
09/13/75	Brooklyn, MI	Michigan International Speedway
09/21/75	Trenton, NJ	New Jersey State Fairgrounds
11/09/75	Phoenix, AZ	Phoenix International Raceway

DATE	LOCATION	TRACK NAME
03/14/76	Phoenix, AZ	Phoenix International Raceway
05/02/76	Trenton, NJ	New Jersey State Fairgrounds
05/30/76	Indianapolis, IN	Indianapolis Motor Speedway

#Race scheduled for 200 laps but halted after 102 laps due to rain.

DATE	LOCATION	TRACK NAME
06/13/76	Milwaukee, WI	Wisconsin State Fairgrounds
06/27/76	Pocono, PA	Pocono International Raceway
07/18/76	Brooklyn, MI	Michigan International Speedway
08/01/76	College Station, TX	Texas World Speedway
08/15/76	Trenton, NJ	New Jersey State Fairgrounds

#Race scheduled for 134 laps but halted after 117 laps by rain.

DATE	LOCATION	TRACK NAME
08/22/76	Milwaukee, WI	Wisconsin State Fairgrounds
09/05/76	Ontario, CA	Ontario Motor Speedway
09/18/76	Brooklyn, MI	Michigan International Speedway

Q	F	OWNER & CAR #	TYPE TRACK	DISTANCE
2	27	#3 McLaren Cars	2.5 Paved	200 Laps
2	7	#3 McLaren Cars	1 Paved	150 Laps
8	6	#3 McLaren Cars	1.5 Paved	134 Laps
25	1	#3 McLaren Cars	2.5 Paved	200 Laps
2	1	#3 McLaren Cars	1 Paved	150 Laps
5	1	#3 McLaren Cars	2.5 Paved	200 Laps
4	4	#3 McLaren Cars	2 Paved	100 Laps
5	5	#3 McLaren Cars	1 Paved	200 Laps
2	9	#3 McLaren Cars	2 Paved	125 Laps
5	4	#3 McLaren Cars	1.5 Paved	100 Laps
4	7	#3 McLaren Cars	1.5 Paved	100 Laps
1	7	#3 McLaren Cars	1 Paved	150 Laps
4	2	#2 McLaren Racing	2.5 Paved	40 Laps
5	17	#2 McLaren Racing	2.5 Paved	200 Laps
2	1	#2 McLaren Racing	1 Paved	150 Laps
7	2	#2 McLaren Racing	1.5 Paved	134 Laps
7	2	#2 McLaren Racing	2.5 Paved	174 Laps#
4	3	#2 McLaren Racing	1 Paved	150 Laps
5	6	#2 McLaren Racing	2.5 Paved	170 Laps#
7	6	#2 McLaren Racing	2 Paved	100 Laps
1	13	#2 McLaren Racing	1 Paved	200 Laps
3	2	#2 McLaren Racing	2 Paved	75 Laps
2	3	#2 McLaren Racing	1.5 Paved	100 Laps
2	11	#2 McLaren Racing	1 Paved	150 Laps
6	18	#2 McLaren Racing	1 Paved	150 Laps
2	1	#2 McLaren Racing	1.5 Paved	134 Laps
1	1	#2 McLaren Racing	2.5 Paved	102 Laps#
5	9	#2 McLaren Racing	1 Paved	150 Laps
15	4	#2 McLaren Racing	2.5 Paved	200 Laps
5	2	#2 McLaren Racing	2 Paved	100 Laps
5	3	#2 McLaren Racing	2 Paved	75 Laps
5	7	#2 McLaren Racing	1.5 Paved	117 Laps#
1	3	#2 McLaren Racing	1 Paved	200 Laps
7	2	#2 McLaren Racing	2.5 Paved	200 Laps
8	11	#2 McLaren Racing	2 Paved	75 Laps

DATE	LOCATION	TRACK NAME
10/31/76	College Station, TX	Texas World Speedway
11/07/76	Phoenix, AZ	Phoenix International Raceway
03/06/77	Ontario, CA	Ontario Motor Speedway
03/27/77	Phoenix, AZ	Phoenix International Raceway
04/02/77	College Station, TX	Texas World Speedway
04/30/77	Trenton, NJ	New Jersey State Fairgrounds
05/29/77	Indianapolis, IN	Indianapolis Motor Speedway
06/12/77	Milwaukee, WI	Wisconsin State Fairgrounds
06/26/77	Pocono, PA	Pocono International Raceway
07/03/77	Mosport, Canada	Mosport Park
07/17/77	Brooklyn, MI	Michigan International Speedway
07/31/77	College Station, TX	Texas World Speedway
08/21/77	Milwaukee, WI	Wisconsin State Fairgrounds
09/04/77	Ontario, CA	Ontario Motor Speedway
09/17/77	Brooklyn, MI	Michigan International Speedway
10/29/77	Phoenix, AZ	Phoenix International Raceway
03/18/78	Phoenix, AZ	Phoenix International Raceway
03/26/78	Ontario, CA	Ontario Motor Speedway
04/15/78	College Station, TX	Texas World Speedway
04/23/78	Trenton, NJ	New Jersey State Fairgrounds
05/28/78	Indianapolis, IN	Indianapolis Motor Speedway
06/11/78	Mosport, Canada	Mosport Park
06/18/78	Milwaukee, WI	Wisconsin State Fairgrounds
06/25/78	Pocono, PA	Pocono International Raceway
07/16/78	Brooklyn, MI	Michigan International Speedway
07/23/78	Atlanta, GA	Atlanta International Raceway
08/06/78	College Station, TX	Texas World Speedway
08/20/78	Milwaukee, WI	Wisconsin State Fairgrounds
09/03/78	Ontario, CA	Ontario Motor Speedway
09/16/78	Brooklyn, MI	Michigan International Speedway
09/23/78	Trenton, NJ	New Jersey State Fairgrounds
10/01/78	Silverstone, England	Silverstone Circuit
10/07/78	Brands Hatch, England	Brands Hatch Circuit
10/28/78	Phoenix, AZ	Phoenix International Raceway
05/27/79	Indianapolis, IN	Indianapolis Motor Speedway
4/13/80	Ontario, CA	Ontario Motor Speedway
5/25/80	Indianapolis, IN	Indianapolis Motor Speedway
6/08/80	Milwaukee, WI	Wisconsin State Fairgrounds
6/22/80	Pocono, PA	Pocono International Raceway

Q	F	OWNER & CAR #	TYPE TRACK	DISTANCE
6	1	#2 McLaren Racing	2 Paved	100 Laps
6	16	#2 McLaren Racing	1 Paved	150 Laps
1	25	#2 Team McLaren	2.5 Paved	80 Laps
1	1	#2 Team McLaren	1 Paved	150 Laps
1	4	#2 Team McLaren	2 Paved	100 Laps
1	8	#2 Team McLaren	1.5 Paved	134 Laps
17	33	#2 Team McLaren	2.5 Paved	200 Laps
2	1	#2 Team McLaren	1 Paved	150 Laps
2	5	#2 Team McLaren	2.5 Paved	200 Laps
2	9	#2 Team McLaren	2.459 Paved RC	75 Laps
2	3	#2 Team McLaren	2 Paved	100 Laps
2	1	#2 Team McLaren	2 Paved	100 Laps
3	1	#2 Team McLaren	1 Paved	200 Laps
1	24	#2 Team McLaren	2.5 Paved	200 Laps
4	2	#2 Team McLaren	2 Paved	75 Laps
3	22	#2 Team McLaren	1 Paved	150 Laps
5	16	#4 Team McLaren	1 Paved	150 Laps
3	13	#4 Team McLaren	2.5 Paved	80 Laps
5	19	#4 Team McLaren	2 Paved	100 Laps
11	10	#4 Team McLaren	1.5 Paved	134 Laps
4	13	#4 Team McLaren	2.5 Paved	200 Laps
6	8	#4 Team McLaren	2.459 Paved RC	76 Laps
5	2	#4 Team McLaren	1 Paved	150 Laps
3	2	#4 Team McLaren	2.5 Paved	200 Laps
2	1	#4 Team McLaren	2 Paved	100 Laps
5	2	#4 Team McLaren	1.5 Paved	100 Laps
4	2	#4 Team McLaren	2 Paved	100 Laps
5	8	#4 Team McLaren	1 Paved	200 Laps
2	11	#4 Team McLaren	2.5 Paved	200 Laps
1	13	#4 Team McLaren	2 Paved	75 Laps
5	11	#4 Team McLaren	1.5 Paved	100 Laps
6	5	#4 Team McLaren	2.932 Paved RC	38 Laps
7	3	#4 Team McLaren	1.2 Paved RC	100 Laps
3	1	#4 Team McLaren	1 Paved	150 Laps
8	18	#4 Team McLaren	2.5 Paved	200 Laps
1	1	#4 Chaparral Racing	2.5 Paved	80 Laps
1	1	#4 Chaparral Racing	2.5 Paved	200 Laps
2	2	#4 Chaparral Racing	1 Paved	150 Laps
5	2	#4 Chaparral Racing	2.5 Paved	200 Laps

DATE	LOCATION	TRACK NAME
07/13/80	Lexington, OH	Mid-Ohio Sports Car Course
05/24/81	Indianapolis, IN	Indianapolis Motor Speedway
05/30/82	Indianapolis, IN	Indianapolis Motor Speedway
05/29/83	Indianapolis, IN	Indianapolis Motor Speedway
05/27/84	Indianapolis, IN	Indianapolis Motor Speedway
05/26/85	Indianapolis, IN	Indianapolis Motor Speedway
05/31/86	Indianapolis, IN	Indianapolis Motor Speedway
05/24/87	Indianapolis, IN	Indianapolis Motor Speedway
05/29/88	Indianapolis, IN	Indianapolis Motor Speedway
05/28/89	Indianapolis, IN	Indianapolis Motor Speedway

#Also drove #14T A. J. Foyt Enterprises machine but blew engine on first qualifying lap.

05/27/90	Indianapolis, IN	Indianapolis Motor Speedway
05/2492	Indianapolis, IN	Indianapolis Motor Speedway
07/9/92	New Bremen, OH	New Bremen Speedway

SPECIAL EVENTS (Championship Car):

04/27/75	Trenton, NJ	Trenton International Speedway

USAC SPRINT CARS

06/25/61	New Bremen, OH	New Bremen Speedway
03/25/62	Reading, PA	Reading Fairgrounds
04/22/62	Rossburg, OH	Eldora Speedway
04/29/62	Salem, IN	Salem Speedway
05/06/62	New Bremen, OH	New Bremen Speedway
05/27/62	Indianapolis, IN	Indianapolis Raceway Park
06/03/62	New Bremen, OH	New Bremen Speedway
09/16/62	Reading, PA	Reading Fairgrounds
09/30/62	Salem, IN	Salem Speedway
10/14/62	Williams Grove, PA	Williams Grove Speedway
11/10/62	Gardena, CA	Ascot Park
04/7/63	Langhorne, PA	Langhorne Speedway

Q	F	OWNER & CAR #	TYPE TRACK	DISTANCE
4	1	#4 Chaparral Racing	2.4 Paved RC	65 Laps
5	32	#1 Chaparral Racing	2.5 Paved	200 Laps
12	8	#5 Chaparral Racing	2.5 Paved	200 Laps
-	-	#40 STP-Patrick	2.5 Paved	200 Laps
30	22	#84 A. J. Foyt Ent.	2.5 Paved	200 Laps
30	6	#21 Alex Morales	2.5 Paved	200 Laps
12	8	#21 Alex Morales	2.5 Paved	200 Laps
8	11	#21 Alex Morales	2.5 Paved	200 Laps
30	22	#17 King-Protofab	2.5 Paved	200 Laps
TS	-#	#98 Team Menard	2.5 Paved	200 Laps
TS	-	#17 Stoops Racing	2.5 Paved	200 Laps
TS	-	#17 Walker Motorsports	2.5 Paved	200 Laps
26	15	#1 Willie Davis	1/2 Dirt	40 Laps
2	1	#2 Team McLaren, Ltd.	3/4 Paved	100 Laps
-	-	#42 Merle Heath	1/2 Dirt	30 Laps
8	11	#63 Dave Beatson	1/2 Dirt	30 Laps
9	5	#63 Dave Beatson	1/2 Dirt	30 Laps
17	-	#63 Dave Beatson	1/2 Paved	30 Laps
10	6	#63 Dave Beatson	1/2 Dirt	30 Laps
15	8	#63 Dave Beatson	5/8 Paved	50 Laps
10	10	#63 Dave Beatson	1/2 Dirt	30 Laps
19	-	#52 Clem Tebow	1/2 Dirt	100 Laps
13	6	#10 Walt Flynn	1/2 Paved	100 Laps
9	7	#10 Walt Flynn	1/2 Dirt	30 Laps
23	-	#70 Harry Miller	1/2 Dirt	30 Laps
14	9	#10 Walt Flynn	1 Dirt	50 Laps

DATE	LOCATION	TRACK NAME
04/07/63	Langhorne, PA	Langhorne Speedway
04/28/63	New Bremen, OH	New Bremen Speedway
06/30/63	Indianapolis, IN	Indianapolis Raceway Park
08/31/63	DuQuoin, IL	DuQuoin State Fairgrounds
09/29/63	Salem, IN	Salem Speedway
01/26/64	Phoenix, AZ	Arizona State Fairgrounds
01/26/64	Phoenix, AZ	Arizona State Fairgrounds
03/29/64	Reading, PA	Reading Fairgrounds
04/05/64	Rossburg, OH	Eldora Speedway
06/14/64	Terre Haute, IN	Terre Haute Action Track
06/28/64	Indianapolis, IN	Indianapolis Raceway Park
07/18/64	Williams Grove, PA	Williams Grove Speedway
08/02/64	Salem, IN	Salem Speedway
08/09/64	Terre Haute, IN	Terre Haute Action Track
08/15/64	Allentown, PA	Allentown Fairgrounds
08/29/64	St. Paul, MN	Minnesota State Fairgrounds
08/30/64	St. Paul, MN	Minnesota State Fairgrounds
10/04/64	Salem, IN	Salem Speedway
10/31/64	Gardena, CA	Ascot Park
06/13/65	Terre Haute, IN	Terre Haute Action Track
06/19/65	Reading, PA	Reading Fairgrounds
07/03/65	Rossburg, OH	Eldora Speedway
07/04/65	Salem, IN	Salem Speedway
07/11/65	Winchester, IN	Winchester Speedway
07/17/65	Reading, PA	Reading Fairgrounds
07/23/65	Kansas City, KS	Lakeside Speedway
08/07/65	Allentown, PA	Allentown Fairgrounds
08/11/65	Allentown, PA	Allentown Fairgrounds
08/15/65	Terre Haute, IN	Terre Haute Action Track
08/28/65	St. Paul, MN	Minnesota State Fairgrounds
08/29/65	St. Paul, MN	Minnesota State Fairgrounds
09/05/65	New Bremen, OH	New Bremen Speedway
09/19/65	Fort Wayne, IN	Baer Field Raceway
09/25/65	Reading, PA	Reading Fairgrounds
10/03/65	Salem, IN	Salem Speedway
10/10/65	Winchester, IN	Winchester Speedway
10/17/65	Rossburg, OH	Eldora Speedway
11/06/65	Gardena, CA	Ascot Park
11/13/65	Gardena, CA	Ascot Park

Q	F	OWNER & CAR #	TYPE TRACK	DISTANCE
9	9	#10 Walt Flynn	1 Dirt	40 Laps
15	7	#10 Walt Flynn	1/2 Dirt	30 Laps
9	6	#1 Harlan Fike	5/8 Paved	50 Laps
5	16	#83 Rufus Gray	1 Dirt	25 Laps
13	14	#83 Rufus Gray	1/2 Paved	100 Laps
5	16	#6 Jack Colvin	1 Dirt	50 Laps
16	4	#6 Jack Colvin	1 Dirt	50 Laps
3	8	#6 Jack Colvin	1/2 Dirt	30 Laps
2	1	#6 Jack Colvin	1/2 Dirt	30 Laps
8	2	#6 Jack Colvin	1/2 Dirt	30 Laps
3	6	#6 Jack Colvin	5/8 Paved	100 Laps
2	11	#6 Jack Colvin	1/2 Dirt	30 Laps
5	6	#6 Jack Colvin	1/2 Paved	30 Laps
1	2	#6 Jack Colvin	1/2 Dirt	30 Laps
15	8	#6 Jack Colvin	1/2 Dirt	30 Laps
6	11	#6 Jack Colvin	1/2 Paved	30 Laps
4	4	#11 Babe Stapp	1/2 Paved	30 Laps
8	5	#11 Babe Stapp	1/2 Paved	100 Laps
4	5	#11 Babe Stapp	1/2 Dirt	30 Laps
6	1	#4 Steve Stapp	1/2 Dirt	30 Laps
1	4	#4 Steve Stapp	1/2 Dirt	30 Laps
6	13	#9 Wally Meskowski	1/2 Dirt	30 Laps
3	3	#9 Wally Meskowski	1/2 Paved	30 Laps
2	1	#9 Wally Meskowski	1/2 Paved	30 Laps
4	1	#9 Wally Meskowski	1/2 Dirt	30 Laps
2	14	#9 Wally Meskowski	1/2 Dirt	30 Laps
18	7	#9 Wally Meskowski	1/2 Dirt	30 Laps
13	3	#9 Wally Meskowski	1/2 Dirt	30 Laps
1	1	#9 Wally Meskowski	1/2 Dirt	30 Laps
1	1	#9 Wally Meskowski	1/2 Paved	30 Laps
2	1	#9 Wally Meskowski	1/2 Paved	30 Laps
1	3	#9 Wally Meskowski	1/2 Dirt	50 Laps
2	3	#9 Wally Meskowski	1/2 Paved	30 Laps
5	3	#9 Wally Meskowski	1/2 Dirt	30 Laps
4	8	#9 Wally Meskowski	1/2 Paved	100 Laps
3	1	#9 Wally Meskowski	1/2 Paved	100 Laps
1	2	#9 Wally Meskowski	1/2 Dirt	30 Laps
9	3	#9 Wally Meskowski	1/2 Dirt	30 Laps
13	14	#9 Wally Meskowski	1/2 Dirt	30 Laps

DATE	LOCATION	TRACK NAME
03/27/66	Reading, PA	Reading Fairgrounds
04/03/66	Rossburg, OH	Eldora Speedway
06/11/67	Terre Haute, IN	Terre Haute Action Track
06/24/67	Granite City, IL	Tri-City Speedway
06/25/67	New Bremen, OH	New Bremen Speedway
07/02/67	Rossburg, OH	Eldora Speedway
07/04/67	Salem, IN	Salem Speedway
07/07/67	Kansas City, KS	Lakeside Speedway
07/08/67	Tulsa, OK	Tulsa Fairgrounds
08/13/67	Terre Haute, IN	Terre Haute Action Track
08/27/67	New Bremen, OH	New Bremen Speedway
08/27/67	New Bremen, OH	New Bremen Speedway

#Second feature.

09/03/67	Dayton, OH	Dayton Speedway
09/17/67	Winchester, IN	Winchester Speedway
10/15/67	Dayton, OH	Dayton Speedway
10/15/67	Dayton, OH	Dayton Speedway

#Second feature.

11/05/67	Altamont, CA	Altamont Speedway
01/14/68	Irwindale, CA	Speedway 605
07/14/68	Oswego, NY	Oswego Speedway
07/14/68	Oswego, NY	Oswego Speedway

#Second feature.

07/20/68	Rossburg, OH	Eldora Speedway
07/26/68	Stafford Springs, CT	Stafford Springs Speedway
07/27/68	Reading, PA	Reading Fairgrounds

#Car qualified by Sonny Ates.

08/11/68	Terre Haute, IN	Terre Haute Action Track

#Larry Dickson drove car in feature and WON.

08/19/68	Granite City, IL	
08/24/68	Hamburg, NY	Erie County Fairgrounds
08/25/68	New Bremen, OH	New Bremen Speedway
09/01/68	Dayton, OH	Dayton Speedway
09/01/68	Dayton, OH	Dayton Speedway

#Did not start 2nd feature.

09/08/68	Terre Haute, IN	Terre Haute Action Track
09/15/68	Winchester, IN	Winchester Speedway
09/29/68	Rossburg, OH	Eldora Speedway

Q	F	OWNER & CAR #	TYPE TRACK	DISTANCE
19	-	#1 Wally Meskowski	1/2 Dirt	30 Laps
8	13	#1 Wally Meskowski	1/2 Dirt	30 Laps
18	-	#17 J. J. Smith	1/2 Dirt	30 Laps
4	-	#17 J. J. Smith	1/2 Dirt	30 Laps
12	-	#17 J. J. Smith	1/2 Dirt	30 Laps
25	16	#17 J. J. Smith	1/2 Dirt	30 Laps
7	9	#22 George Snider & Harold Murrell	1/2 Paved	30 Laps
11	14	#17 J. J. Smith	1/2 Dirt	30 Laps
22	-	#17 J. J. Smith	1/2 Dirt	30 Laps
12	6	#1 Mutt Anderson	1/2 Dirt	50 Laps
14	5	#1 Mutt Anderson	1/2 Dirt	50 Laps
-	17#	#1 Mutt Anderson	1/2 Dirt	50 Laps
21	-	#1 Mutt Anderson	1/2 Paved	30 Laps
11	16	#63 Clyde Gutzweiler	1/2 Paved	100 Laps
21	10	#99 Gene Besecker	1/2 Paved	33 Laps
-	16#	#99 Gene Besecker	1/2 Paved	33 Laps
1	14	#51x Don Peabody	30 Laps	
2	3	#51 Don Peabody	1/2 Paved	30 Laps
2	8	#27 Steve Stapp	5/8 Paved	50 Laps
-	11#	#27 Steve Stapp	5/8 Paved	50 Laps
16	9	#27 Steve Stapp	1/2 Dirt	30 Laps
5	10	#27 Steve Stapp	1/2 Paved	30 Laps
25#	15	#11 Walt Winterbotham	1/2 Dirt	50 Laps
14	-#	#27 Steve Stapp	1/2 Dirt	30 Laps
2	7	#27 Steve Stapp	1/2 Dirt	30 Laps
-	-	#3 Ken Lay	1/2 Dirt	30 Laps
18	-	#3 Ken Lay	1/2 Dirt	50 Laps
27	11	#15 Wally Meskowski	1/2 Paved	33 Laps
-	-#	#15 Wally Meskowski	1/2 Paved	33 Laps
9	7	#15 Wally Meskowski	1/2 Dirt	50 Laps
13	16	#15 Wally Meskowski	1/2 Paved	100 Laps
4	-	#15 Wally Meskowski	1/2 Dirt	30 Laps

DATE	LOCATION	TRACK NAME
10/26/68	Gardena, CA	Ascot Park
11/10/68	Clovis, CA	Clovis Speedway
06/29/69	New Bremen, OH	New Bremen Speedway
10/05/69	Salem, IN	Salem Speedway
10/26/69	Syracuse, NY	New York State Fairgrounds
10/26/69	Syracuse, NY	New York State Fairgrounds
#Second feature.		
08/09/70	Terre Haute, IN	Terre Haute Action Track
08/15/70	Rossburg, OH	Eldora Speedway
08/16/70	New Bremen, OH	New Bremen Speedway
09/13/70	Terre Haute, IN	Terre Haute Action Track
10/25/70	Salem, IN	Salem Speedway
06/12/71	Rossburg, OH	Eldora Speedway

SPECIAL EVENTS (Sprint):

DATE	LOCATION	TRACK NAME
10/20/74	Pocono, PA	Pocono International Raceway

Q	F	OWNER & CAR #	TYPE TRACK	DISTANCE
12	-	#28 Don Peabody	1/2 Dirt	30 Laps
4	-	#28 Don Peabody	1/2 Dirt	30 Laps
30	-	#22 George Snider	1/2 Paved	30 Laps
15	13	#47 Glen Niebel	1/2 Paved	30 Laps
11	4	#47 Glen Niebel	1 Dirt	50 Laps
-	9#	#47 Glen Niebel	1 Dirt	50 Laps
16	11	#15 Wally Meskowski	1/2 Dirt	40 Laps
1	-	#15 Wally Meskowski	1/2 Dirt	40 Laps
19	12	#15 Wally Meskowski	1/2 Paved	40 Laps
4	9	#15 Wally Meskowski	1/2 Dirt	40 Laps
2	4	#60 Niebel & Mead	1/2 Paved	50 Laps
1	16	#14 Willard Coil	1/2 Dirt	40 Laps

Q	F	OWNER & CAR #	TYPE TRACK	DISTANCE
12	12	#26 C & S Racing	3/4 Paved	50 Laps

CART CAREER SUMMARY

DATE	LOCATION OF TRACK	S	F
03/11/79	Phoenix, AZ	3	3
04/22/79	Atlanta, GA	1	1
04/22/79	Atlanta, GA	1	1
05/27/79	Indianapolis, IN	8	18
06/10/79	Trenton, NJ	5	15
06/10/79	Trenton, NJ	15	3
07/15/79	Brooklyn, MI	10	3
07/15/79	Brooklyn, MI	3	11
08/05/79	Watkins Glen, NY	7	15
08/19/79	Trenton, NJ	6	5
09/02/79	Ontario, CA	13	4
09/15/79	Brooklyn, MI	4	4
09/30/79	Atlanta, GA	5	11
10/20/79	Phoenix, AZ	6	6

Finished 4th in points—Led 13 times for 129 laps completing 2224.344 miles

04/13/80	Ontario, CA	1	1
05/25/80	Indianapolis, IN	1	1
06/08/80	Milwaukee, WI	2	2
06/22/80	Pocono, PA	5	2
07/13/80	Mid-Ohio, OH	4	1
07/20/80	Brooklyn, MI	2	1
08/03/80	Watkins Glen, NY	5	5
08/10/80	Milwaukee, WI	1	1
08/31/80	Ontario, CA	3	2
09/20/80	Brooklyn, MI	3	4
10/26/80	Mexico City, Mexico	4	10
11/08/80	Phoenix, AZ	2	13

Finished 1st in points——Led 27 times for 448 laps completing 2899.056 miles— Prize monies, $503,595

03/22/81	Phoenix, AZ	3	1
05/24/81	Indianapolis, IN	5	32
06/07/81	Milwaukee, WI	4	6
06/21/81	Pocono, PA		
06/28/81	Atlanta, GA	1	2
06/28/81	Atlanta, GA	2	3
07/25/81	Brooklyn, MI	2	22
08/30/81	Riverside, CA	6	21

OWNER & CAR#	TRACK TYPE	MILES
McLaren/Cosworth #4	1Mile-PO	150
McLaren/Cosworth #4	2 Mile-PO	125
McLaren/Cosworth #4	2 Mile-PO	125
McLaren/Cosworth #4	2.5 Mile-PO	500
McLaren/Cosworth #4	1.5 Mile-PO	100
McLaren/Cosworth #4	1.5 Mile-PO	100
McLaren/Cosworth #4	2 Mile-PO	126
McLaren/Cosworth #4	2 Mile-PO	126
McLaren/Cosworth #4	2.45 Mile-RC	150
McLaren/Cosworth #4	1.5 Mile-PO	150
McLaren/Cosworth #4	2.5 Mile-PO	500
McLaren/Cosworth #4	2 Mile-PO	150
McLaren/Cosworth #4	1.5 Mile-PO	150
McLaren/Cosworth #4	1 Mile-PO	150
Chaparral/Cosworth #4	2.5 Mile-PO	200
Chaparral/Cosworth #4	2.5 Mile-PO	500
Chaparral/Cosworth #4	1 Mile-PO	150
Chaparral/Cosworth #4	2.5 Mile-PO	500
Chaparral/Cosworth #4	2.4 Mile-RC	156
Chaparral/Cosworth #4	2 Mile-PO	200
Chaparral/Cosworth #4	2.45 Mile-RC	150.536
Chaparral/Cosworth #4	1 Mile-PO	200
Chaparral/Cosworth #4	2.5 Mile-PO	500
Chaparral/Cosworth #4	2 Milc-PO	150
Chaparral/Cosworth #4	2.48 Mile-RC	148.8
Chaparral/Cosworth #4	1 Mile-PO	150
Chaparral/Cosworth #1	1 Mile-PO	150
Chaparral/Cosworth #1	2.5 Mile-PO	500
Chaparral/Cosworth #1	1 Mile-PO	150
Chaparral/Cosworth #1	2.5 Mile-PO	500
Chaparral/Cosworth #1	1.5 Mile-PO	126.326
Chaparral/Cosworth #1	1.5 Mile-PO	126.326
Chaparral/Cosworth #1	2 Mile-PO	500
Chaparral/Cosworth #1	2.6 Mile-RC	313.5

DATE	LOCATION OF TRACK	S	F
09/05/81	Milwaukee, WI	1*	4
09/20/81	Brooklyn, MI	4	20
10/04/81	Watkins Glen, NY	4	2
10/18/81	Mexico City, Mexico	7	26
10/31/81	Phoenix, AZ	2	21

Finished 5th in points—-Led 13 times for 231 laps completing 1426.495 miles
*record—135.890mph

03/28/82	Phoenix, AZ	6	4
05/30/82	Indianapolis, IN	12	8
06/13/82	Milwaukee, WI	6	15
07/14/82	Cleveland, OH	16	23
07/18/82	Brooklyn , MI	10	28
08/01/82	Milwaukee, WI	9	17
08/15/82	Pocono, PA	3	12
08/29/82	Riverside, CA	16	3
09/19/82	Elkhart Lake, WI	18	12
09/26/82	Brooklyn, MI	-	-
10/06/82	Phoenix, AZ	9	21

Finished 12th in points—-Led 5 times for 24 laps completing 1312.320 miles.
Jim Hall retired team.

04/17/83	Atlanta, GA	2	18
08/14/83	Pocono, PA	7	21
09/18/83	Brooklyn, MI	2	23
10/08/83	Las Vegas, NV	23	24
10/29/83	Phoenix, AZ	6	20

Finished 37th in points—-Led 1 time for 6 laps completing 452.173 miles.
Left the team @ end of season.

05/27/84	Indianapolis, IN	30	22
07/22/84	Brooklyn, MI	10	7
08/19/84	Pocono, PA	12	28
09/09/84	St. Pie, Canada	10	5
09/24/84	Brooklyn, MI	1*	14
10/14/84	Phoenix, AZ	3	11

Finished 22nd in points—Led 1 time for 46 laps completing 1498.524 miles
*New World Record - Indy Cars 215.189mph

OWNER & CAR#	TRACK TYPE	MILES
Chaparral/Cosworth #1	1 Mile-PO	200
Chaparral/Cosworth #1	2 Mile-PO	148
Chaparral/Cosworth #1	2.45 Mile-RC	202.62
Chaparral/Cosworth #1	2.48 Mile-RC	147.5
Chaparral/Cosworth #1	1 Mile-PO	150
Chaparral/Cosworth #5	1 Mile-PO	150
Chaparral/Cosworth #5	2.5 Mile-PO	500
Chaparral/Cosworth #5	1 Mile-PO	150
Chaparral/Cosworth #5	2.48 Mile-StC	310
March/Cosworth #5	2 Mile-PO	500
March/Cosworth #5	1 Mile-PO	200
March/Cosworth #5	2.5 Mile-PO	500
March/Cosworth #5	2.6 Mile-RC	313.5
March/Cosworth #5	4 Mile-RC	200
2 Mile-PO	150	
March/Cosworth #5	1 Mile-PO	150
Patrick #40	1.5 Mile-PO	200
Patrick #40	2.5 Mile-PO	500
Patrick #40	2 Mile-PO	200
Patrick #40	1.125 Mile-MO	200.25
Patrick #40	1 Mile-PO	150
A. J. Foyt # 84	2.5 Mile-PO	500
A. J. Foyt #84	2.5 Mile-PO	500
A. J. Foyt #84	2.5 Mile-PO	500
Penske #6	.8264 Mile PO	185.85
Penske #6	2 Mile-PO	200
Penske #6	1 Mile-PO	150

DATE	LOCATION OF TRACK	S	F
04/14/85	Long Beach, CA	20	10
05/26/85	Indianapolis, IN	30	6
06/02/85	Milwaukee, WI	7	23
06/16/85	Portland, OR	20	9
06/30/85	Meadowlands, NJ	24	14
07/07/85	Cleveland, OH	25	15
07/28/85	Brooklyn, MI	6	4
08/04/85	Elkhart Lake, WI		DNS
08/18/85	Pocono, PA	5	14
09/01/85	Mid-Ohio, OH	21	22
09/08/85	St. Pie, Canada	12	1
09/22/85	Brooklyn, MI	14	9
10/06/85	Laguna Seca, CA	20	21
10/13/85	Phoenix, AZ	14	26
11/09/85	Miami, FL	24	19

Finished 11th in points—-Led 6 times for 36 laps completing 2698.744 miles

DATE	LOCATION OF TRACK	S	F
04/06/86	Phoenix, AZ	11	5
04/13/86	Long Beach, CA	21	9
05/31/86	Indianapolis, IN	12	8
06/08/86	Milwaukee, WI	2	4
06/15/86	Portland, OR	17	15
06/29/86	Meadowlands, NJ	19	7
07/06/86	Cleveland, OH	18	10
07/20/86	Toronto, ONT, Canada	22	10
08/02/86	Brooklyn, MI	14	1*
08/17/86	Pocono, PA	2	18
08/31/86	Mid-Ohio, OH	21	8
09/07/86	St. Pie, Canada	14	16
09/28/86	Brooklyn, MI	5	9
10/04/86	Elkhart Lake, WI	21	14
10/12/86	Laguna Seca, CA	17	12
10/19/86	Phoenix, AZ	9	9
11/09/86	Miami, FL	24	12

Finished 11th in points—-Led 5 times for 105 laps completing 3540.530 miles
*Oldest driver to win a 500 mile race.

DATE	LOCATION OF TRACK	S	F
04/05/87	Long Beach, CA	22	23
04/12/87	Phoenix, AZ	10	9
05/24/87	Indianapolis, IN	8	11

OWNER & CAR#	TRACK TYPE	MILES
Morales #21	1.67 Mile-StC	150.3
Morales #21	2.5 Mile-PO	500
Morales #21	1 Mile-PO	200
Morales #21	1.915 Mile-RC	200
Morales #21	1.682 Mile-StC	168.2
Morales #21	2.48 Mile-StC	218.24
Morales #21	2 Mile-PO	500
Morales #21	4 Mile-RC	200
Morales #21	2.5 Mile-PO	500
Morales #21	2.4 Mile-RC	200.5
Morales #21	.8264 Mile-PO	185.85
Morales #21	2 Mile-PO	250
Morales #21	1.9 Mile-RC	186.20
Morales #21	1 Mile-PO	150
Morales #21	1.784 Mile-StC	199.8
Morales #21	1 Mile-PO	200
Morales #21	1.67 Mile-StC	158.65
Morales #21	2.5 Mile-PO	500
Morales #21	1 Mile-PO	200
Morales #21	1.915 Mile-RC	200
Morales #21	1.682 Mile-StC	168.2
Morales #21	2.48 Mile-StC	218.24
Morales #21	1.78 Mile-StC	183
Morales #21	2 Mile-PO	500
Morales #21	2.5 Mile-PO	500
Morales #21	2.4 Milc-RC	200.5
Morales #21	.8264 Mile-PO	185.85
Morales #21	2 Mile-PO	250
Morales #21	4 Mile-PO	200
Morales #21	1.9 Mile-RC	186.2
Morales #21	1 Mile-PO	150
Morales #21	1.784 Milc-StC	199.8
Morales #21	1.67 Mile-StC	158.65
Morales #21	1 Mile-PO	200
Morales #21	2.5 Mile-PO	500

DATE	LOCATION OF TRACK	S	F
05/31/87	Milwaukee, WI	14	9
06/14/87	Portland, OR	17	7
06/28/87	Meadowlands, NJ	15	11
07/06/87	Cleveland, OH	19	9
07/19/87	Toronto, ONT, Canada	19	21
08/02/87	Brooklyn, MI	10	28
08/16/87	Pocono, PA	12	26
08/30/87	Elkhart Lake, WI	21	24
09/06/87	Mid-Ohio, OH	22	12
09/20/87	Nazareth, PA	13	20
10/11/87	Laguna Seca, CA	23	15
11/01/87	Miami, FL	27	16

Finished 18th in points—-completed 2155.214 miles
Morales retired the race team at end of season.

DATE	LOCATION OF TRACK	S	F
05/29/88	Indianapolis, IN	30	22
08/07/88	Brooklyn, MI	13	18

Finished 43rd in point—completed 525.5 miles

DATE	LOCATION OF TRACK	S	F
05/28/89	Indianapolis, IN-qualified but was bumped from the field		
08/06/89	Brooklyn, MI	21	10
08/20/89	Pocono, PA	24	13
09/24/89	Nazareth, PA	DNS	Machinist #11

Finished 27 in points—completed 957.5 miles

NASCAR CAREER SUMMARY

DATE	LOCATION	TRACK	Q
02/22/63	Daytona Beach, FL	Daytona International	4 *
	Led 6 laps		
02/24/63	Daytona Beach, FL	Daytona International	4

*New Track & World's Record for stock cars on a closed course—165.183mph

DATE	LOCATION	TRACK	Q
02/21/64	Daytona Beach, FL	Daytona International	11
02/23/64	Daytona Beach, FL	Daytona International	36
07/04/64	Daytona Beach, FL	Daytona International	21
04/11/65	Hampton, GA	Atlanta Int'l Speedway	24
02/25/66	Daytona Beach, FL	Daytona International	14
02/27/66	Daytona Beach, FL	Daytona International	42

OWNER & CAR#	TRACK TYPE	MILES
Morales #21	1 Mile-PO	200
Morales #21	1.915 Mile-RC	200
Morales #21	1.682 Mile-StC	168.2
Morales #21	2.48 Mile-StC	196.4
Morales #21	1.78 Mile-StC	183
Morales #21	2 Mile-PO	500
Morales #21	2.5 Mile-PO	500
Morales #21	4 Mile-RC	200
Morales #21	2.4 Mile-RC	200.5
Morales #21	1 Mile-PO	200
Morales #21	1.9 Mile-RC	186.2
Morales #21	1.784 Mile-StC	183.7
King-Protofab #17	2.5 Mile-PO	500
A. J. Foyt #14	2 Mile-PO	500
Stoops #17	2 Mile-PO	500
Stoops #17	2.5 Mile-PO	500
1 Mile-PO	200	

F	OWNER & CAR#	TRACK TYPE	LAPS
1	Smokey Yunick Chevy #13	2 Paved	40
9	Smokey Yunick Chevy #13	2 Paved	200
18	Bud Moore Mercury #01	2 Paved	40
26	Bud Moore Mercury #01	2 Paved	200
7	Holman-Moody Ford #0	2 Paved	160
13	Bondy Long Ford #77	1.522 Paved	328
23	C.Sadderfield Chevy #33	2 Paved	40
28	C.Sadderfield Chevy #33	2 Paved	200

DATE	LOCATION	TRACK	Q
11/12/72	College Station, TX	Texas World Sp.	9
10/21/73	Rockingham, NC	N.C. Motor Speedway	22
02/17/74 *Led 2 laps*	Daytona Beach, FL	Daytona International	17
07/04/74	Daytona Beach, FL	Daytona International	37
10/06/74 *Led 1 lap*	Charlotte, NC	Charlotte Motor Sp.	17
02/16/75	Daytona Beach, FL	Daytona International	11
03/23/75	Hampton, GA	Atlanta Int'l Speedway	20
07/04/75	Daytona Beach, FL	Daytona International	21
10/05/75	Charlotte, NC	Charlotte Motor Sp.	10
07/04/76	Daytona Beach, FL	Daytona International	21
10/10/76	Charlotte, NC	Charlotte Motor Sp.	20
02/20/77	Daytona Beach, FL	Daytona International	40
03/20/77	Hampton, GA	Atlanta Int'l Speedway	23
08/07/77	Talladega, AL	Alabama Int'l Motor Sp.	12
02/15/81	Daytona Beach, FL	Daytona International	35
03/01/81	Rockingham, NC	N.C. Motor Speedway	28
03/15/81	Hampton, GA	Atlanta Int'l Speedway	33
04/12/81	Darlington, SC	Darlington Raceway	24
06/21/81	Brooklyn, MI	Michigan Int'l Speedway	18
07/04/81	Daytona Beach, FL	Daytona International	9
08/16/81 *Led 5 laps*	Brooklyn, MI	Michigan Int'l Speedway	18
09/07/81	Darlington, SC	Darlington Raceway	25
09/13/81	Richmond, VA	Richmond Fairgrounds	24
10/11/81	Charlotte, NC	Charlotte Motor Speedway	27
11/01/81	Rockingham, NC	N.C. Motor Speedway	11
11/08/81	Hampton, GA	Atlanta Int'l Speedway	27
11/06/88	Phoenix, AZ	Phoenix Int'l Raceway	34
12/18/88	Melbourne, Australia	Calder Park Thunderdome	3

1963–1988 : 36 races, 10,000 miles, $60,000 prize. Led 4 races for 14 laps

SPECIAL EVENTS (Stock):

DATE	LOCATION	TRACK	Q
04/27/75	Trenton, NJ	Trenton International Speedway	10

F	OWNER & CAR#	TRACK TYPE	LAPS
26	J. Donlevey Ford #90	2 Paved	250
13	Don Bierechwale Chevy #61	1.017 Paved	492
24	Don Bierechwale Chevy #61	2 Paved	200
39	Don Bierechwale Chevy #61	2 Paved	160
24	Junior Johnson Chevy #1	1 Paved	334
27	DiGard Chevy #08	2 Paved	200
32	Norris Reed Chevy #83	1.522 Paved	328
40	Norris Reed Chevy #83	2 Paved	160
34	Norris Reed Chevy #83	1 Paved	334
20	Johnny Ray Chevy #77	2 Paved	160
31	Johnny Ray Chevy #77	1 Paved	334
41	Johnny Ray Chevy #77	2 Paved	200
40	Johnny Ray Chevy #77	1.52 Paved	328
21	AJFoyt Enterprises Chevy#41	2.66 Paved	188
10	Ron Benfield Pontiac#98	2 Paved	200
12	Ron Benfield Pontiac#98	1.017 Paved	492
12	Ron Benfield Pontiac#98	1.522 Paved	328
28	Ron Benfield Pontiac#98	1.366 Paved	367
17	Ron Benfield Pontiac#98	2 Paved	200
5	Ron Benfield Pontiac#98	2 Paved	160
13	Ron Benfield Pontiac#98	2 Paved	200
33	Ron Benfield Pontiac#98	1.366 Paved	367
31	Ron Benfield Pontiac#98	.542 Paved	400
27	Ron Benfield Pontiac#98	1 Paved	334
29	Ron Benfield Pontiac#98	1.017 Paved	492
37	Ron Benfield Pontiacc#98	1.522 Paved	328
39	Clark Motorsports Olds#31	1 Paved	312
17	Clark Motorsports Olds#31	1.123 Paved	280

F	OWNER & CAR#	TRACK TYPE	LAPS
6	#9 Steve Drake	3/4 Paved	100 Laps

INTERNATIONAL RACE OF CHAMPIONS (IROC)

Invited to race in 1975-77-78-79-80-84

DATE	RACE#	LOCATION
09/14/74	IROC2-#1	Michigan Int'l Speedway
10/26/74	IROC2-#2	Riverside Int'l Raceway
10/27/74	IROC2-#3	Riverside int'l Raceway
02/14/75	IROC2-#4	Daytona Int'l Speedway

Final standing 9th of 12

09/18/76	IROC4-#1	Michigan Int'l Speedway*
10/16/76	IROC4-#2	Riverside Int'l Raceway
10/17/76	IROC4-#3	Riverside Int'l Raceway
02/18/77	IROC4-#4	Daytona Int'l Speedway

Final Standing 4th of 12
*Record——25 lead changes

09/17/77	IROC5-#1	Michigan Int'l Speedway
10/15/77	IROC5-#2	Riverside Int'l Raceway
10/16/77	IROC5-#3	Riverside Int'l Raceway
02/17/78	IROC5-#4	Daytona Int'l Speedway

Final standing 9th

09/16/78	IROC6-USAC	Michigan Int'l Speedway

New format—must finish 4th or better in oval or road course qualifiers to advance to final

09/15/79	IROC7-CART	Michigan Int'l Speedway
10/28/79	IROC7-ROAD	Riverside Int'l Raceway
03/15/80	IROC7-OVAL	Atlanta Int'l Raceway

Final standing 6th

06/16/84	IROC8-#1	Michigan Int'l Speedway
07/07/84	IROC8-#2	Burke Lakefront Airport
07/28/84	IROC8-#3	Talladega Superspeedway
08/11/84	IROC8-#4	Michigan Int'l Speedway

Final standing 8th

S	F	TRACK/TYPE	LAPS
12	8	2 mile-paved oval	50/50
5	9	2.54 mile-road course	30/30
4	7	2.54 mile-road course	30/30
9	9	2.5 mile-paved oval	3/40
9	2	2 mile-paved oval	50/50
4	5	2.54 mile-road course	30/30
7	7	2.54 mile-road course	30/30
4	5	2.5 mile-paved oval	40/40
10	8	2 mile-paved oval	50/50
7	7	2.54 mile-road course	30/30
6	9	2.54 mile-road course	30/30
—	9	2.5 mile-paved oval	23/40
8	6	2 mile-paved oval	2/50
1	4	2 mile-paved oval	50/50
12	6	2.54 mile-road course	30/30
6	3	1.522 mile-paved oval	66/66
10	6	2 mile-paved oval	50/50
7	9	2.48 mile-road course	30/30
5	4	2.66 mile-paved oval	38/38
8	9	2 mile-paved oval	50/50

SPECIAL EVENTS (IROC):

DATE	LOCATION	TRACK NAME
09/14/74	Brooklyn, MI	Michigan International Speedway
09/18/76	Brooklyn, MI	Michigan International Speedway
09/17/77	Brooklyn, MI	Michigan International Speedway
09/16/78	Brooklyn, MI	Michigan International Speedway

IMSA CAMEL GT:

DATE	LOCATION/RACE	CAR &CLASS
11/27/77	Daytona Finale	Porsche 934-GTO
02/05/78	Daytona 24 Hour	Porsche 935-GTX
04/02/78	Talladega 6 Hour	Porsche 935-GTX
07/15/78	Watkins Glen 6 Hour	Porsche 935-GTX
02/04/79	Daytona 24 Hour	Porsche 935-GTX
03/22/80	Sebring 12 Hour	Porsche 935-GTX
08/17/80	Mosport 1000 K	Porsche 935-GTX

Not a complete listing

FORMULA 5000:

DATE	LOCATION	TRACK NAME
09/01/74	Ontario, CA	Ontario Motor Speedway
10/13/74	Monterey, CA	Laguna Seca Raceway

MIDGETS:

DATE	LOCATION	TRACK NAME
10/20/62	Gardena, CA	Ascot Park
04/26/63	Toronto, Canada	C.N.E. Fairgrounds
07/19/63	Indianapolis, IN	Indianapolis Speedrome
08/09/63	Indianapolis, IN	Indianapolis Speedrome
10/06/63	Terre Haute, IN	Terre Haute Action Track
06/03/64	Louisville, KY	Fairgrounds Motor Speedway
06/19/64	Toronto, Canada	C.N.E. Fairgrounds
11/27/65	Gardena, CA	Ascot Park
03/25/66	Dallas, TX	Devil's Bowl
10/21/67	Fresno, CA	Kearny Bowl
11/12/67	El Cajon, CA	El Cajon Motor Speedway
01/28/68	Irwindale, CA	Speedway 605

Q	F	OWNER & CAR #	TYPE TRACK	DISTANCE
12	8	#9 Chevy Camaro	2 Paved	50 Laps
9	2	#6 Chevy Camaro	2 Paved	50 Laps
10	8	#7 Chevy Camaro	2 Paved	50 Laps
8	6	#8 Chevy Camaro	2 Paved	50 Laps

S	F	LAPS	STATUS	CO-DRIVERS
10	31	6/65	DNF	D.Barbour
8	2	650/680	Run	Barbour/Schurti
3	3	161/175	Run	D.Barbour
16	4	-----	Run	D.Barbour
12	4	529/684	DNF	Mendez/Miller
9	7	224/253	Run	Heimrath/Horam
7	12	127/245	DNF	L. Heimrath

Q	F	OWNER & CAR #	TYPE TRACK	DISTANCE
22	9	#3 Hogan Racing	2.9 Paved RC	34 Laps
11	9	#3 Hogan Racing	1.9 Paved RC	50 Laps

Q	F	OWNER & CAR #	TYPE TRACK	DISTANCE
NA	15	#26 Bob Hansen	1/2 Dirt	40 Laps
33	20	#55 Leon Mensing	1/4 Paved	200 Laps
4	7	#8 Dick Kincaid	1/5 Paved	50 Laps
6	4	#8 Dick Kincaid	1/5 Paved	50 Laps
21	22	#2 Lloyd Rahn	1/2 Dirt	100 Laps
15	13	#8 Dick Kincaid	1/4 Paved	50 Laps
22	12	#8 Dick Kincaid	1/4 Paved	200 Laps
22	22	#32 Robert Weaver	1/2 Dirt	150 Laps
18	8	#14 Jack Cunningham	3/8 Dirt	40 Laps
12	8	#18 Frank Berlott	1/4 Paved	50 Laps
15	6	#50 Jim Gary	1/3 Paved	50 Laps
9	7	#5 Jim Gary	1/2 Paved	40 Laps

DATE	LOCATION	TRACK NAME
02/04/68	El Cajon, CA	El Cajon Motor Speedway
04/05/68	Tucson, AZ	Corona Speedway
04/06/68	Phoenix, AZ	Manzanita Park
08/16/68	Springfield, IL	Springfield Speedway
11/16/68	Phoenix, AZ	Manzanita Park
03/08/69	Houston, TX	Astrodome
03/09/69	Houston, TX	Astrodome
03/28/69	Tucson, AZ	Corona Speedway
03/29/69	Phoenix, AZ	Manzanita Park
10/25/69	Wichita Falls, TX	Wichita Speedway
03/14/70	Houston, TX	Astrodome
04/17/70	Navasota, TX	Moody-Clary Speedway
04/19/70	Lawton, OK	Lawton Motor Speedway
07/16/70	Indianapolis, IN	Indianapolis Raceway Park
03/27/71	Phoenix, AZ	Manzanita Park
03/11/72	Houston, TX	Astrodome
07/22/72	Philadelphia, PA	John F. Kennedy Stadium
09/17/72	Trenton, NJ	Trenton International Speedway
09/17/72	Trenton, NJ	Trenton International Speedway

#Did not start second feature event.

DATE	LOCATION	TRACK NAME
08/20/75	Indianapolis, IN	Indianapolis Raceway Park
11/30/75	Irwindale, CA	Speedway 605
06/15/77	Indianapolis, IN	Indianapolis Raceway Park
08/02/77	Cedar Rapids, IA	Hawkeye Downs
08/10/77	Indianapolis, IN	Indianapolis Raceway Park
09/11/77	Terre Haute, IN	Terre Hate Action Track
10/22/77	Seattle, WA	Kingdome
11/24/77	Gardena, CA	Ascot Park

SPECIAL EVENTS (Midget)

DATE	LOCATION	TRACK NAME
10/20/74	Pocono, PA	Pocono International Raceway
01/04/86	Indianapolis, IN	Hoosier Dome

Q	F	OWNER & CAR #	TYPE TRACK	DISTANCE
17	12	#5 Jim Gary	1/3 Paved	50 Laps
23	-	#66 Scott Hunter	1/4 Dirt	40 Laps
6	11	#66 Scott Hunter	1/2 Dirt	40 Laps
19	-	#66 Scott Hunter	1/4 Dirt	50 Laps
12	6	#66 Scott Hunter	1/2 Dirt	40 Laps
48	-	#66 Scott Hunter	1/5 Dirt (Indoor)	100 Laps
35	16	#66 Scott Hunter	1/5 Dirt (Indoor)	100 Laps
15	14	#66 Scott Hunter	1/4 Dirt	50 Laps
25	-	#66 Scott Hunter	1/2 Dirt	40 Laps
27	-	#66 Scott Hunter	1/4 Dirt	40 Laps
32	-	#66 Scott Hunter	1/5 Dirt	100 Laps
14	-	#66 Scott Hunter	1/4 Dirt	40 Laps
19	-	#66 Scott Hunter	1/4 Dirt	40 Laps
21	-	#2 Don Kenyon	5/8 Paved	30 Laps
13	10	#66 Stan Lee	1/2 Dirt	40 Laps
-	17	#32 T.D. Enterprises	1/5 Dirt	100 Laps
-	17	#82 Harry Turner	1/4 Paved	100 Laps
-	29	#90 Dyno Stargate Racing	1.5 Paved	34 Laps
-	-#	#90 Dyno Stargate Racing	1.5 Paved	34 Laps
8	7	#98 Linne Enterprises	5/8 Paved	30 Laps
19	11	#22 Shannon Brothers	1/2 Paved	100 Laps
9	4	#28 Bob Lithgow	5/8 Paved	30 Laps
11	20	#28 Bob Lithgow	1/2 Dirt	50 Laps
25	-	#89 Robert Mahalik	5/8 Paved	30 Laps
-	-	#2 Doug Caruthers	1/2 Dirt	100 Laps
6	8	#2x Doug Caruthers	1/5 Paved	100 Laps
3	5	#2 Doug Caruthers	1/2 Dirt	100 Laps

Q	F	OWNER & CAR #	TYPE TRACK	DISTANCE
7	5	#4 Shannon Brothers	3/4 Paved	50 Laps
-	20	#21 Charlie Patterson	1/6 P (Indoor)	100 Laps

SILVER CROWN

DATE	LOCATION	TRACK NAME
06/20/71	Nazareth, PA	Nazareth Speedway
08/22/71	Springfield, IL	Illinois State Fairgrounds
09/06/71	DuQuoin, IL	DuQuoin State Fairgrounds
09/11/71	Indianapolis, IN	Indiana State Fairgrounds
08/20/72	Springfield, IL	Illinois State Fairgrounds
09/04/72	DuQuoin, IL	DuQuoin State Fairgrounds

#Race scheduled for 100 laps but halted after 52 laps due to rain.

09/09/72	Indianapolis, IN	Indiana State Fairgrounds
08/19/73	Springfield, IL	Illinois State Fairgrounds
09/03/73	DuQuoin, IL	DuQuoin State Fairgrounds
09/08/73	Indianapolis, IN	Indiana State Fairgrounds

#Qual. 9/8 and raced 9/15. George Snider drove the car on 9/15.

08/31/75	St. Paul, MN	Minnesota State Fairgrounds
09/10/77	Indianapolis, IN	Indiana State Fairgrounds

Q	F	OWNER & CAR #	TYPE TRACK	DISTANCE
12	16	#18 Tim DelRose	1.125 Dirt	89 Laps#
4	17	#18 Tim DelRose	1 Dirt	100 Laps
14	8	#18 Tim DelRose	1 Dirt	100 Laps
12	20	#18 Tim DelRose	1 Dirt	100 Laps
13	4	#15 Doug Caruthers	1 Dirt	100 Laps
9	7	#36 Don Rogala	1 Dirt	52 Laps#
-	-	#36 Don Rogala	1 Dirt	100 Laps
21	12	#73 Lee Elkins	1 Dirt	100 Laps
21	10	#18 T.D. Enterprises	1 Dirt	100 Laps
25	-#	#18 T.D. Enterprises	1 Dirt	100 Laps
12	11	#15 Doug Caruthers	1/2 Paved	200 Laps
41	-	#15 Kurtz/DiGeronimo	1 Dirt	100 Laps

USAC DIVISIONAL POINT RANKINGS

YEAR	CH	ST	SC	SP	M	F5	
1962	25	-	-	19	-	-	
1963	10	-	-	14	67	-	
1964	21	21	-	5	103	-	
1965	12	-	-	1	153	-	
1966	-	-	-	-	-	-	
1967	22	-	-	29	71	-	
1968	18	-	-	27	52	-	
1969	11	-	-	21	112	-	
1970	12	48	-	30	-	-	
1971	19	74	19	-	110	-	
1972	7	-	7	57	124	-	
1973	3	32	16	-	-	-	
1974	2	65	-	-	-	22#	#Tied with 3 drivers.
1975	2	48	29	-	84	-	
1976	2	94	-	-	-	-	
1977	3#	-	-	-	40	-	#Tied with A. J. Foyt.
1978	4	-	-	-	-	-	
1979	-	-	-	-	-	-	
1980	1	-	-	-	-	-	
1981	-	-	-	-	-	-	
1982	-	-	-	-	-	-	
1983	-	-	-	-	-	-	
1984	25	-	-	-	-	-	
1985	6	-	-	-	-	-	
1986	8	-	-	-	-	-	
1987	11	-	-	-	-	-	
1988	22	-	-	-	-	-	
1989	-	-	-	-	-	-	
1990	-	-	-	-	-	-	
1992	-	-	-	-	-	-	

INDY CAR RECORDS

YEAR	STARTS	1st	2nd	3rd	4th	5th	6-10	PURSES
1962	4	-	-	-	-	-	1	$ 2,225
1963	12	-	-	-	1	1	5	16,091
1964	11	-	-	-	-	1	1	10,568
1965	15	1	-	-	1	1	3	28,729
1966	1	-	-	-	-	-	-	144
1967	16	-	-	-	-	1	2	18,848
1968	17	-	-	-	1	3	1	26,889
1969	14	-	-	-	2	2	1	30,792
1970	14	-	-	1	1	1	1	45,629
1971	10	-	-	-	-	-	4	45,029
1972	9	-	1	1	-	1	2	84,209
1973	13	2	2	1	2	2	1	109,904
1974	13	4	-	-	2	1	5	382,925
1975	12	1	4	2	-	-	2	161,137
1976	13	3	2	2	1	-	2	378,238
1977	14	4	1	1	1	1	2	148,051
1978	18	2	4	1	-	1	3	247,478
1979	14	2	-	3	2	1	1	113,598
1980	12	5	3	-	1	1	1	503,595
1981	12	1	2	1	1	-	1	160,320
1982	10	-	-	1	1	-	1	116,484
1983	5	-	-	-	-	-	-	29,064
1984	6	-	-	-	-	1	1	115,758
1985	14	1	-	-	1	-	4	378,519
1986	17	1	-	-	1	1	8	549,868
1987	15	-	-	-	-	-	4	347,775
1988	2	-	-	-	-	-	-	116,907
1989	2	-	-	-	-	-	1	40,458
TOTALS	315	27	19	14	19	20	58	$4,209,232

INDY RECORDS

-Ranks 4th in number of races run (24)
-2nd in number of wins (3)
-4th in number of pole position (3)

500 MILE RACE STANDINGS

—4th in most 500 mile starts (59)
—5th in most 500 mile wins (5)
—6th in 500 mile pole positions(4)

ALL TIME LIST FOR INDY CARS

—6th in wins (27)
—6th in pole positions (23)
—12th on All-Time Earnings list (4,209,232)
—4th in All-Time Starts with 315
—3rd in Top-Ten Finishes in 59 "500" mile race starts (25)
—Longest duration between first win and most recent win 21 years

FIRSTS

1965   Atlanta 250
1973   Ontario 100, Michigan 125
1974   Ontario 100, Indy 500, Milwaukee 150, Pocono 500
1975   Phoenix 150
1976   Trenton 200, Indy 500, Texas 200
1977   Phoenix 150, Milwaukee 150, Texas 200, Milwaukee 200
1978   Michigan 200, Phoenix 150
1979   Atlanta 125 (2)
1980   Ontario 200, Indy 500, Mid-Ohio 156, Michigan 200, Milwaukee 200
1981   Phoenix 150
1985   Montreal 187
1986   Michigan 500

POLES (23)

1963   Phoenix
1964   Langhorne
1973   Indy 500, Ontario
1974   Ontario, Phoenix

1975	Milwaukee
1976	Indy 500, Milwaukee
1977	Ontario, Phoenix, Texas, Trenton, Ontario 500
1978	Michigan
1979	Atlanta (2)
1980	Ontario, Indy 500, Milwaukee
1981	Atlanta, Milwaukee
1984	Michigan

POINTS (STANDING)

1962	80 (25TH)
1963	640 (10TH)
1964	270 (21ST)
1965	993 (12TH)
1966	0 (55TH)
1967	290 (22ND)
1968	890 (17TH)
1969	1,130 (11TH)
1970	960 (12TH)
1971	570 (19TH)
1972	1,620 (7TH)
1973	2,595 (3RD)
1974	3, 650 (2ND)
1975	2,900 (2ND)
1976	4,220 (2ND)
1977	2, 840 (3RD)
1978	3, 067 (4TH)
1979	2, 163 (4TH)
1980	4, 723 (1ST)
1981	120 (5TH)
1982	62 (12TH)
1983	0 (37TH)
1984	20 (22ND)
1985	51 (11TH)
1986	78 (11TH)
1987	23 (18TH)
1988	0 (43RD)
1989	3 (27TH)

INDY 500 RECORD

Year	Car	Qual. Speed	Start	Finish	Laps	Status
1963	U.S. Equipment Co.	148.063	26	29	43	Transmission
1964	Bardahl	151.400	15	27	2	Accident
1965	Racing Associates	156.291	11	31	15	Rear end
1967	Weinberger Homes	162.859	19	25	103	Accident
1968	City of Seattle	163.830	21	18	125	Fuel surge tank
1969	Patrick Petroleum	166.628	17	29	24	Oil leak
1970	Patrick Petroleum	170.213	2	18	135	Broken header
1971	Patrick Petroleum	171.151	24	18	128	Engine
1972	Patrick Petroleum	183.234	8	27	55	Connecting rod
1973	Gulf McLaren	198.413	1	9	124	Running
1974	McLaren	190.446	25	1	200	Running (158.589)
1975	Gatorade McLaren	185.998	7	2	174	Running
1976	HyGain McLaren	188.957	1	1	102	Running (148.725)
1977	1st Natl. McLaren	197.325	17	33	12	Tagged valves
1978	1st Natl. McLaren	197.098	4	13	180	Running
1979	Budweiser McLaren	188.137	8	18	168	Running
1980	Pennzoil Chaparral	192.256	1	1	200	Running (162.016)
1981	Pennzoil Chaparral	195.387	5	32	25	Fuel pump
1982	Pennzoil Chaparral	197.066	12	8	187	Engine
1984	Gilmore/Greer/Foyt	202.062	30	22	116	Engine
1985	Vermont American	208.254	30	6	198	Running
1986	Vermont American	210.220	12	8	198	Running
1987	Vermont American	208.296	8	11	171	Running
1988	MacTools	208.442	30	22	107	Accident

Michigan 500 Record

Year	Car	Qual. Speed	Start	Finish	Laps	Status
1981	Pennzoil Chaparral	200.892	2	22	112	Cut tire
1982	Pennzoil Chaparral	196.084	10	28	54	Piston
1984	Gilmore-Calumet Farms	203.580	10	7	249	Running
1985	Vermont American	209.290	6	4	248	Running
1986	Vermont American	212.578	14	1	250	Running (137.139)
1987	Vermont American	210.225	10	11	171	Running
1988	Copenhagen-Gilmore	208.938	13	18	129	Fire
1989	Stoops Freighliner	208.303	21	10	240	Running

Pocono 500 Record

Year	Car	Qual. Speed	Start	Finish	Laps	Status
1971	Patrick Petroleum	165.809	12	7	198	Running
1972	Therma King	176.872	13	2	200	Running
1973	Gulf McLaren	188.216	7	5	195	Running
1974	McLaren	181.424	5	1	200	Running (156.701)
1975	Gatorade McLaren	181.214	5	6	168	Running
1976	HyGain McLaren	Drew	15	4	200	Running
1977	1st Natl. McLaren	189.255	2	5	193	Running
1978	1st Natl. McLaren	188.937	3	2	200	Running
1980	Pennzoil Chaparral	182.315	5	2	200	Running
1982	Pennzoil Chaparral	194.843	3	12	137	Accident
1983	Sea Ray Boats	186.393	7	21	91	Accident
1984	Gilmore-Calument	195.029	12	28	75	Exhaust
1985	Vermont American	201.378	5	14	134	Accident
1986	Vermont American	203.114	2	18	48	Accident
1987	Vermont American	192.308	12	26	0	Accident
1989	Stoops Freightliner	192.209	24	13	191	Running

California 500 Record

Year	Car	Qual. Speed	Start	Finish	Laps	Status
1970	Michner Petroleum	176.375	3	31	5	Blown engine
1971	Patrick Petroleum	178.890	5	26	54	Pit fire
1972	Thermo King	196.624	24	10	178	Differential
1973	Gulf McLaren	197.190	4	31	13	Accident
1974	McLaren	185.989	2	27	49	Piston
1975	Gatorade	192.513	5	17	86	Piston
1976	HyGain McLaren	186.732	7	2	200	Running
1977	1st Natl. McLaren	195.111	1	24	46	Valve
1978	1st Natl. McLaren	199.734	2	11	129	Engine
1979	Budweiser McLaren	193.849	13	4	199	Running
1980	Pennzoil Chaparral	189.685	3	31	200	Running